AS MINORITY
BECOMES
MAJORITY

Recent Titles in
Contributions in Women's Studies

The Second Assault: Rape and Public Attitudes
Joyce E. Williams and Karen A. Holmes

Oppression and Resistance: The Struggle of Women
in Southern Africa
Richard E. Lapchick and Stephanie Urdang

Against All Odds: The Feminist Movement in Mexico to 1940
Anna Macias

Pariahs Stand Up! The Founding of the Liberal Feminist Movement
in France, 1858-1889
Patrick Kay Bidelman

Separated and Divorced Women
Lynne Carol Halem

Female Soldiers—Combatants or Noncombatants? Historical and
Contemporary Perspectives
Nancy Loring Goldman, editor

A Woman's Issue: The Politics of Family Law Reform in England
Dorothy M. Stetson

"Traitors to the Masculine Cause": The Men's Campaign
for Women's Rights
Sylvia Strauss

Women in the Resistance and in the Holocaust:
The Voices of Eyewitnesses
Vera Laska, editor

Saints and Shrews: Women and Aging in American Popular Film
Karen M. Stoddard

Women of the English Renaissance and Reformation
Retha M. Warnicke

Face to Face: Fathers, Mothers, Masters, Monsters—
Essays for a Nonsexist Future
Meg McGavran Murray, editor

AS MINORITY
BECOMES
MAJORITY

Federal Reaction
to the Phenomenon
of Women in
the Work Force,
1920-1963

JUDITH SEALANDER

Contributions in Women's Studies, Number 40

GREENWOOD PRESS
Westport, Connecticut • London, England

Library of Congress Cataloging in Publication Data

Sealander, Judith.
  As minority becomes majority.

  (Contributions in women's studies, ISSN 0147-104X ;
no. 40)
  Bibliography: p.
  Includes index.
    1. Women—Employment—United States—History—20th
century. 2. Women—Government policy—United States—
History—20th century. 3. Labor policy—United States—
History—20th century. I. Title. II. Series.
HD6095.S43   1983   331.4'125'0973   82-15820
ISBN 0-313-23750-6 (lib. bdg.)

Library of Congress Catalog Card Number: 82-15820
ISBN: 0-313-23750-6
ISSN: 0147-104X

First published in 1983

Greenwood Press
A division of Congressional Information Service, Inc.
88 Post Road West
Westport, Connecticut 06881

Printed in the United States of America

10 9 8 7 6 5 4 3 2 1

for
Steve Nowka

Contents

Acknowledgments

No scholarly work reaches completion without the help of friends and colleagues. I take pleasure in this ritual of thanking a few of those people.

I have profited greatly from the suggestions of archivists and manuscript librarians throughout the country. I am particularly indebted to the staff of the Social and Industrial Division of the National Archives and to the archivists at the Schlesinger Library in Cambridge, Massachusetts. Several former employees of the Women's Bureau and the Labor Department generously gave of their time and granted me interviews. Ethel Erickson, Mary Cannon, and Esther Peterson were particularly helpful.

The skeleton of this book first emerged at Duke University, where Anne Scott and William Chafe asked sharp and good questions. My wonderful former colleagues in the History Department at Kansas State University deserve many thanks. Several chapters of this book began as papers delivered to noon hour faculty seminars at KSU. Many of my colleagues took these first rough drafts seriously, skewering prose style and penning all sorts of improvements in the margins. Joe Hawes and Don Mrozek deserve special gratitude.

My chairperson at Wright State University, Carl Becker, and Dean of Liberal Arts, Eugene Cantelupe, have devoted time to helping me garner University money for the completion of this project. Both a Wright State University Research Council stipend and an award from the Liberal Arts Research Committee helped me with travel and typing costs.

I would like to express thanks to Timothy Walch for his permission to use parts of my article, "In the Shadow of Good Neighbor: The Women's Bureau and Latin America," which appeared in *Prologue: The Journal of the National Archives* in 1979. Oliver Ferguson has also kindly agreed to permit me to use some quotations that I earlier used to illustrate my article, "Feminist Against Feminist: The First Phase of the Equal Rights Amendment Debate," which appeared in the *South Atlantic Quarterly* in 1982.

In an odd way, my greatest professional debt is owed to a man who has had little to do with this particular manuscript. Willard Gatewood, my undergraduate mentor at the University of Arkansas, delivered wonderful lectures in American history that left my head spinning. His kind interest and contagious enthusiasm convinced me to take the study of history seriously. I have yet to meet his match as a teacher.

Frank Costigliola, Michael Pritchard, Pat Nolan, and Bobbe Nolan buoyed my spirits. John Sealander provided a bemused introduction to the ways of academe. My greatest personal debt is to my husband, Steve Nowka. His editorial sense improved the manuscript. His common sense improves my life.

Abbreviations

UAW	United Auto Workers
USES	United States Employment Service
WAC	Women's Advisory Committee
WMC	War Manpower Commission
WPA	Works Progress Administration
WPB	War Production Board
WCTU	Women's Christian Temperance Union
WTUL	Women's Trade Union League
YWCA	Young Women's Christian Associations

ABBREVIATIONS USED IN THE NOTES

CL	Manuscript Room, Butler Library, Columbia University, New York, New York
COHC	Oral History Collection, Butler Library, Columbia University, New York, New York
CORNELL	Labor Management Documentation Center, School of Industrial and Labor Relations, Cornell University, Ithaca, New York
DU	Manuscript Room, Perkins Library, Duke University, Durham, North Carolina
FDR Lib	Franklin D. Roosevelt Presidential Library, Hyde Park, New York
KL	The John F. Kennedy Presidential Library, Boston, Massachusetts
LC	Manuscript Division, Library of Congress, Washington, D.C.
NA	National Archives, Washington, D.C.
SHC	Southern History Collection, University of North Carolina at Chapel Hill, Chapel Hill, North Carolina
SL	Arthur and Elizabeth Schlesinger Library on the History of Women in America, Radcliffe College, Cambridge, Massachusetts
SS	Sophia Smith Collection, Smith College, Northampton, Massachusetts

WB	Office of Information—Records Files, Women's Bureau, Department of Labor Building, Washington, D.C.
WI	Manuscript Division, The Wisconsin State Historical Society, Madison, Wisconsin
WS	Wayne State Labor Archives, Wayne State University, Detroit, Michigan

AS MINORITY
BECOMES
MAJORITY

Introduction

In 1920, the year Congress established the United States Women's Bureau in the Department of Labor to "investigate and improve the condition of working women," Secretary of Labor William Wilson wrote in explanation, "We are safeguarding the mothers of tomorrow. All will agree that women in industry would not exist in an ideal scheme."[1] Secretary Wilson's "ideal scheme" had, in fact, never existed. American women had always worked in a variety of occupations. A few colonial women, aided by a relatively fluid social structure, a shortage of labor, and the absence of formal training for the professions, had worked as millers, carpenters, pewterers, shipwrights, lawyers, and shopkeepers.[2]

Throughout the nineteenth century, women workers had been young, single, poor, largely unorganized, badly trained, and ill-paid. Most worked as domestic servants, tobacco processors, or garment workers. Almost all labored long hours. Those who worked outside their homes frequently risked their health in unsanitary and dangerous factories. Clearly, the nineteenth-century literary image of women as delicate, retiring, religiously devout creatures unsuited for paid labor was idealized. Though marriage, not employment, remained the focus of most women's lives and usually ended outside employment, by mid-century tens of thousands of single women had contributed six to eight years of wages to their families before leaving full-time employment to become wives.

By 1870, one of every four nonagricultural workers was a woman. Even unmarried women of the middle class had begun seeking work as schoolteachers, librarians, secretaries, and clerks. And, for many, paid labor did not end with marriage. Though few married women of any class earned wages outside their homes, only upper-class women enjoyed leisure. To increase the family income, working-class married women routinely took in laundry, operated boarding houses, or did piecework such as making silk flowers.[3]

At the outset of the twentieth century, women workers, especially those who left the home to work, illustrated the changes brought by industrialization. These changes were harbingers of the kinds of major economic shifts that would result in the twentieth century from the increasing importance of the clerical and service sectors. In 1870, 70 percent of all working women were domestic servants. By 1920, that percentage had fallen to 18.2 percent. In contrast, the percentage of women working in factories increased from 17.6 percent in 1870 to 23.8 percent in 1920. Over one-quarter of employed women were in offices in 1920. Only 5 percent had worked as clerks in 1870. In sum, by 1920, women in significant numbers were already working in occupations that were to expand rapidly in the coming fifty years.[4]

Public concern for women workers had preceded the twentieth century government efforts that will be the subject of this study. Throughout the nineteenth century, philanthropists and social activists saw working women as risks both to themselves and to a social order that idealized the woman as wife, mother, and defender of the home. Dozens of private organizations such as the New York Female Moral Reform Society, the Charity Organization Society, and the Florence Crittendon Mission sought to establish homes to reclaim and uplift destitute working girls or prostitutes, to educate immigrant girls, and to provide wholesome recreation for women factory workers.

The early twentieth-century movement generally called Progressivism included a search by reformers for different means to achieve similar ends of education, protection, and uplift for women workers. Still interested in wholesome recreation and proper environments for women whose idealized role was that of wife and mother, Progressives concerned with the issues raised by women workers demanded that state action supplement or, in some cases, supersede the work of private charities. Secretary Wilson's explanation that organizing a Women's Bureau was "protecting the mothers of tomorrow" accurately reflected a Progressive ethos which argued that, through regulation and investigation, public institutions could safeguard the family assaulted by rapid economic and social change. The Women's Bureau, a victory for Progressive social reformers, was the brainchild of social activists who also lobbied successfully for a federally funded infant and maternal health care program, for a Children's Bureau, and for compulsory education laws to keep children in school and out of factories. These programs were of an intellectual piece, government action to protect actual or potential families.[5]

The Women's Bureau, the core of the federal program for female workers until the 1960s, was a Progressive legacy steeped in the Progressive idea that women workers needed a government advocate to help keep them fit for present or future domestic obligations. The fact that the agency lobbied for equal pay as well as for special job restrictions and protection for women workers meant that a self-contradiction stayed at the center of federal policy for decades.

The Bureau's adherence to scientific management and data collection, and its advocacy of protective labor legislation and government investigations of the health and home life conditions of women workers linked the Progressive and Eisenhower eras. Any study analyzing federal policy on women workers from the 1920s through the early 1960s should view the Women's Bureau as a central, though not necessarily powerful, federal voice. Bureau employees consorted with or battled against other officials or bodies that were temporarily assigned some supervision of working women from 1920 to 1963.

The present study will explain federal reaction to female wage earning from 1920 to 1963 by looking at the Women's Bureau as primary and by interpreting other temporary federal responses to problems encountered by women wage earners as secondary. The New Deal Schools and Camps for Unemployed Women, the Women's Advisory Committee to the World War II War Manpower Commission, and the Kennedy Presidential Advisory Commission on the Status of Women serve as examples of other federal policies and programs not engineered in the offices of the Women's Bureau. Why federal executive policy toward female workers during this forty-year period merits attention is a question easily answered. Four major reasons emerge.

First, a study of federal responses to female wage earning illustrates twentieth-century government response to a phenomenon of major social and economic importance. Columbia University economist Eli Ginzberg argued in 1977 that of all events affecting Western societies from the early to the mid-twentieth century changes in female employment patterns—not the atomic bomb, not the Russian Revolution—had proved most "revolutionary."[6] In unprecedented ways, the composition of the American female labor force had changed dramatically. In 1920, the average woman worker resembled her nineteenth-century counterpart. She was young, single, and working-class. By 1963, she was middle-aged, married—and when her income was combined with her husband's—middle-class. The results of these changes would be difficult to overstate.

One image used to illustrate federal bureaucratic growth in the twentieth century fits new government agencies with extended octopus-like tentacles which for the first time probed every corner of American society to investigate and regulate social and economic behavior. The federal effort to monitor and supervise the phenomenon of paid female labor during this period of significant changes provides a good example through which to examine the strength or even the existence of those tentacles.

Second, a study of federal involvement with the female labor question during these years will illustrate the complex connections between women's and reform organizations and the government. Emboldened by the suffrage victory and the significant wartime contributions women had made, Progressives, especially women Progressives, led a successful campaign to transform the World War I Woman-in-Industry Service into a permanent agency named the Women's Bureau. Other reformers, men and women, in such organizations as the League of Women Voters, the Women's Trade Union League, and the National Consumers' League, continued through four decades to support the Women's Bureau and other temporary or subsidiary federal responses. The link between these groups was a belief in the value of gradual reform and the use of the apparatus of the existing political structures to achieve it. A history of federal response can provide a focus for studying government relationships with unions, workers, employers, and the numerous organizations interested in the welfare of women workers.

Third, the work histories of members of the Women's Bureau and other temporary agencies implementing federal policy provide material for an analysis of women government professionals over a period of years. Although women led such agencies as the Children's Bureau in the Department of Labor and the Bureau of Home Economics in the Department of Agriculture, these women directed agencies less exclusively and consistently staffed by women. While other male-led and staffed agencies investigated traditional "women's" issues—among them child health, child labor, food purity, and the safety of products used in the home—the "woman-worker" issue, the one with the greatest social and economic implications, was the issue most clearly relegated to the woman government professional.[7]

The mandate given the Women's Bureau in 1920 to "investigate and improve" the condition of women workers implied an advocacy of reform. Indeed, that problem—how to urge reform from within the government—provides the fourth major justification for this inquiry into federal reaction to female wage earning.

From the 1920s through the mid-1960s, most federal bureaucrats concerned with the problems of working women dealt in influence, not power. Most were advisors, without enforcement authority. They could not compel industries to obey their recommendations. Nor could they force male-led unions to treat women workers fairly. Yet the majority of these bureaucrats in the Women's Bureau and in other programs appeared sincerely to desire to reform a system that damned women workers to low pay and little advancement. Although often patronizing, their concern, especially for blue-collar women forced into the labor market by economic circumstances, was genuine.

Working with the status quo, federal bureaucrats sought to improve the position of working women. That status quo forced most women workers during the four decades examined here to labor under unfair conditions. Federal bureaucrats paid to catalog problems facing working women, paid to write reports, summarize statistics, and supervise programs, sometimes saw themselves as paid to advocate improvements for working women. These bureaucrats were women workers themselves, but for the most part their perception of improvements meant changes in working conditions for women of a different class, a different professional and educational status. Women's Bureau members, indeed, were frequent spokespersons for the need for adequate seating in Delaware canneries and for proper toilet facilities in Ohio bakeries.

These bureaucrats, as reformers within government, were, to use Peter Gay's phrase, "Outsiders as Insiders." Though they often attacked an economic system that made women the cheapest source of labor even in good times, as "Insiders" they did not advocate major structural changes. Agents of the Women's Bureau and allied smaller programs could not do so; they were part of the system they received pay to investigate. They were middle-class working women who sought not a revolution in women's roles but programs and legislation that they justified primarily as being in the best interests of lower-class women. As "Insiders," these federal bureaucrats defended some traditional notions of special female roles. They argued, for instance, that their defense of the right of married women to work did not impugn the traditional duties of wives. As "Outsiders," however, Bureau members and others were gadflies, criticizing inequities in industry and unions and unfair practices that were condoned by other, more powerful, federal agencies. Perhaps more interestingly, the administrators of the committees and bureaus to be studied here clearly recognized that better conditions for working women could never be achieved solely through government efforts. In fact, Women's Bureau members continually urged women to organize and to lobby on their own behalf, correctly implying that without organized support, the Bureau would have little influence. In 1920, Mary Anderson, head of the new Women's Bureau, urged women to form a "universal union" concerned with hours, wages, conditions, and equal pay.[8] In 1936, Assistant Director of the Women's Bureau Bertha Nienburg counseled:

Men are busy reshaping man's world in a man's way. . . . Men will not reshape the world for women. Women themselves must bring into play the humanizing factors which will affect economic forces. They must determine the part women are to play in the country's economic life of tomorrow.[9]

And in 1947, new Director Frieda Miller argued:

In the final analysis working women realize that they must turn to other women for the help they need for attainment of their post-war objectives. To be sure, understanding and fairness are needed in other quarters from employers, city planners, and key individuals in every locality of the nation. For the real impetus to their post-war drive, however, they must look to other women.[10]

But a "universal union" of women never emerged. Women workers did not vote as a bloc. They provided no powerful lobby, either for themselves or for the work of the Women's Bureau.

And that work provoked criticism both from those, including some women workers, who argued that the Bureau and its allies supported a discriminatory political system and from those who argued that they sought to undermine the system. For quite different reasons, many saw the Women's Bureau as a Fifth Column. Forced to straddle fences, it and other agencies proved easy targets.

Befitting an "Outsider" status, all the federal efforts here examined remained small, poorly funded, or temporary—losers in a broker state best attuned to the needs of powerful constituencies. During the years 1920-1963, the Bureau never exceeded seventy-five employees, or a yearly budget of $200,000, though the same years saw the proliferation of other agencies and greatly expanded federal budgets.[11] In light of such facts, for four decades the Women's Bureau's instructions to "formulate standards and policies to promote the welfare of wage-earning women, to improve their working conditions, and increase and advance their opportunities for profitable employment" were primarily statements of federal concern about the social and economic problems faced by many working women. Focusing on the theme of Outsider-Insider, this study grapples with the inherent limits of such concern.

The year 1963 is a watershed date and marks a convenient chronological end to this study. In 1963, Congress finally passed an Equal Pay Act requiring that women receive equal pay for equal work. The act signaled a major change in the federal posture toward female workers and was the first of several national laws forbidding sex discrimination and establishing the means to enforce that prohibition. Analysis of these laws is beyond the bounds of this study. The four decades between the establishment of the Women's

Bureau and the passage of the Equal Pay Act stand in recent American history not merely as time before the Divide but as a period during which federal officials accepted certain ideas about government responsibilities toward working women. These ideas led to decades of support for protective labor legislation. The histories of the government agencies and programs to be analyzed here not only trace forty years of government policy but also raise questions about definitions of and conditions for government-imposed reform.

NOTES

1. William Wilson, "Explanations for the Women's Bureau" (memorandum copy) , 1920, Records of the Women's Bureau, "Secretaries of Labor Files," R.G. 86, National Archives, Washington, D.C. (hereafter cited as WB, NA).

2. See Julia Spruill, *Women's Life and Work in the Southern Colonies* (Chapel Hill: University of North Carolina Press, 1938); Sophie Drinker, "Women Attorneys of Colonial Times," *Maryland Historical Magazine,* 56 (December 1961).

3. See United States Bureau of the Census, *Comparative Occupation Statistics for the United States 1870-1940* (Washington, D.C.: Government Printing Office, 1943); for further information about female work patterns, see Gerda Lerner, "The Lady and the Mill Girl," *Mid-Continent American Studies Journal,* 10 (1969); Mary Ryan, "American Society and the Cult of Domesticity, 1830-1860" (Ph.D. dissertation, University of California at Santa Barbara, 1971); Carl Degler, *At Odds: Women and the Family in America from the Revolution to the Present* (New York: Oxford University Press, 1980); Tamara Hareven, ed., *Transitions: The Family and the Life Course in Historical Perspective* (New York: Academic Press, 1978); Alice Kessler-Harris, "Women's Wage Work as Myth and History," *Labor History,* 19:2 (Spring 1978), pp. 287-307.

4. For discussion of theories about female labor force trends, see Valerie Oppenheimer, *The Female Labor Force in the United States, Demographic and Economic Factors Governing its Growth and Changing Composition,* Population Monograph Series, 5 (University of California, Berkeley, 1970); Richard Edwards, Michael Reich, David Gordon, *Labor Market Segmentation* (New York: Lexington, 1975).

5. For an introduction to historical interpretations of the Progressive years, see Robert Wiebe, "The Progressive Years," in William Cartwright and Richard Watson, *The Reinterpretation of American History and Culture* (Washington, D.C.: National Council for the Social Studies, 1973),

pp. 425-443. Sheila Rothman's *Woman's Proper Place: A History of Changing Ideals and Practices, 1870 to the Present* (New York: Basic Books, 1978) provides a good introduction to Progressive definitions of "woman's proper place." Rothman persuasively argues that Progressive policies could be called an ideology of "educated motherhood," with a woman's present or future duties to family paramount.

6. Quoted in *The New York Times,* November 29, 1977.

7. "Survey of Women in Public Office," Comp. LWV (mimeograph, typescript), Bx. 834, WB, NA.

8. "Women's Future Position in Industry," *American Industries,* 3 (Summer 1920), p. 28.

9. Bertha Nienburg, "The Role of Women in the Nation's Wealth Production," speech before Board of Directors of the General Federation of Women's Clubs, January 15, 1936, "Speech File #341-S-147," WB, NA.

10. Frieda Miller, address before 21st Woman's Patriotic Conference on National Defense at the Hotel Statler, Washington, D.C., January 25, 1947 (typescript), Frieda Miller Papers, Folder 199, Schlesinger Library (hereafter cited as SL).

11. These figures have been calculated using figures taken from *Annual Reports of the Secretaries of Labor 1920-63* (Washington, D.C.: Government Printing Office, 1921-64).

Progressivism and the Female Labor Question: The Birth of the Women's Bureau

2

In 1921, Mary Anderson, director of the newly established Women's Bureau within the Department of Labor, assessed the future position of women in industry and the need for her agency by remarking:

> I think of Mrs. Poyser and the cat. "I ain't one to see a cat walking into a dairy and wonder what she's come after." Women have walked into the great industrial concerns. If at first they took the skim milk jobs, the cream of the jobs should as naturally be theirs as the men's.[1]

The cream of the jobs, however, did not come to women. As an unorganized and largely powerless group, women wage earners routinely labored for low wages at repetitive jobs that carried no responsibility. Many worked in dangerous or unsanitary places.

The woman worker was an underdog, forced by circumstances to work inefficiently for an inadequate return. Few working women held jobs requiring professional degrees or apprenticeship training. Few had significant opportunities for job advancement. Few worked at the same job for many years.[2] The idea that a federal bureau could improve working conditions for these women through collecting data, exposing abuse, and advising standards, was one far more natural to the era than was Anderson's idea that good jobs should naturally be shared with women. The Women's Bureau

that Progressive reformers urged was to be a symbol of government awareness of the special problems caused by women in the
labor force, especially those problems perceived as actual or potential threats to the family or to the future health of the nation. The
number and percentage of women at work had grown dramatically
since the late nineteenth century. From 1870—when federal census
figures for women workers began to be kept—until World War I,
percentage increases among women workers far outstripped the
growth of the female population.[3] Almost one-fifth of all workers
by the turn of the century, employed women were typically young—
in their teens or twenties. The general press picture of the working
woman as a young girl, a "typewriter," carefree in Gibson shirt-
waist, or as a sweatshop seamstress, begrimed in immigrant's shawl,
was not completely inaccurate. The Progressive reformer saw her
as a figure needing supervision and protection, provided by government, not by private organizations.[4]

Reconstructing early twentieth century public reaction to the
problems encountered by working women is difficult. Reconstructing the reactions of community leaders, politicians, and reformers
is less so. Progressives voiced alarm about the damaged health of
women workers and the future chances of weak babies, diminished
birth rates, and "race suicide." Government action would be in
women's interests and in the nation's interests. The idea that the
federal government had a duty to regulate dangerous and unhealthy
industrial conditions and a duty to ensure the welfare of those who
could not protect themselves was an essential part of the Progressive
vision. So, too, was the belief that efficient and scientifically
planned government fact-finding could solve problems as varied
as productivity in canneries and ill health among the poor. Indeed,
the Progressive movement was not so much an easily identifiable
political or social program as a collection of causes with one common goal: a safer and more orderly society. Social reformers concerned about the dangers that industrialization and urbanization
posed to traditional family patterns demanded a variety of kinds of
state intervention. Pure food and drug regulation, mandatory public
schooling, laws to govern child labor were other items on an agenda
that included statements of the need for a government agency to
campaign for the proper protection of women. As such, the establishment of a federal Women's Bureau was one objective of activists

primarily intent on protecting children and families, not on changing the social roles given women.[5]

In 1905, Mary McDowell and her co-workers Edith Abbott and Sophonisba Breckenridge, all prominent Progressives connected with the University of Chicago Settlement House, began to campaign for a federal agency to "collect data of national scope on the problems of working women."[6] Within months, the Chicago Settlement House had recruited the support of the Women's Trade Union League (WTUL) and had established a committee made up of McDowell, Jane Addams, Margaret Dreier Robins, and Lillian Wald to lobby for a survey of women in industry and for the eventual establishment of a federal Women's Bureau. In the fall of 1905, McDowell and Addams journeyed to Washington to petition President Theordore Roosevelt. In response to their plea for a systematic investigation of the status of women in industry, he responded, "Of course we should have it. I'll do what I can. You get the women's clubs behind you."[7] Aptly, President Roosevelt counseled the two Chicago women to contact the women's clubs because middle-class "ladies bountiful," together with professional social workers, led the campaign for the Women's Bureau. The fact that the WTUL helped initiate the drive for a Women's Bureau and remained its staunch ally for decades illustrates the power balance within the League, not a classic trade union but a hybrid of educated middle-class "allies" and actual women workers. The middle-class leadership of the WTUL proposed the Women's Bureau as an investigatory tool, an agency through which to educate the public about the needs of women workers, not an agency that would participate in a grass roots union organization or support the principle of a union shop.[8] Main-line unions expressed little interest. In 1900, fewer than 3 percent of all women workers belonged to American Federation of Labor (AFL) affiliates. Trade union leaders perceived women as poorly paid, temporary workers, not worth recruiting, and as potential job threats whose real place was in the home as wives and mothers. Few AFL officials thought a permanent Women's Bureau necessary.[9]

Since female trade unionists exercised little power and male union leaders lent little enthusiasm, Mary McDowell and her committee threw a wide net in search of support. Civic organizations like the National Consumers' League (NCL), which had battled since the

1890s for the improvement of working conditions for women, joined in the appeal, which was finally successful in 1910, for a thorough Congressional investigation of conditions faced by working women. From 1910 to 1912, Charles Neill of the Department of Commerce and Labor directed a survey whose results filled nineteen volumes. This survey showed that women toiled as an exploited, indeed sweated, group earning, on average, one-third to one-half of male wages in horrendous factory conditions guaranteed to produce exhaustion and illness.[10]

One outcome of the Neill investigation was the establishment of a Women's Division within the Bureau of Labor Statistics. Unfortunately, the Women's Division was an unqualified failure. Its female agents were paid disproportionately low wages, and the director of the Bureau of Labor Statistics frequently diverted money from the Division's meager budget to other Bureau investigations. The women agents responsible for writing a report on unemployment among women in the retail stores of Boston charged that their statistics had been tampered with by the time the study reached print and so refused to sign the completed copy. In 1915, only four years after its inception, all the women in the Division had resigned, citing unfair wages and the sabotage of their work. The Bureau hired no replacements, and the Division died.[11]

Despite such a dismal precedent, a coalition of women's and consumer's groups continued to lobby actively for a permanent and separate Women's Bureau within the newly established Department of Labor. The AFL, which had given the campaign that resulted in the Neill survey at least a lukewarm endorsement, remained cool to the idea of a permanent Women's Bureau, even though WTUL organizers made repeated efforts to win AFL support. Mary Anderson, who was soon to leave her work as an organizer for the WTUL to begin a career of government service, encountered typical resistance at the AFL national convention in 1916. When she asked for support for a resolution favoring a federal Women's Bureau, one delegate, John Ramsay, rose to reply. "I shall be brief," he said, "but I am opposed to this resolution for the purpose of giving some hi-falutin lady an opportunity to make surveys and find out how cold a working woman's feet are in a department where she is employed. I am sick and tired of this idea of having some of these silk stocking hi-falutin uplifters telling the working women how cold their feet are." To no avail, Anderson responded that no such women would end up heading a Women's Bureau. Members of the AFL vetoed support for the resolution despite Anderson's plea that "You men know as well as I do that our women are going into the factories and taking the places of men for half the wages. We have to find out what is happening."[12]

Senator Wesley Jones, Republican from the state of Washington, introduced a bill in 1916 calling for the creation of a Woman's Bureau in the Department of Labor, separate from the Bureau of Labor Statistics, with adequate salaries and independent appropriations. Despite a vigorous letter-writing campaign led by the NCL, the bill remained buried in committee.[13]

With organized labor unsupportive and Congress apathetic, the Women's Bureau forces appeared stymied. World War I broke that stalemate. Harriet Stanton Blatch, suffragist and writer, exclaimed, "War compels women to work. . . . That is one of its merits . . . the rapidly increasing employment of women today then is the usual and happy accompaniment of war."[14] Three million men entered military service; women quickly filled their places, working in heretofore male-dominated fields, as electricians, mechanics, carpenters, farmers, bus drivers, and train operators. They were working at jobs unusual for women, but few were working at paid employment for the first time. A retrospective Women's Bureau survey estimated that sixty-five percent had come from other factories, 25 percent from household service, 5 percent from laundries, and that only 5 percent had entered the work force for the first time during the war.[15]

The jobs were new, even if the workers were seasoned, yet the network of planning agencies spawned by the war emergency gave only scant attention to women workers. The Council of National Defense (CND) did establish a women's committee that sent investigators to war production plants, shipyards, and armories and advised the government on how best to utilize and accommodate women workers. The Women's Committee took such work seriously, and many members resented the fact that most members of the CND saw it as frivolous. For example, when members of the Women's Committee learned that the CND had originally sought the actress Lillian Russell to lead the women's effort, they protested vigorously. As a result, Dr. Anna Howard Shaw took the chair instead. Members also resented the lack of funds, especially for any investigative work, and continually petitioned Congress to establish a separate agency to advise on questions of female wartime industrial service. A few wartime departments such as the Ordnance Department established special sections to deal with problems encountered by women workers, but Congress did not fund a separate Woman-in-Industry Service until July 1918, a few months before the Armistice.[16]

The end of the war threatened the existence of the Woman-in-Industry Service, which, as a war emergency agency, received money only for the duration of the war. In 1919, however, Congress voted to extend the Service for one year to smooth the transition back to peacetime industrial conditions. Then, in 1920, Senator William Kenyon of Iowa co-sponsored a bill with Congressman Philip Campbell of Kansas to make the Woman-in-Industry Service a permanent Women's Bureau within the Department of Labor, mandated "to formulate standards to promote the welfare of wage earning women, to improve their working conditions, increase their efficiency and advance their opportunities for profitable employment."[17]

Congressman John Raker, Democrat from California, also submitted a bill to establish a permanent Women's Bureau during the 1920 Congressional session, and the Joint Committee on Labor Hearings debated the merits of both bills. Raker's testimony stressed the theme of the hearings: the need of the woman worker for wise and benevolent state protection. As Raker put it, "The delicate character of women is such that it is incumbent upon us to look out for them. When they leave their work, they must leave it with strong, healthy minds and bodies, so that they may do their functions as American citizens and contribute to the vitality of coming generations."[18] Although Raker supported most of the wording of the Kenyon/Campbell measure and agreed that the bills were similar, he took pains to note that in his proposal a federal Women's Bureau would specifically supervise the adjustment of modern industrial management to the "nervous organization" of women and investigate the influence of industrial employment upon the subsequent home life of wage-earning women. In fact, Raker went on to propose that Women's Bureau agents make long-range studies that would follow working women even after they left the labor force to see whether their experiences as wage earners had harmful effects on the home.[19] In a heated exchange, Joint Committee member Congressman John MacCrate of New York criticized Raker's suggestion as dangerous, setting government agents on the loose, "permitted to go into every home in the country and ask questions."[20] Raker, interrupting MacCrate, answered, "My dear sir, where else can you get better first hand information than to go to the homes? Is it not what this legislation is primarily for: the benefit of a woman after she leaves her work as well as while she works?"[21] MacCrate, himself interrupting, replied, "Of course not. Women are in industries, and are going in in greater numbers. A great many women do not want a man but prefer work. They are the objects of this legislation."[22] Unconvinced, Raker shouted, "99% of women have the desire to marry."[23] Eventually, the Joint Committee approved the more strictly worded Kenyon/Campbell bill, which instructed the proposed Women's Bureau to investigate conditions under which women worked, rather than Raker's more ambitious scheme to examine conditions while working and conditions after working "to try and keep a healthy race."[24] The transcripts kept of the hearings reveal, however, that Raker's concern for the sanctity of the home and the health of future mothers surfaced again and again among supporters of the proposed Bureau. In no real way was the final approval of the more narrowly worded Kenyon/Campbell bill a repudiation of Raker's classically Progressive concern for "educated motherhood."

A union representative, Henry Sterling, for instance, was equally concerned about social stability and the nervous temperaments of women. He argued, "There are women in industry, and a very great number of them work under conditions that are deplorable. They need the mothering that women can bring them, that men cannot."[25] Many at the hearings to lobby for the establishment of a permanent Women's Bureau agreed with Sterling. An agency established to protect the downtrodden, to lobby for safe conditions in industry, and to help guarantee the vitality of the race by encouraging a wholesome product and a healthy worker would fulfill several Progressive objectives at once.

Echoing Progressive concerns for scientific management and efficiency, many Congressmen demanded assurance that a separate Women's Bureau would not duplicate effort at the Department of Labor. Dr. Royal Meeker, commissioner of the Bureau of Labor

Statistics, testified that, while cooperating government bureaus always risked that problem, no such waste had occurred between his bureau and the already established Woman-in-Industry Service. He also agreed with members of the Women's National Committee of the National Democratic Committee and with Mary Van Kleeck, former head of the Woman-in-Industry Service, that, while other departments of the government collected information that dealt with women workers, the Women's Bureau could act to coordinate and interpret such information as well as collect additional information.[26]

To MacCrate's question, "Is it not a matter of fact that the establishment of all these bureaus draws good brains from production and puts them to card indexing here in Washington?" Mary Van Kleeck responded that Women's Bureau workers would not confine themselves to pushing papers.[27] Moreover, she noted acidly, "The people who manage the card indexes here have not generally figured in manufacturing."[28]

Whether the Women's Bureau would draw talented women away from more productive work was an issue that remained moot. Many who testified agreed, however, that an independent Women's Bureau would be more likely to attract "good brains," women of training and ability, than those with subordinate status. In doing so, more witnesses placed emphasis on the need for a woman-staffed agency than they did on the possibilities that an independent bureau would bring for recruiting women of ability. Mary Stewart, executive secretary of the Women's Committee of the National Republican Committee, asked, "Can you conceive of a Department of Labor manned entirely by women studying the conditions that affect the men in this country?"[29] Indeed, the testimony of many witnesses emphasized not just the need for talented female economists and statisticians, but the need for an element which, for lack of a better term, might be called the female presence. This was best summed up in Dr. Royal Meeker's explanation of the significance of a Women's Bureau, "You cannot make a man into a woman; you cannot make a woman into a man."[30]

Once out of committee, the bill was easily passed through Congress, and the Bureau officially began life in June 1920, within weeks of the ratification of the Nineteenth Amendment.[31] Though touted in the press as an example of the changes to be wrought by voting women, the Bureau was not well financed, and annual appropriations remained small for decades. Women statisticians and other professionals within the Bureau received lower salaries than did men doing comparable work in other bureaus and divisions within the Department of Labor, and the Civil Service Reclassification Act of 1923 did not remedy the inequity.[32]

Still, World War I and the immediate postwar years were years of excitement for the "Woman Citizen." Both a permanent Women's Bureau and woman suffrage were victories that had been accelerated by the Great War. Women officials from both the Democratic and Republican parties appeared to testify at the Congressional hearings for the establishment of a Women's Bureau, and significantly each party's representatives threatened female voter reprisal should plans for the Bureau be scotched.[33]

Writers of the 1920s saw the American woman emerging from World War I into a New Era of expanded economic opportunities. Louis Dublin, chief statistician for the Metropolitan Life Insurance Company restated many popular assumptions when he wrote: "The whole aspect of a woman's life has been changed, and community life has been correspondingly transformed."[34]

Women active as lobbyists for government protection of women workers reflected some of the enthusiasm. Indeed, a few argued that the proposed Women's Bureau could eventually relinquish most of its guardian functions as women achieved economic equality; they argued against too close an alliance with its already established sister agency, the Children's Bureau. Children would always be dependent creatures. Such status was temporary simply because children became adults. But women workers were adults. Mary Van Kleeck, formerly of the Women-in-Industry Service, cited instance after instance where untrained or poorly trained women had replaced experienced men at jobs during the war emergency only to quickly match or outproduce previous records. Women had "proved themselves at the drill presses and lathes." They deserved opportunities to train as permanent, skilled workers for these and other nontraditional tasks. They deserved equal consideration for entrance into the professions. A Women's Bureau, as fact finder and policy maker, could provide the necessary guidance as women entered new careers. The women workers so helped would soon require no further government supervision at all.[35] Van Kleeck's arguments were those of a minority, however. They were not the arguments that persuaded Congress to authorize the Bureau. Van Kleeck herself had resigned from government service at the end of the war.

Despite Louis Dublin's assessment, community life was not transformed by women's activities during the 1920s. The women who had driven taxis, piloted trains, laid bricks, and made bullets during World War I soon returned to their traditional, low-paying jobs. And those women who had indeed proved themselves at drill presses and lathes received few opportunities to increase their skills. A number of organizations such as the NCL and the WTUL that had fought for the Women's Bureau lost membership and funding in the 1920s. Others, including the Daughters of the American Revolution (DAR), shifted from supporting the Women's Bureau to making false accusations that it provided a haven for Reds and support for socialist doctrine.[36] Progressive programs supported by allies of the Women's Bureau met defeat. In 1921, the Sheppard Towner Act authorized the first federally funded public health program to provide states with matching funds to establish infant and maternity care centers. By 1929, bowing to pressure from the American Medical Association, which wanted all medical practice private, Congress killed the program. Organized labor experienced hard times in the 1920s, with unsuccessful strikes, adverse court decisions, open shops, and other developments leading to debilitating losses in membership. Often shunned by male-dominated unions— and on the bottom of the wage ladder in most industries—female workers proved to be a most vulnerable segment of the labor force.[37]

The Women's Bureau, then, began poorly funded, understaffed, in most ways ill-equipped to make significant efforts to "promote the welfare of wage-earning women" in the face of such overwhelming problems. The Progressive reform impulses that had created the Bureau, however, did not die in the 1920s. The very fact that the Bureau continued to exist provided one tangible proof of that. The agency organized conferences attended by employers, trade unionists, middle-class reformers, and women's organizations of widely differing ideologies. Its agents investigated factories, compiled statistics, interviewed workers, and published the results in a steady stream of Women's Bureau *Bulletins.* The Bureau provided information, counsel, and leadership to other federal committees and temporary agencies.

It sought to help women workers by campaigning for industrial standards that included equal pay for equal work, but it also campaigned for special protection for women workers, for night-work prohibitions, for an eight-hour day and six-day week, for weight-lifting limits, and for special facilities in factories that employed women so that, in effect, large numbers of women would not perform their duties under circumstances that were likely to be construed as equal work. Given the weak and unorganized position of women wage earners and the burden of their domestic duties, the Women's Bureau argued, they were unable to bargain equally with men for their rights as workers, even if they were granted legal equality in all spheres through constitutional amendment. Promoting themselves as protectors of working women and advocates of their economic advance, the members of the Women's Bureau were disciples of the self-contradictory Progressive philosophies that had prompted the federal government to institutionalize a recognition of working women.

NOTES

1. "The Future Position of Women in Industry," *American Industries,* December 1921, p. 28.

2. A whole series of contemporary books and studies documented the appalling conditions under which women labored. See Louise Bosworth, *The Living Wage of Women Workers, Incomes of 450 Women Workers in Boston* (Philadelphia: Women's Educational and Industrial Union, 1911); H. B. Wolfe, "Wartime Industrial Employment of Women in the United States," *Journal of Political Economy,* 27 (October 1919); Elizabeth Butler, *Women and the Trades, Pittsburgh, 1907-08* (New York: International Pub., 1926).

3. Decennial Census, *Data on the Female Labor Force,* 1870-1960, 1960 Census of Population, v. 1, *Characteristics of the Population,* pt. 1., U.S. Summary Table, p. 195; Alba Edwards, *Comparative Occupational Statistics for the United States,* 1870-1940, Bureau of the Census (Washington, D.C.: Government Printing Office, 1943); A. J. Jaffe, "Trends in the Participation of Women in the Working Force," *Monthly Labor Review,* 79 (May 1956), p. 560; Robert Smith, "The Female Labor Force: A Case Study in the Interpretation of Historical Statistics," *Journal of the American Statistical Association,* 55 (March 1960), pp. 71-79.

4. Hadley Cantril, *Public Opinion* (Princeton: Princeton University Press, 1951), pp. 35-60.

5. Samuel Haber, *Efficiency and Uplift, Scientific Management in the*

Progressive Era (Chicago: University of Chicago Press, 1964); Robert Wiebe, *The Search for Order,* 1877-1920 (New York: Hill and Wang, 1967); Robert Bremner, *From the Depths, The Discovery of Poverty in the United States* (New York: New York University Press, 1956); Peter Filene, "An Obituary for the Progressive Movement," *American Quarterly* (Spring 1970), pp. 20-34; Sheila Rothman, *Woman's Proper Place* (New York: Basic Books, 1978). Rothman, in a very interesting chapter, ties together Progressive programs designed to affect women, using the term "educated motherhood."

6. McDowell, quoted in Howard Wilson, *Mary McDowell, Neighbor* (Chicago: University of Chicago Press, 1928), p. 125.

7. Roosevelt, quoted in Wilson, *Mary McDowell,* p. 126.

8. William Chafe, *The American Woman, Her Changing Social, Economic, and Political Role, 1920-1970* (New York: Oxford University Press, 1972), pp. 71-79; Allen F. Davis, "The W.T.U.L.—Origins and Organization," *Labor History,* 5 (Winter 1964).

9. J. Stanley Lemons, *The Woman Citizen, Social Feminism in the 1920s* (Urbana: University of Illinois Press, 1973), p. 26; Katherine Fisher, "Women Workers and the AF of L," *New Republic,* August 3, 1921, p. 265; John Andrews, "History of Women in Trade Unions," v. 10, U.S. Department of Labor, *Report on the Condition of Women and Child Wage Earners in the United States,* S. Doc. 645, 61st Cong., 2nd Sess. (Washington, D.C.: Government Printing Office, 1910-1912).

10. U.S. Department of Labor, *Report on the Condition of Women and Child Wage Earners,* 19 v., 1910-1913.

11. "What Uncle Sam Does Not Do for Women," *New Republic,* 7 (July 29, 1916), p. 324.

12. Transcript of Minutes (fragment) AFL National Convention, Baltimore, MD, November 23, 1916, Bx. 21, Women's Trade Union League Papers, Library of Congress, Washington, D.C. (hereafter cited as WTUL, LC).

13. National Consumers League Papers at the Library of Congress include thick files of letters written by chapters across the country requesting congressmen to endorse Jones' bill, S. 5408. NCL Papers, L.C., Bx. C-63 (hereafter cited as NCL, LC).

14. "Mobilizing Women Power" (New York: Women's Press, 1918), quoted in Lemons, *The Woman Citizen,* p. 15.

15. "The New Position of Women in American Industry," Women's Bureau *Bulletin #12* (Washington, D.C.: Government Printing Office, 1920), p. 17.

16. Typed transcript (unpaginated), taped interview, between Esther Peterson and Mary Anderson (Washington, D.C., April 24, 1964), Women's Bureau Files, Office of Information, Department of Labor, Washington,

D.C.; Valborg Fletty, "Public Services of Women's Organizations" (Ph.D. dissertation, Syracuse University, 1952); Valerie Conner, " 'The Mothers of the Race' in World War I: The National War Labor Board and Women in Industry," *Labor History* (Winter 1979-80), pp. 32-40.

17. Women's Bureau Hearings, House Committee on Labor, March 4, 1920, S. 4002, H.R. 1134, 66th Cong., 2nd Sess., v. 235, pp. 2, 3, 1 (hereafter cited as Hearings).

18. Hearings, p. 11.

19. Hearings, p. 11.

20. Hearings, p. 76.

21. *Ibid.*

22. *Ibid.*

23. *Ibid.* The word *shouted* appears in the published transcript of the Hearings.

24. Hearings, p. 77.

25. Hearings, pp. 45-46, 63-64.

26. Hearings, p. 64.

27. *Ibid.*

28. Hearings, p. 48.

29. Hearings, p. 40.

30. *Ibid.*

31. Taped interview, typed transcript, Esther Peterson and Mary Anderson, April 24, 1964.

32. Women's Bureau *Bulletin #53,* "The Status of Women in Government Service in 1925" (Washington, D.C.: Government Printing Office, 1926).

33. Hearings, p. 43.

34. "Homemaking and Careers," *Atlantic Monthly* (September 1926), p. 336.

35. "What Women Can Do," *Proceedings of the Academy of Political Science,* v. 8 (February 1919), p. 3.

36. For analyses of women's economic opportunities in the New Era, see Chafe, *The American Woman,* pp. 48-65; Lemons, *The Women Citizen,* pp. 1-115; Sophonisba Breckenridge, *Women in the Twentieth Century* (Recent Social Trends Monograph, New York: McGraw-Hill, 1933).

37. Lemons, *The Woman Citizen,* pp. 118-149; Dorothy Johnson, "Organized Women and National Legislation, 1920-1944" (Ph.D. dissertation, Western Reserve University, 1960); Dorothy Johnson, "Organized Women as Lobbyists in the 1920's," *Capital Studies,* 1 (Spring 1972), pp. 41-58. See also Records of the Women's Joint Congressional Committee (WJCC), Bx. 6-9, "Minutes of Meetings," MSS. Division, Library of Congress, Washington, D.C.

The "New Woman" and the Woman Worker: The Shaping of Government Policy During the New Era

3

The buoyant optimism that had characterized feminists and reformers in 1920 had faded by the end of the decade. Prospects for dramatic social change in the decade many contemporaries called the New Era had dimmed. The observation of Henry George that "those bent on raising wages by moral suasion alone are likely those who would tell you of tigers that live on oranges" succinctly describes the dilemma faced by the United States Women's Bureau soon after its establishment.[1] Despite its yearly efforts to lobby within the Department of Labor and before Congress for increased legal authority and bigger budgets, the Bureau remained small and at the edges of power a fate established in the 1920s that was to last for the next four decades.

Nevertheless, the Women's Bureau remained the principal federal response to the phenomenon of paid female labor until the 1960s. Two patterns emerging in the 1920s provide keys to understanding federal policy for the forty-year period, 1920-1963. The first concerns the nature of sponsorship for federal policies affecting women workers. The specialists in the Women's Bureau developed warm, supportive work relationships with their advocates within social reform and women's organizations. Hostility, however, characterized the exchanges between these same federal woman-worker experts along with their colleagues in the government bureaucracy, and the leaders of businesses and national labor unions. Lacking strong support from industrialists, bureaucratic superiors, or national union bosses, Women's Bureau agents established a network of mutually supportive relationships with women's and social reform clubs. The network, no matter how helpful, condemned the Bureau to the outer circles of power. Without the sponsorship of business, labor, or high-level government officials, the Women's Bureau had no chance to effect improvements in the working conditions of the woman worker.

Staffing and hiring practices begun in the 1920s at the Women's Bureau formed a second durable pattern. The typical Bureau agent was a white, well-educated economist. She was more likely to have seen the drawing room of the Henry Street Settlement House in New York City than to have seen a corporate boardroom or union executive's office. Few agents had personal entree with leaders of either management or labor. The confidential telegrams they sent begging for help went to the president of the League of Women Voters not to the president of the National Association of Manufacturers. Because so many of the women professionals who staffed the Women's Bureau remained loyal to their beleaguered agency, staying until forced to retire in the 1950s, they helped shape the nature of federal programs for the entire four decades.

The economists, social workers, teachers, statisticians, writers, and lawyers who arrived in Washington in 1919 and 1920 to work for the Women's Bureau inspected factories, compiled statistics, and submitted reports. From the Bureau's inception, these reports focused attention on poorly paid female industrial work. *Bulletins* published in the first few years of the Bureau's existence summarized investigations of such topics as "Women in the Candy Industry in Chicago," "Health Problems of Women in Industry," and "Lost Time and Labor Turnover in Cotton Mills."[2] An emphasis on low-skilled factory, clerical, or sales work persisted for almost four decades. An examination of the sponsorship and staffing of the Bureau helps to explain this consistency in federal reaction to women workers during years when the nature of the female labor force itself changed dramatically.

The labor specialists in the Women's Bureau found their advocates and sponsors, indeed found their unpaid co-workers, in a network of women's clubs, not within bureaucratic, industrial, or union hierarchies. An explanation of this alliance provides a matrix to use to analyze the committees, commissions, and specific programs of the Depression, war, and postwar years. An investigation of the nature of the Bureau's sponsorship also provides an opportunity to analyze its interactions with unions and management. Here again, patterns established in the 1920s proved lasting, though these latter patterns were ones of confrontation, not alliance.

Although that network of women's organizations that had agitated for a Women's Bureau continued to rise to the Bureau's defense, not all national women's organizations supported the Women's Bureau in the 1920s. In fact, the uneasy coalition of radical women's groups like the Woman's Party and moderate ones led by the National American Women's Suffrage Association that had shared the common goal of a woman suffrage amendment split apart during the 1920s, to remain disunited through the next four decades. Those groups that sponsored the Bureau were moderates, members of organizations labeled by several historians as social feminist, inheritors of suffrage campaign rhetoric that argued women wanted the vote because of their special interest in home and family rather than because they wanted to share equally in the political fray with men. By 1900, moderate leaders of the woman suffrage campaign had reorganized their strategy to focus on one key argument: Women needed the vote to protect the home. Jane Addams contended that "city housekeeping has failed partly because women, the traditional housekeepers, have not been consulted." Suffrage leaders, in effect, promised that enfranchised women would be interested in traditional women's concerns. When the feared women's bloc vote proved to be a chimera, these women's groups lost an ace they had used in the suffrage fight. Unaffiliated with other powerful business or trade organizations, they had no other cards to play.

Generally, the moderate reform groups supporting the Women's Bureau emphasized genteel behavior, in preference to hard-ball politics. The League of Women Voters, for instance, rather than seeking to act as a national pressure group for the interests of women voters, proclaimed its intention objectively to study the issues. In fact, members who wanted to run for political office had to resign from the League so as not to impugn its nonpartisan character. Militant groups like the Woman's Party, no longer tied in fragile alliance by the vision of suffrage, completely broke with moderate women's organizations, arguing that an Equal Rights

Amendment was more important than a Child Labor Amendment. Other formerly militant suffragists became adherents of international pacifism and socialism through organizations like the Women's International League for Peace and Freedom.[3]

Women's organizations moved to the right as well as to the left. By the end of the decade, the Daughters of the American Revolution found evidence of Communism almost everywhere, including the Women's Bureau. Mary Anderson, head of the Bureau, became tired of the annual DAR blacklists. She dreaded the annual DAR convention, held only blocks away from the Department of Labor Building in Washington, D.C., and called it the "Damned Annual Row."[4]

Therefore, the sponsors of the Women's Bureau were not all women's organizations, but organizations claiming the political center. Together, these organizations had many thousands of members. Their interest in close cooperation with the Women's Bureau expanded the agency's ability to do research and share information. Their interest also helped to ensure the Bureau's political survival. But these women's organizations, representing no unified women's movement with the threatened power of millions of votes and isolated from real centers of political power themselves, could not ensure that the Women's Bureau would be given serious attention in the boardrooms or cloakrooms.

The historian Estelle Freedman argues that the separate women's network that had sustained nineteenth-century women's participation in social reform and politics had begun to fall apart by 1920. The new rhetoric emphasized the rejection of separate women's spheres in politics in favor of promises of integration into male institutions. Although Freedman exaggerates the cohesive nature of nineteenth-century women's organizational networks, she correctly identifies the absence of female bloc voting and the disunity within women's groups in the 1920s as major impediments to expansion of the political gains for women signified by the Nineteenth Amendment.[5]

The extensive cooperation between the Bureau and its sponsors among women's organizations, however, provides an interesting illustration of the persistence of a form of women's network, albeit one with greatly diminished power, compared to the dreams of suffrage reformers of millions of women voting and working together as a self-consciously female political unit.

Still, Women's Bureau agents and organizational club women

certainly were women working together for political goals such as the passage of protective labor legislation. Organizations such as the Young Women's Christian Association (YWCA), the League of Women Voters (LWV), the American Association of University Women (AAUW), the Women's Christian Temperance Union (WCTU), the National Council of Catholic Women, and the National Council of Women established close and mutually productive relationships with the Women's Bureau.

Several of these groups provided detailed assistance with Bureau surveys. American Association of University Women members in several states helped canvass workers' homes and compiled cost-of-living schedules. Staff members of the AAUW began a practice that continued through the 1950s of volunteering to write the texts of some Bureau reports. The YWCA regularly offered the Women's Bureau the use of relevant records. Because many factory women and shop girls participated in YWCA educational and recreation programs, the organization often made its own extensive surveys, conducting home interviews and visiting factories. The Bureau did, in fact, use some of the YWCA's statistics and suggested joint projects such as a 1928 study of both black and white women industrial workers in Richmond, Virginia [6]

The League of Women Voters often compiled information used in Bureau surveys of women in public office and government service. Its officers helped plan Bureau campaigns during the 1920s to persuade the Bureau of the Census to revive its abandoned custom of taking the Census of Manufacturers by sex.[7] The Bureau copied a great number of speeches supplied by the League for its research files.[8]

In turn, the Women's Bureau offered help and advice. It tabulated some of the data for a League revision of outdated government surveys on the legal status of American women.[9] The WCTU distributed Women's Bureau literature when its members asked questions about problems encountered by women in industry and relied for decades on the Women's Bureau files rather than on establishing a separate department covering the problems of women in industry.[10] For all groups, the Bureau encouraged joint cooperation and "mutual aid," offering statistics, speech outlines, books, and mailing lists.[11]

The relationship between the Women's Bureau and the National Women's Trade Union League was a classic one of a close, dedicated mutual support that began in the 1920s and extended through three decades until the effective death of the WTUL in the 1950s. Some officials in the two agencies, in effect, married careers in the Women's Bureau and the WTUL.[12] Mary Anderson herself came to Washington during World War I after having spent years as an organizer for the National WTUL.[13] Elizabeth Christman, who capped decades of informal advice with work as a special Bureau agent during World War II, returned to her duties as secretary-treasurer of the WTUL only after it informed her that she was indispensable.[14]

The WTUL consistently supported the Bureau. Agnes Nestor, who, as chairperson of the National Legislation Committee of the WTUL testified in support of the establishment of a federal Women's Bureau in 1920 before the House-Senate Committee on Labor, accurately predicted decades of close cooperation between the two organizations.[15] As far back as 1909, a national convention of the WTUL had passed a resolution urging the establishment of a national Women's Bureau within the Department of Labor and Commerce.[16] A resolution in support of the Women's Bureau became, after 1920, a ritual at WTUL conventions.[17] The WTUL faithfully lobbied for the Women's Bureau. It sent yearly petitions to Congress urging an increase in the Bureau's appropriation and also sent petitions to the Democratic and Republican National Platform Committees urging statements supporting the inclusion of the Women's Bureau in the presidential campaign platforms.[18] When rumors circulated during the 1930s that Congress or the Secretary of Labor wished to dissolve the Bureau, WTUL members wrote letters of vigorous protest.[19]

Members of the Women's Bureau clearly reciprocated such support. Mary Anderson solicited funds for the WTUL, writing to such potential benefactors as Mrs. John D. Rockefeller, Jr., on behalf of her "old friends and co-workers."[20] Mary Anderson was not the only Women's Bureau member to support the organization. The Women's Bureau Archives record at least one instance of a Bureau employee sending money she had made on Bureau time to the WTUL. Mary Robinson of the Bureau research division wrote to Elizabeth Christman:

> You may be surprised and probably pleased to receive an additional check contributed by me to the exchequer and work

of the WTUL. It was a check which I received for an article written partly on Women's Bureau time, and as I wanted to give it to a cause Miss Anderson and I, in talking over the matter, decided that you could doubtless put it to good use.[21]

Of course, many male trade unionists disliked the WTUL's lace-collar image. The Women's Trade Union League allowed both women workers and middle-class "allies" to join. Until its decline in the 1950s, WTUL leaders tended to be middle-class women reformers, not women workers. An emphasis on moral uplift, education, and protective labor laws, not on strikes and aggressive bargaining, resulted. Samuel Gompers, for one, scoffed at the membership rules and made no secret of his dislike for the WTUL leaders whom he had once damned as "intellectuals on a sociology slumming tour."[22] In February 1924, Gompers attended a conference on the woman worker sponsored by the AFL. When Gompers' turn came to speak he condemned the WTUL as "inadequate to the task" and "academic."[23] Less than three weeks after the February conference, Gompers sent an emissary, Florence Thorn, to Mary Anderson's office. The Women's Bureau director quickly sent a letter describing the visit to Elizabeth Christman. Thorn had come to find out "if the League could be persuaded to go out of business," if the AFL established its own Women's Bureau.[24]

The League did not "go out of business," though organized labor's contempt helped cripple its effectiveness. In fact, the separate and isolated nature of not just the WTUL but of many other women's organizations illustrated the political marginality of women during the New Era. The fact that the Women's Bureau received sponsorship primarily from these women's and reform groups guaranteed that its members would find themselves similarly isolated from real power.

The proposed AFL Women's Bureau never became a reality, for it could not survive the disinterest of union leaders. Indicative of the apathy of the national unions, the scheduling of the 1924 AFL Executive Council conference on organizing women workers conflicted with another Council meeting called to discuss the problems of competition from prison contract labor. Most international officers chose to debate the prison labor issue rather than to hear the advice of Mary Anderson and others.[25] Thus, unions were not to be active sponsors of federal action to investigate and improve the lot of women workers. The pattern of fruitful cooperation between government woman-worker experts and members of women's organizations, started in the 1920s, helped shape federal policy toward female labor. A pattern of union hostility, also born in the 1920s, exercised another kind of shaping force, this time to limit, not expand, federal efforts. Hostile encounters with the male hierarchy of the country's major labor organizations limited Bureau effectiveness during the agency's first decade and set a precedent for troubled relations. By the 1920s, over 3 million women worked at trades within the jurisdiction of national and international organizations affiliated with the AFL, but AFL records show that no more than 200,000 of this number were AFL members. Many unionists considered women workers as transient, unreliable, and not worth the trouble to recruit. Most union leaders, in fact, agreed with Samuel Gompers that unions should focus on higher wages for men so that men could keep their women at home.[26] As a result, Women's Bureau members rightly charged that male unionists too frequently ignored or belittled the problems of women workers. When William Green, president of the AFL, wrote to Mary Anderson in 1925 asking her to write a series of articles for the *American Federationist,* she took the opportunity to deliver a lecture. She would, she said, be happy to write the articles since many labor papers republished material from the *Federationist,* and the Women's Bureau would thus have an opportunity to deliver its message to a larger audience. She continued:

> I feel strongly that the spokesmen for labor in the American trade union movement have not realized fully the importance of the problems of women in industry, both to the women themselves and to the effects upon the labor movement that this problem presents.[27]

Anderson also instructed her staff to "keep at" specific unions that blatantly discriminated against women: "Send letters . . . keep letting them know where we stand."[28] One such letter, written in 1921 by Anderson to A. J. Berre, secretary of the Metal Trades Department of the AFL, condemned the International Molders Union's practice of expelling any member who instructed any woman in foundry work. Anderson warned Berre that such practices were not only shortsighted, but counterproductive. Women, she prophesied, would continue to enter the trades; men should realize that an effective organization among women could benefit them as well.[29] In 1926, the Women's Bureau began to investigate and keep lists of unions that barred women from membership. The Bureau found, typically, that if the work done by the union was not conventional woman's work, or if the work was physically taxing, women had trouble gaining union acceptance. Many unionists argued that a number of positions could never be held by women, despite the success women had had performing many of these proscribed jobs during World War I. The Women's Bureau investigators were told by L. M. Robe of the Upholsterers' Union that he had no interest in organizing women. "The work," he said, "is too hard for them."[30]

Without the encouragement, and certainly without the sponsorship, of union leaders, woman-worker experts in the Women's Bureau nonetheless advocated union activity as one avenue for the improvement of female labor conditions. Memoranda to the Women's Bureau field staff encouraged traveling agents to keep notes of their impressions of union attitudes toward women in addition to the special *Bulletin* assignments on which they might be working. Bureau investigators were advised to observe the number of women at union meetings and to notice whether women unionists tried to elect women to union office.[31] The information was not only to be sent back to Washington. Rachel Nyswander wrote to the field staff, "Information about success of women in one local union can be carried to another and thus ideas can be planted where they didn't exist before."[32]

Thus, although male unionists showed little interest in cultivating women members, Women's Bureau agents were nonetheless the advocates of trade unions. Mary Anderson argued that "Our [women] workers must learn to achieve full industrial citizenship. Trade unionism is part of the essential machinery to attain such goals," and she warned, "women should not let union participation stop with passive dues payments; they should attend meetings, run for office, participate in grievance delegations and help formulate policies which will take their own special interests into account."[33]

Ironically, the Bureau's advocacy of union membership for

women jibed poorly with its advocacy of protective labor legislation. Both solutions for problems experienced by women workers
uneasily coexisted as Bureau campaigns for decades. Bureau members who wrote angry letters to union bosses who forbade women
apprentices in foundries and other dangerous trades were the same
Bureau members who argued that women workers needed more
protective labor legislation such as restrictions on night work and
work involving physical dangers. Unions not only used that legislation to justify their lack of interest in wooing women as members
but also, quite logically, used it to justify their own internal job and
apprentice restrictions. The self-contradictions came from the
Women's Bureau, not from the International Molders Union.

Neither union chiefs nor company executives found it necessary
to sponsor the Women's Bureau. The interactions of the Women's
Bureau staff with management formed another negative shaping
pattern. The law setting up the Women's Bureau did not compel
employers to cooperate in any way. Those who did won Bureau
praise. Many published studies echo the tone of thanks registered in
Bulletin #30:

> Too much credit can hardly be given to the manufacturers
> whose cooperation made it possible to get this information.
> They permitted agents of the Women's Bureau to interview
> their employees during working hours and gave much assistance
> in securing information from pay rolls.[34]

Field agents reporting back to Washington cited the names of
particularly helpful employers.[35] More frequently, however, Bureau
file reports noted confrontations. Despite Bureau assurances of
confidentiality, many firms wrote the Women's Bureau expressing
fear that the government agency would take advantage of their
cooperation and misuse divulged information.[36] In 1927, Ethel
Erickson wrote a long letter to Mary Anderson reporting a "stormy
session" with James Dougherty, director of industrial relations at
General Motors. Dougherty at first refused to sanction Erickson's
visits to local plants as an agent of the Women's Bureau, as he said
he had a written agreement with Secretary of Labor James Davis
that all labor statistics given the federal government would be
cleared through the Bureau of Labor Statistics. Erickson reported:

His secretary spent almost an hour hunting up this correspondence [with Davis], and in the meantime he had a grand time
giving vent to his opinion of all studies and investigations and
those of the government in particular.[37]

By 1926, Mary Anderson, in an address to the National Association of Manufacturers, felt compelled to outline an edgy definition of the agency's proper relationship with employers:

(There) are still so many employers who sit back until compelled by legislation or by a strike . . . that we must keep on
discussing and criticizing instead of giving praise, or the large
numbers of women employed under poor working conditions
will be forgotten.[38]

Unions and corporations often ignored Women's Bureau con-
demnations of union discrimination or corporate sweatshops. Federal
administrators expressed, at best, gelid support for those bureaucrats
paid to study and advise them concerning the female labor question.
Bureaucratic apathy was the fourth and final element in the shaping
of federal policy toward women workers. Once again, a lack of
active sponsorship exercised a deeply negative influence.

In 1920, Senator Lee Overman from North Carolina had opposed
the establishment of a Women's Bureau on grounds that "all bureaus
after creation . . . quickly expand. The staff increases, and the
appropriation mounts. What the appropriation for the Women's
Bureau will quickly be no one knows."[39] The senator need not have
worried. The Women's Bureau did not expand. Clearly, more
money would not have guaranteed greater Bureau success in helping women workers advance. But the small appropriations the
Bureau did receive reduced the scope of its investigations, the size
of its staff, and the number of its opportunities to present information about women workers. When Congress began hearings in
1919 on the efficacy of continuing the Women-in-Industry Service
as a permanent agency, the House Committee on Labor first proposed an annual budget of $40,000. The Women's Trade Union
League convincingly denounced that appropriation, calling it ridiculous: "It is less than what would be slotted for a small-town post
office."[40] Eventually, the Bureau received a $75,000 budget, less

than one-half of that requested by the Department of Labor.[41] Mary Anderson expressed the bitterness felt by many advocates of working women when she testified before the hearings held to consider establishing the Bureau: "In the past two years Congress has approved $600,000 for the prevention of hog cholera and $1,500,000 for the eradication of tuberculosis in animals, and now you resist a meager grant of $75,000 to improve the cause of working women."[42]

Anderson's contributions to the *Annual Reports* issued by the Secretary of Labor repeatedly detailed projects stymied for lack of funds.[43] For instance, the Bureau director wrote, in the *Annual Report* for 1922, "With staff and money limitations once again the Bureau has attempted to extract data from a single city, Passaic, New Jersey. . . . It has a manageable population and a large number of working women."[44] Indeed, Passaic, easily reached by train, became a stamping ground.

Bureau correspondence with sympathetic organizations detailed battles waged and lost with the Bureau of the Budget. In private letters to trusted friends, Anderson outlined the financial woes of her Bureau and blamed some of her difficulties on the lack of support within the Department of Labor. She complained, "While the Secretary [James Davis] sent over our estimate, he certainly did not make any effort to get us any money."[45] Indeed, Women's Bureau interaction with a series of secretaries of labor pointed up an overwhelming problem for a Bureau established out of Progressive concern not to put more women into the work force but to protect those already there and to work for a society where most women were free to be full-time wives and mothers. As a rule, secretaries of labor gave only token support for the need to consider the problems encountered by women workers. Most felt uneasy with the phenomenon of spiraling numbers of women at work. William Doak and James Davis spoke in awed terms of the obligations of motherhood and the hearth. In a perfect world, the Women's Bureau would not need to exist at all. Of course, not even Women's Bureau agents argued that a woman's ideal role was as a wage laborer. The stage was set for a later battle of wills between Mary Anderson and Frances Perkins, the first woman Cabinet officer.

Like Mary Anderson, the first two secretaries of labor, William Wilson and James Davis, had immigrated to America, had received almost no formal education, had worked as child laborers, and had come to the Department of Labor after many years in the trade union movement. Such similar antecedents did not, however, strengthen ties between the Women's Bureau chief and these secretaries of labor. Indeed, both Wilson and Davis reflected instead the traditional unwillingness of the male unionist to organize women workers. William Wilson, given the authority in 1918 to organize a War Labor Administration, set up the War Labor Board to coordinate labor's involvement with the nation's war effort. The Board, in turn, established a women's committee but gave it only advisory status. The members of this advisory committee charged Secretary Wilson with an unwillingness to take the problems of working women seriously.[46] James Davis, who took office in 1921, held "excessively sentimental" views about women in industry.[47] When he discussed working women, Davis favored speeches that concluded with tributes to "those best managers of all . . . the women who tend the home."[48] In a speech given in 1923 he argued:

> Ever since woman was first admitted to a place in industry, there has been a controversy as to the right of women to take part in the gainful vocations. This question the Women's Bureau does not attempt to solve. . . . Still all would agree women in industry would not exist in an ideal [society]. Women have a higher duty and a higher sphere in life. It was for Adam to protect Eve and provide for their posterity. There is no vocation higher than that assigned by God: women have been called to the care of children, the future society of the world.[49]

William Doak, who replaced Davis in 1930, shared his predecessor's attitudes about working women. Doak, a one-time official in the Brotherhood of Railroad Trainmen, lauded the "important work" of the Women's Bureau, which he defined as having the potential "to help unite women and the family in times of economic crisis and change."[50] But like his predecessors, he refused to support Anderson's pleas for more money. Clearly, no secretary of labor viewed women workers as powerful constituents to be wooed by amply funded programs.

By the end of the 1920s, another important pattern had emerged: Those women who staffed federal programs concerned with women workers were to be moderate reformers, well educated but politically uninfluential career civil servants.

Lacking sponsors among union, federal, and business leaders, the Bureau turned for support to allies within the network of social reform and women's clubs. This, of course, was the same network from which Bureau staffers had come. Most of the female professionals who came to Washington to staff the Women's Bureau in the 1920s had little entree to the organizations that they most needed as advocates. Lacking political connections, they brought bags of oranges to tigers.

Because many charter-member Women's Bureau agents stayed until their retirements in the 1950s and influenced the selection of members of temporary New Deal and World War II agencies concerned with women workers, they left an important legacy for federal policy making through the 1960s. Personnel files kept for Bureau employees reveal them to be white, educated women, idealistic about the possibilities for accomplishing something worthwhile in their jobs, intrigued with the principles of scientific management and efficiency, eager to achieve better conditions for women workers by investigating and publicizing their problems. They were professionals: statisticians, writers, publicists, economists, union advisors, former teachers, and social workers. Most were single. Many had already worked in state or local government and had come to Washington as seasoned bureaucrats. Members of a small agency that never employed more than eighty individuals at one time, Bureau staff members frequently saw themselves as embattled reformers, arrayed against foes both in union hierarchies and in Wall Street offices. In a fascinating contradiction, the majority were career women committed to their jobs, working for an agency whose main argument for four decades was that women usually worked out of economic necessity and wished to leave work for marriage. Not until the 1950s did Women's Bureau agents begin to advocate an expanded vision of preferred roles for women beyond the domestic circle. Their own correspondence reveals that their jobs brought them a sense of satisfaction, a vocation, and independence, not just income. It is extremely doubtful that many were bitter spinsters, denied the right man. They were middle-class women workers who, consciously or not, excluded themselves from the advice they repeated in *Bulletin* after *Bulletin*.[51]

Asked to describe the spirit in the Women's Bureau, Field Agent Ethel Erickson recalled, "It may seem naive and simple now, but it [the Bureau] was a cause. So much was wrong . . . girls so many places getting seven cents an hour . . . we felt we had to reform the world." Erickson, who studied with Paul Douglas at the University of Chicago, obtained a master's degree in economics and taught at a small college in Minnesota before coming to the Bureau in 1923 to begin a thirty-year career as a field agent, remembered that on her first factory inspection trip, she visited the homes of dozens of cannery workers in Delaware. She ended up taking one woman to a movie since the woman had told her she really wanted to see the movie but had no money, and eating lunch in a coffee shop with another woman who confided to her that one of the things she had yearned to do for years was to eat in a restaurant. "I just wanted to help them all . . . so badly . . . but you get hardened to the poverty."[52]

Mary Cannon did not begin work as director of the Women's Bureau's International Division until the early 1940s, but she maintained that this reformist spirit of idealism lingered even then among some of the Bureau staff.[53] When discussing her colleagues, Ethel Erickson repeatedly remarked, "We were naive, so naive."[54] If, by naive, Erickson meant a boundless faith in the power of government to bring about significant changes in industry and society, then the Bureau members were initially naive. They were certainly not timid. Many Women's Bureau members traveled frequently on speech-making, advisory, or inspection trips. Most traveled alone, on very tight budgets. Caroline Manning's memoranda to her field agents were at times eloquently understated sermons on frugality: In one, she advised agents of the benefits to their health to be derived from walking rather than from taking buses or taxis.[55] Both Ethel Erickson and Mary Elizabeth Pidgeon—longtime chief of the Research Division of the Women's Bureau and like Erickson an economist trained at the University of Chicago—recalled facing down owners of southern mills when they tried to investigate charges that the owners were keeping double or triple books.[56]

The independence that Women's Bureau agents displayed may have derived in part from the fact that few came directly from college. Most were seasoned workers when they arrived in Washington. The first major Bureau turnover of professional personnel occurred in the 1950s simply because so many had reached retirement age. Although the correspondence of several agents reveals measures of commitment and satisfaction with work at the Bureau, the very low job turnover doubtlessly stemmed in part from the restricted job opportunities for women professionals within the federal bureaucracy.

The historian Susan Ware argues that the period 1933-1945 offered "greatly expanded opportunities" for women in public life. She credits a "women's network" headed by powerful figures like Molly Dewson, leader of the Women's Division of the Democratic Party, First Lady Eleanor Roosevelt, and Secretary of Labor Frances Perkins with the increased influence of women in the Democratic Party and in New Deal social welfare programs. Ware lists Mary Anderson as a member of this women's network. In truth, Anderson's feud with Frances Perkins limited her influence and probably diminished the opportunities available to members of her Bureau. Ware acknowledges that the network she describes did not exist in the 1920s and had "ceased to function after 1945."[57] By the time Franklin Roosevelt arrived in Washington, many Bureau agents, who had begun federal service during World War I, were mature women in their late fifties or sixties, nearing retirement. Perhaps their age deterred some at that point from aggressively seeking new bureaucratic job opportunities. Their successors would have to wait for the Johnson Administration for government job opportunities that matched those available during the peacetime New Deal.

And their successors would have been younger when the 1960s brought a second New Deal for women government professionals. In fact, many agents were already mature women with fifteen or twenty years of work experience by the time they began long careers in the Women's Bureau. Agnes Peterson, who served for sixteen years as assistant director of the Bureau, had earlier worked as superintendent of the Division of Women and Children within the Minnesota department of labor.[58] Arcadia Near Phillips, who worked during the 1930s as chief of the Statistical Division, received a master's degree in statistics at Columbia University, then served as a statistical economist in the Children's Bureau before transferring to the Women's Bureau in 1930.[59] Elizabeth Hyde, who headed the Editorial Division of the Bureau for twenty-three years, had previously worked as an editor for the United States Immigration Commission.[60] Ethel Best, Women's Bureau industrial supervisor from 1920 to 1941, worked for the New York Woman-in-Industry Service before coming to Washington.[61] Caroline Manning received a master's degree in English from Radcliffe in 1906, then worked for the Women's Educational and Industrial Union in Boston before moving to Minnesota to work for Agnes Peterson in the Bureau of Women and Children of the Minnesota department of labor. She came to Washington, D.C., in 1918 to work as an investigator for the Children's Bureau, transferring to the Women's Bureau in 1920 to work again under Peterson.[62] Mary Robinson, chief of the Division of Public Information, also came to the Bureau from the Children's Bureau.[63] Other Bureau members came with administrative experience as national or regional executives for such organizations as the YWCA and the League of Women Voters.[64]

These women were products of their times and sometimes wrote reports that accepted contemporary racial and ethnic stereotypes. Field Agent Jean Brown, for example, circulated a staff memorandum describing her research on the increasing numbers of black women working in laundries during the years 1910-1927:

> Some writers attribute this substitution largely to the willingness of Negro women to work for smaller wages than whites, but the fact is washing and ironing is a traditional employment of the race. Negro women ordinarily do it well and willingly, and they are better able than white women to work easily under conditions of excessive heat.[65]

Jean Brown and others in the Bureau acknowledged in their published studies that black women were at the bottom of the economic ladder, exploited by long hours, poor working environments, and inadequate pay. Such discrimination would lessen, they contended, when black women "prove themselves capable of steady work habits." Mary Anderson summarized much of the Bureau's approach when she noted, "The Negro woman, if she would advance, must first show that she is worthy of the opportunity."[66] The Bureau director once complained to a friend about a black typist she had hired who was a "fine girl when we first got her, but some of our people who get very tender about the colored people, I think, spoiled her a little."[67] The information that Bureau agents sent to organization allies sometimes lapsed into stereotypes describing ethnic women: Italians were devout; Jews boisterous and eager to join trade unions.[68] Until the 1950s, the Bureau focused on blue-collar women workers. Agents often wrote of such workers with well-meant condescension.

The fact that Bureau agents did not transcend the prejudices of their times and associates does not condemn all their efforts. It does, however, illustrate their status as Progressives, with commonly held Progressive prejudices.

Agents shared an esprit de corps, a similar view of the world, seen not just in their views about minorities. It was a view shaped in the settlement houses and women's colleges of the late nineteenth and early twentieth centuries. Most were college educated, with some training in economics. A striking number had connections with settlement houses in either Chicago or New York City. An applicant for a position as a field agent or supervisor was required to have three years of experience as a factory inspector or employment manager, or "as a wage earner in close and continuous contact with the problems of women."[69] If the applicant had a college degree, however, preferably a degree in economics, one year of experience would suffice. Moreover, any college work toward a master's degree could substitute for industrial work experience. For most Bureau agents, college education substituted for industrial work experience, though a substantial minority had arrived in Washington with factory inspection experience from previous jobs. Several Bureau positions required college education. Applicants for work in the research and editorial divisions of the Women's Bureau, for instance, were required to have a college degree.[70]

Not surprisingly—given a camaraderie born of years of shared work, shared education, and shared experience—many close friendships developed. For almost twenty years, Louise Stitt, Ethel Erickson, Mary Anderson, and Agnes Peterson dined together and played canasta whenever all four were in town. Women's Bureau members frequently took holidays together. Thanksgiving and Christmas were often celebrated with the "[Women's Bureau] girls getting together."[71] Esther Peterson, director of the Women's Bureau from 1961 to 1964 and former assistant secretary of labor, argued in an interview that close bonds of personal friendship were a leitmotiv for the Women's Bureau, even through the 1960s, when, following national trends, increasing numbers of Bureau members were married, with commitments to husbands and children. Though Anderson and her successor, Frieda Miller, were single, Bureau directors after 1952 were married. Peterson argued that these close personal ties helped explain the Bureau's vehement resistance to efforts to reorganize the Department of Labor and consolidate it with other bureaus and agencies.[72]

Ties linking women government professionals extended beyond the Bureau. Agents expressed interest in the activities of other women, in the legislative and judicial branches as well as within the executive bureaucracy. For instance, Opal Gooden noted:

> The House yesterday finally passed a bill permitting WAVES to serve overseas. The men advanced some screwy arguments against it. The Navy was all for it, but had to push hard. The women in Congress were at last united, in disgust with their male colleagues and their arguments.[73]

Mary Anderson ritually sent letters congratulating female appointees to prominent government positions, often saying, as she wrote to Florence Allen when Allen received an appointment as federal judge of the Sixth Circuit District, "Thousands of women will rejoice."[74] But these women's networks were not those with which a militant feminist would have felt comfortable. Its own press releases and radio talks presented members of the Women's Bureau as "real women," even though prevailing social expectations still said that "real women" married and stayed home. A Bureau press release assured:

> Despite her efficiency and devotion to duty, Mary Anderson is not a machine, but a real human being, with hosts of friends, both men and women. Mary Anderson is also a real woman when it comes to dress. She likes pretty clothes and always has them. Around Washington she has the reputation of being dressed stylishly and of being extremely well-groomed.[75]

A radio talk portrayed Elizabeth Christman as a woman "with a strong preference for the prettiest and most feminine of hats."[76]

The personality and direction of Mary Anderson helped to shape this equivocal spirit within the Bureau. Anderson began work for the Woman-in-Industry Service in 1918, during World War I; she retired in 1944 as World War II waned.[77] Anderson differed in striking ways from most members of her professional staff. Coming to America as an impoverished Swedish immigrant, Anderson spent her teens and early twenties working as a domestic servant and factory laborer in the boot and shoe trade, rather than studying for a college degree. Though she was to be the recipient of an honorary degree from Smith College, she never finished high school and never lost her Swedish accent.[78]

Her position within the Bureau was a complicated one. On one level, she functioned as a kind of national symbol: a sensible, unsophisticated, earthy, workers' advocate. Molly Dewson remembered, "the quaint ungrammatical things she was always saying . . . what was it now? 'Man' for 'men'?"[79] At a remembrance service held after her death in 1964, Senator Wayne Morse from Oregon lauded her ability to "know without theoretical agonizing."[80] Anderson indeed labeled herself in a taped interview with Esther Peterson as "not the kind of person who could do research or anything. I just knew what was needed."[81]

In fact, Anderson did not know what was needed. Her style never really suited her position. She had many allies in reform and women's organizations, but she was not a charmer or an adept politician. She remembered as a high point in her life the strikes, marches, and hostile confrontations with police that marked her early years as a union organizer.[82] Mary Anderson's combative personality, her dogged insistence on the moral correctness of her stances, even when they were contradictory, and her inability to learn how to thrive in a government structure that demanded the skills of a horse-trader, marred her success. Mary Robinson, of the Bureau's Research Division, once called her boss the "symbol for a cause."[83] The description fit, especially if that cause was adherence to a Progressive ideology of protection of women workers. Symbols for causes often lack the skill in bartering needed to deal with the federal structure. Mary Anderson left office after World War II a discouraged and embittered woman, still stymied by problems first encountered in the 1920s. Her inability to compromise contributed to the problems of the Bureau, although it is unlikely that any person could have transformed her agency into a locus of power.

The Bureau's support groups outside government, a corollary to its influence inside, certainly never exercised that kind of lobbying clout.

Despite its efforts to reach an audience through radio programs, a plethora of *Bulletins,* publication of a newsletter, and frequent speechmaking, the Women's Bureau never had the staff, enforcement power, funding, or sponsorship to become truly effective in fulfilling its mandate to study and improve conditions under which women worked. Women's Bureau members certainly realized the extent of their invisibility. Many made a habit of good-humoredly starting speeches with anecdotes describing public confusion about the functions of the Bureau. Most agents had at least one story about an encounter with a young man seeking a date with a nice girl. The Women's Bureau, in fact, kept a file of letters from men writing for names of suitable wives from a government agency they assumed to be a matrimonial service. Frequently the Bureau received inquiries from people seeking missing women.[84]

By the time the Wall Street Crash spectacularly ended the New Era, patterns for federal involvement with problems caused by paid female work had been established. Without powerful advocates, government experts in women's work issues would find their advice ignored, their studies uncirculated, and their feet weary from walking the streets of Passaic, New Jersey. Patterns of sponsorship or lack of sponsorship persisted for decades, dooming federal programs for women workers to haphazard funding and relative indifference. Patterns of staffing remained stable, and Bureau staff members persisted, too, in self-contradictory patterns of advice: urging both employers and unions to grant women equal status as well as special protective considerations. For federal policy towards women workers, at least, the Progressive legacies of the New Era endured into the Eisenhower era.

NOTES

1. Henry George, *The Condition of Labor* (New York: The United States Book Company, 1891).

2. The following are representative *Bulletins* from the 1920s. Women's Bureau *Bulletin #10,* "Hours and Conditions of Work for Women in Industry in Virginia," (Washington, D.C.: Government Printing Office,

1920); Women's Bureau *Bulletin #11,* "Women Street Car Conductors and Ticket Agents" (Washington, D.C.: Government Printing Office, 1921); Women's Bureau *Bulletin #13,* "Industrial Opportunities and Training for Women and Girls" (Washington, D.C.: Government Printing Office, 1920); Women's Bureau *Bulletin #24,* "Women in Maryland Industries" (Washington, D.C.: Government Printing Office, 1922); Women's Bureau *Bulletin #25,* "Women in the Candy Industry" (Washington, D.C.: Government Printing Office, 1923); Women's Bureau *Bulletin #21,* "Women in Rhode Island Industries" (Washington, D.C.: Government Printing Office, 1922); Women's Bureau *Bulletin #45,* "Home Environment and Opportunities of Women in Coal-Mine Worker's Families" (Washington, D.C., Government Printing Office, 1925); Women's Bureau *Bulletin #47,* "Women in the Fruit-Growing and Canning Industries in the State of Washington" (Washington, D.C.: Government Printing Office, 1926); Women's Bureau *Bulletin #52,* "Lost Time and Labor Turnover in Cotton Mills" (Washington, D.C.: Government Printing Office, 1926); Women's Bureau *Bulletin #55,* "Women in Mississippi Industries" (Washington, D.C.: Government Printing Office, 1926); Women's Bureau *Bulletin #57,* "Women Workers and Industrial Poisons" (Washington, D.C.: Government Printing Office, 1926). For a complete list, see Appendix B.

3. Quote from Jane Addams, *A Centennial Reader* (New York: Macmillan, 1960), p. 115. For a review of women's organizations in the 1920s, see J. Stanley Lemons, *The Woman Citizen: Social Feminism in the 1920s* (Urbana, Ill.: University of Illinois Press, 1973); Lois Scharf, *To Work and To Wed: Female Employment, Feminism and the Great Depression* (Westport, Conn.: Greenwood Press, 1980), chaps. 1-2; Estelle Freedman, "The New Woman: Changing Views of Women in the 1920's," *Journal of American History* 61 (September 1974), pp. 372-393; Estelle Freedman, "Separatism as Strategy: Female Institution Building and American Feminism, 1870-1930," 5 *Feminist Studies* (Fall 1979), pp. 512-529; Martin Gruberg, *Women in American Politics* (Oshkosh, Wis.: Academia Press, 1968); Patricia Hummer, *The Decade of Elusive Promise: Professional Women in the United States, 1920-1930* (Ann Arbor: UMI Research Press, 1979). For information on the Woman's Party, see "The Alice Paul Oral History," (typescript—Regional Oral History Office, Bancroft Library, University of California at Berkeley, 1976; interviewer, Amelia Fry) (hereafter cited as Alice Paul Oral History); Susan Becker, "An Intellectual History of the National Woman's Party, 1920-40" (Ph.D. dissertation, Case Western Reserve University, 1975); Susan Becker, *Origins of the Equal Rights Amendment: American Feminism Between the Wars* (Westport, Conn.: Greenwood Press, 1981).

4. Mary Anderson, *Woman at Work, the Autobiography of Mary Anderson as Told to Mary Winslow* (Minneapolis: University of Minnesota

Press, 1951) p. 190; see also clipping file in Mary Anderson Papers, Folders 6 and 7, Schlesinger Library (hereafter cited as SL).

5. Estelle Freedman, "Separatism as Strategy," pp. 512-529.

6. See "Cost of Living Schedules—To be Sent to Participating A.A.U.W. Chapters," 1923-1940 (typescript), "Organizations File: A.A.U.W.," Records of the Women's Bureau, R.G. 86, The National Archives, Washington, D.C. (hereafter cited as WB, NA). For copies of some YWCA materials used by the Bureau, see "Organizations File: Y.W.C.A.," WB, NA; Bertha Nienburg, assistant director of WB, to Vera Woods, industrial secretary, YWCA: March 19, 1944, "Correspondence—Organizations File: Y.W.C.A.," WB, NA: "I am sure that your reports covering a larger number of cities than we will take in our home visits will be very helpful to us." Further information about shared data can be found in records of the YWCA, Bx. 1-6, Sophia Smith Collection, Smith College, Northampton, Mass. (hereafter cited as SS).

7. Staff members of the NLWV, for instance, helped rewrite the text of Women's Bureau *Bulletin #53*, "The Status of Women in Government Service" (Washington, D.C.: Government Printing Office, 1926); Mary Anderson to Gladys Harrison, executive secretary of the NLWV, August 8, 1929, "Correspondence—Organizations File: N.L.W.V.," WB, NA.

8. The speech topics ranged widely. For example, Anderson to Anne Johnstone, October 5, 1939, "Correspondence—Organizations File: N.L.W.V.," WB, NA: "I am returning the speech on the legal status of women in the Philippines by Prof. Bamboa, which we have had copied for our research files."

9. Anderson to Baldwin, November 11, 1935, "Correspondence—Organizations File: N.L.W.V.," WB, NA.

10. Elizabeth Smart to Frieda Miller, December 3, 1946, "Correspondence—Organizations File: W.C.T.U.," WB, NA.

11. For a more complete list, see "Organizations File: Y.W.C.A.," WB, NA. For example, in 1922 the Bureau worked with the YWCA on a survey of state fire hazard laws applying to factories where women worked; in 1938 it cooperated with the YWCA on a study of the leisure-time activities of business girls, Mary Anderson to Martha Geeslin, August 29, 1938, "Correspondence—Organizations File: Y.W.C.A.," WB, NA; the Women's Bureau prepared a pamphlet to be distributed by the YWCA, "Minimum Wage Budgets for Women," in cooperation with the YWCA and the Bureau of Home Economics, Department of Agriculture, February, 1939; Mrs. Frank Letzig, AAUW representative, Little Rock, Arkansas, to Mary Anderson, January 15, 1942, "Correspondence—Organizations File: A.A.U.W.," WB, NA.

12. Anderson, *Woman at Work,* pp. 32-70.

13. See Mary Winslow Papers, Folder 1-3, SL.

14. Anderson to Rose Schneiderman, February 18, 1943, WB, NA, "Correspondence—Organizations: W.T.U.L.," Bx. 851, WB, NA; see also Women's Trade Union League Papers, Bx. 12, The Library of Congress, Manuscript Division, Washington, D.C. (hereafter cited as LC).

15. Women's Bureau Hearings, House Committee on Labor, March 4, 1920, S. 4002; H.R. 1134, 66th Cong., 2nd Sess., v. 235, pp. 22-25, Hearings.

16. Hearings, p. 23.

17. "Correspondence—Organizations: W.T.U.L.," Bx. 851, WB, NA.

18. See Records of the National Women's Trade Union League, Container 21, LC.

19. See, for example, Mary Winslow to Frances Perkins, January 15, 1937, Folder 28, Anderson Papers, SL; Rose Schneiderman to Frances Perkins, November 10, 1943, Folder 38, Anderson Papers, SL; Frances Perkins to Rose Schneiderman, November 12, 1943, Folder 38, Anderson Papers, SL.

20. Anderson to Rockefeller, Anderson Papers, March 18, 1925, Folder 17, SL.

21. Robinson to Christman, "Correspondence—Organizations: W.T.U.L.," Bx. 851, WB, NA.

22. Samuel Gompers, "They Don't Suit the Intellectuals," *American Federationist,* 20 (February 1913), p. 132; see also WTUL Papers, Bound Volumes, Bx. 1, Gompers Address, Berkeley Lyceum, March 24, 1905, SL.

23. Notes of session taken by Ethel Smith, letter, Smith to Mary Anderson, Anderson Papers (undated, 1924?).

24. Florence Thorn acted as secretary and advisor to Gompers. Despite Gompers' expressed opinions about the WTUL, members of the League respected Thorn. Elizabeth Christman in a letter to Mary Anderson wrote that Gompers' association with Thorn and his use of her as emissary "indicates that he had discrimination as to who can think straight and whose judgment can be depended upon." Anderson Papers, March 29, 1924, Folder 15, SL; Anderson to Elizabeth Christman, Anderson Papers, March 21, 1924, Folder 15, SL.

25. *Report on American Federation of Labor Conference for the Organization of Women Workers,* February 14, 1924, in Anderson Papers, Folder 15, SL.

26. *Ibid.*

27. Anderson to Green, March 20, 1925, Bx. 863, WB, NA.

28. Anderson: Memorandum to Staff, "Union Participation," April 1921.

29. Anderson to Berre, June 15, 1921, Bx. 863, WB, NA.

30. Bx. 860-863, WB, NA.

31. "File—Correspondence with Field Agents—1925-1935": See memos by Bertha Nienburg, Rachel Nyswander, and Caroline Manning, WB, NA.

32. "File—Correspondence with Field Agents," February 26, 1944, Bx. 1407, WB, NA.

33. Anderson, "Speech File #341-S-250," May 18, 1942, Commonwealth Club, San Francisco, WB, NA.

34. U.S. Women's Bureau, *Bulletin #30,* "The Share of Wage Earning Women in Family Support" (Washington, D.C.: Government Printing Office, 1923), p. 37.

35. See, for representative letters, Ethel Best to Mary Anderson, 12 November 1926, Bx. 47, WB, NA; Caroline Manning, Memo to Staff, 27 November 1926, Bx. 47, WB, NA.

36. Emphasized in staff instructions: See memorandum signed by Assistant Director Bertha Nienburg,, 19 July 1935, Bx. 1280, WB, NA: "Remember the Bureau never allows the names of parties furnishing facts to be given in its reports. Thus confidence is secured, from the knowledge that in none of the reports have private interests been endangered. Through this confidence, management in this and other countries have opened their books of account, their pay rolls, and their records to the agents of the Bureau."

37. Erickson to Anderson, 26 February 1927, Bx. 46, WB, NA.

38. "Address by Mary Anderson at the Annual Conference of the National Association of Manufacturers," 5 October 1926, Bx. 69, WB, NA.

39. *U.S. Congressional Record,* 66th Cong., 2nd Sess., 1920, 59, pt. 8, p. 8087.

40. The WTUL papers at the Library of Congress contain a file of the letter campaigns mounted in support of the Women's Bureau. The Women's Trade Union League Papers, Bx. 21, LC.

41. Typescript pamphlet, March 21, 1920, WTUL papers, Bx. 21, LC.

42. Hearings, pp. 2, 3, 46.

43. *Third Annual Report of the Women's Bureau,* 1921 (Washington, D.C.: Government Printing Office, 1922), pp. 20-21 (see following table). One should mention the fact that the Department of Labor as well as the Bureau suffered Congressional appropriations cutbacks and massive loss of prestige. See Grossman, *The Department of Labor,* pp. 58-65; Francis Rourke, "The Reorganization of the Department of Labor" (Ph.D. dissertation, University of Minnesota, 1952); *Annual Report of the Secretary of the Department of Labor,* 1920-1950, "Office of the Chief Clerk: Division of Budgets and Accounts: Financial Statement of the Department of Labor" (Washington, D.C.: Government Printing Office, 1921-1951); *The Annual Reports of the Secretary of the Department of Labor* (Washington, D.C.: Government Printing Office, 1950-1961); O. L. Harvey, ed., *The Anvil and the Plow: A History of the Department of Labor,* 1913-1963 (Washington, D.C.: Government Printing Office, 1963).

Date	Women's Bureau Budget	Department of Labor Budget
1920	$ 40,000	$ 6,944,000
1921	75,000	6,661,000
1922	77,000	6,677,000
1923	100,000	7,484,000
1924	105,000	7,913,000
1925	107,000	8,675,000
1926	105,000	9,185,000
1927	100,000	9,537,000
1928	100,000	10,190,000
1929	108,000	11,501,000
1930	108,000	11,322,000
1931	158,000	12,897,000
1932	180,000	15,015,000
1933	160,000	13,571,000
1934	147,000	16,627,000
1935	152,000	22,253,000
1936	154,000	32,229,000
1937	153,000	39,650,000
1938	136,000	31,581,000
1939	143,000	30,131,000
1940	187,000	30,936,000
1941	155,000	24,698,000
1942	155,000	24,145,000
1943	175,000	25,331,000
1944	240,000	72,036,000
1945	245,000	70,829,000
1946	206,000	112,895,000
1947	305,000	115,424,000
1948	314,000	200,262,000
1949	289,000	224,055,000
1950	340,000	235,634,800
1951	389,000	*
1952	379,000	*
1953	350,000	261,708,539
1954	350,000	351,811,749
1955	371,000	447,167,843
1956	403,000	469,872,346
1957	462,000	435,886,013
1958	504,000	1,185,597,400
1959	509,000	1,219,063,105
1960	554,000	*

*The *Annual Reports* for the years 1951, 1952, and 1960 did not tabulate a comprehensive Labor Department budget.

44. *Annual Report of the Secretary of the Department of Labor* (Washington, D.C.: Government Printing Office, 1923).

45. Mary Anderson to Mollie Carroll (Chairperson of the Women-in-Industry Committee of the League of Women Voters), December 17, 1924, WB, NA.

46. Typed transcript (unpaginated), taped interview between Esther Peterson and Mary Anderson (Washington, D.C., April 24, 1964), Women's Bureau Files, Office of Information, Department of Labor, Washington, D.C.

47. Mary Anderson (with Mary Winslow), *Woman at Work, the Autobiography of Mary Anderson* (Minneapolis: University of Minnesota Press, 1951), p. 181.

48. "The Woman in Industry," speech quoted in *The Christian Statesman* (May 1923), p. 12.

49. *Ibid.*

50. Speech delivered at Appalachian Tri-state Fair, Johnson City, Tennessee, September 7, 1931, Bx. 1281, WB, NA.

51. During the years 1920-1960, at least 217 persons worked for the Bureau; biographical information exists in the records of the Women's Bureau on at least 102 of these people, 27 of whom married. There is, of course, a chance that more of the female clerical workers were married, but, being low on the staff totems, they were less likely to show up in Bureau records or biographical sketches than would division chiefs, field agents, and economic experts. The marriage rate, then, may be skewed by the nature of hierarchical record keeping. The small proportion of married women parallels the relatively low proportion of married women in the general labor force before 1945 and the even smaller proportion of married women with professional jobs. It should be noted that the years 1947-1962, which witnessed such great increases among married female workers, were years when the Bureau staff, first beleaguered and then deprived of agency independence within the Department of Labor, was not typical of changes taking place in the professional work force. Tabulations made by author, "Personnel Information Files," WB, NA.

52. Ethel Erickson, interview with author, January 6, 1976, Washington, D.C.

53. Mary Cannon, interview with author, January 15, 1976, Washington, D.C.

54. Ethel Erickson, interview with author, January 6, 1976.

55. Memorandum to Regional Field Agents, June 3, 1941, WB, NA.

56. Ethel Erickson, interview with author, January 6, 1976; Mary Winslow Papers, Folder 1, SL; "Article File #341-A-108," Bx. 56, WB, NA.

57. Susan Ware, *Beyond Suffrage: Women in the New Deal* (Cambridge, Mass.: Harvard University Press, 1981). Ware's interesting book provides a partial refutation to Estelle Freedman's conclusion that the

"self-consciously" female community of nineteenth-century women reformers that helped sustain women's participation in political activism had largely disintegrated in the 1920s. Estelle Freedman, "Separatism as Strategy," pp. 513-514.

58. Memorandum to Field Staff, Rachel Nyswander, March 11, 1944, Bx. 1407, WB, NA.

59. Eleanor Nelson (comp.), "Staff Qualifications," "Article File #341-A-331," November 11, 1933, Bx. 56, WB, NA (hereafter cited as "Staff Qualifications," Bx. 56).

60. *Ibid.*

61. *Ibid.*

62. *Ibid.*

63. *Ibid.*

64. *Ibid.*

65. Memorandum, "Article File #341-A-244" (includes typescript draft for article, unpaginated), April 30, 1931, Bx. 70, WB, NA.

66. Mary Anderson, "The Place of Negro Women in Industry," Conference on Interracial Problems, Atlanta, Georgia, March 17, 1931, "Speech File #341-S-92, WB, NA; for published Bureau evaluations of the problems, see "Negro Women in Industry in Fifteen States," Women's Bureau *Bulletin #70* (Washington, D.C., Government Printing Office, 1921); "The Negro Woman Worker," Women's Bureau *Bulletin #165* (Washington, D.C., Government Printing Office, 1965); "The Negro Woman War Workers," Women's Bureau *Bulletin #205* (Washington, D.C., Government Printing Office, 1945).

67. Mary Anderson to Elizabeth Magee, Anderson Papers, November 20, 1942, Folder 34, SL.

68. Records of the National Consumers' League, Containers D4-D5, LC; "Report of the Special Advisory Conference to the Women's Bureau," January 10, 1950, Frieda Miller Papers, Folder 204, SL.

69. Press releases, July 6, 1925 (typescript, unpaginated), Bx. 69, WB, NA.

70. *Ibid.*

71. Dr. Stella Warner to Mary Anderson, Anderson Papers, December 27, 1942, Folder 34, SL.

72. Esther Peterson, interview with author, January 13, 1976, Landover, Maryland.

73. Gooden to Cannon, June 9, 1943, Bx. 913, WB, NA.

74. Anderson to Allen, Anderson Papers, June, 1934, Folder 25, SL.

75. Quoted in "Article File #341-A-363," April 15, 1935, WB, NA.

76. Typed transcript (unpaginated), July 15, 1942, WB, NA.

77. Anderson, *Woman at Work,* pp. 1-84.

78. Anderson Papers, June 16, 1941, Folder 1, SL.

79. Mary Dewson to Mary Winslow, Winslow Papers, January 26, 1945, Folder 4, SL.

80. Tape of memorial service held in chapel of AFL-CIO Building, Washington, D.C., March 4, 1964, Office of Information, Women's Bureau, U.S. Department of Labor, Washington, D.C.

81. Typed transcript (unpaginated), taped interview between Esther Peterson and Mary Anderson (Washington, D.C., April 24, 1964), Women's Bureau Files, Office of Information, Department of Labor, Washington, D.C. (It should be noted that the transcript that remains in the Office of Information files is dated April 1964. That must mean that it was typed in April 1964, since Anderson was then dead. The transcript does not give the exact date for the taping, though internal evidence would indicate Peterson and Anderson talked in the winter 1963-1964.)

82. Anderson, *Woman at Work,* pp. 1-78.

83. Press release, Bx. 1405, WB, NA.

84. Typed transcript (unpaginated), "Speech File #341-S-125," June 1, 1934, WB, NA; Mary Anderson, speech before the Milwaukee Business and Professional Women's Clubs, March 11, 1941, "Speech File #341-S-219," Bx. 76, WB, NA.

The New Deal and the Woman Worker: Federal Policy During the Great Depression

4

In 1928, Mary Anderson closed a speech with a quotation from Aldous Huxley: "Women will be found to be fearfully weighted in the race for life. The duty of man is to see that not a grain is piled upon that load beyond what nature imposes."[1] With the coming of the Depression, Anderson's warnings proved prophetic. Women workers indeed found themselves fearfully weighted. Few desperate out-of-work women sent letters directly to the Women's Bureau, but thousands sent appeals addressed simply, "Roosevelt" or "The President" or "Washington." Vaguely formed public images of the working woman crystallized into a caricature as millions experienced panic and unemployment. She was a villain, invading an overburdened labor market to steal jobs from indigent men. At a time when women workers took out sheets of butcher paper and wrote "Washington" to testify that they had fainted from hunger or that they had worked eight-hour days and made "less than a quarter," federal reactions vacillated, and no clear policy emerged.[2] Federal response to female workers during these years of economic crisis and dramatic bureaucratic change can be illustrated by examining three controversies that raged during the peacetime New Deal: the right of married women to work, the role of government in worker-education camps and schools, and the value of the Equal Rights Amendment versus protective labor legislation.

"Dr. New Deal" prescribed the proliferation of federal agencies.

Members of the Women's Bureau correctly perceived that many of the new alphabet agencies would have to cope with the problem of female labor. Mary Anderson felt that her agency, staffed with seasoned experts, could act as the central coordinator.[3] Her staff worked harder than ever, but though the Bureau's workload increased, its budget and its influence did not, and it continued on the edges of power, its advice ignored or accepted without acknowledgment. Despite its congressional mandate to do so, the Women's Bureau did not "set policy to improve the position of women wage earners." Some of the federal agencies spawned by the New Deal had a peripheral interest in women workers. As the agencies grew like "Topsy," the Bureau correctly attacked the uncoordinated nature of federal policy. In spite of protest, no agency or single individual played a policy-making or supervisory role.

As final recipients of tens of thousands of desperate letters, economists in the Women's Bureau wrote letters and memoranda arguing that able-bodied, experienced women, deprived of the opportunity to support themselves and their families, felt betrayed. They had a right to work and were not glutting the system. In fact, the major economic problem was not overproduction but underconsumption. The wages of a considerable proportion of the population had been allowed to slide so low that the economy had become seriously imbalanced. Women, a traditional source of the cheapest labor even in flush times, "through no fault of their own" encouraged the downward spiral. Fair wages for women made economic as well as ethical good sense.[4]

Public opinion did not support the Bureau's defense of female work in time of a depression. The attacks on working women, especially married women, were formidable.[5] With too few jobs to go around, some legislators and employers sought to forbid married women the right to work if their husbands had work. Section 213 of the 1932 Federal Economy Act, for example, required that one spouse resign if both husband and wife worked for the federal government. Technically, the assault fell on both marriage partners, yet more than 75 percent of the spouses who did resign were women.[6] Section 213 remained on the books until 1937. Throughout the 1930s, dozens of state legislators considered bills overtly discriminating against married women. In 1938, for instance, twenty-eight states debated married women's bills. Most of the bills tried to reduce unemployment by removing married women from jobs controlled by the state and by making these positions available to unmarried women and to men, married or unmarried. Many such bills did not pass. State supreme courts ruled others unconstitutional. However, executive orders restricted state employment of married women in Alabama, Idaho, Indiana, Pennsylvania, and Rhode Island.[7]

The private sector followed suit. Thousands of industries across the country fired married women.[8] Public, if not legal, opinion lent broad support to attempts to restrict the employment opportunities of married women. George Gallup in November 1936 announced the results of a national poll asking the question, "Do you approve of a married woman earning money in industry or business if she has a husband capable of supporting her?" Eighty-two percent of the 100,000 persons questioned answered no. Women themselves were opposed by seventy-nine percent.[9]

In the face of such developments, the Women's Bureau waged a counterattack and set itself in opposition to Congress and to many bureaucrats in other administrative agencies. Married women formed a minority in the labor force. "Which minority might next become a target?" the Bureau Director asked.[10] Restrictions might spread to other groups. "Marriage has not the remotest connection to fitness qualifications. It would be just as logical to inject the questions of race, religion, or nationality."[11] All employed persons, the Bureau argued, would soon have to prove that their need for jobs was genuine. Young people should stay at home if their fathers could support them, and businessmen with savings should accept forced retirement. This, of course, would be action "without precedent" or place in American history.[12] In fact, denying married women work opportunity smacked of Communism.[13] Laws restricting the employment of married women made need rather than ability the basic qualification for employment and placed restrictions on the right of persons freely to seek work.[14]

Even before the onset of the Depression, the Bureau had challenged a prevailing view that many married women worked for pin money and luxuries at the expense of their families' happiness.[15] It launched a series of radio talks in the 1920s on the theme "The Domestic Revolution and the Industrial Revolution."[16] The radio broadcasts argued that married women and mothers had always participated in economic production. "Women used to rock the cradle with one foot and operate a spinning wheel with the other."[17] With industrialization, married women simply had to follow their work out to factories, mills, and workshops: "Men transported jobs from firesides into factory . . . out from the hands of women into the control of men."[18] When financial consultant Roger Babson wrote in a *Washington Post* column that "unemployment would drop by a full million tomorrow"[19] if working wives were fired, Mary Anderson angrily responded, "Men have been taking away women's jobs for a century. Some women have followed their jobs outside. That is all."[20]

Moreover, most married women worked of necessity and not by choice. The dismissal of factory women and others whose low wages provided the economic margin for family survival would bring even more people to public charity.[21] A Bureau study of Section 213, published in 1936, argued that some 80 percent of the married women dismissed from their work belonged to the lowest paid income groups in government service. Some married women who lost work because of Section 213 had husbands earning subsistence wages, which did not support their wives, as enlisted men in the military. Since these men could not resign, their wives found themselves forced to go on relief. So even in terms of dollars, it made little sense to dismiss married women. Moreover, Bureau members asserted, the issue itself was an economic red herring, for women and men rarely competed for the same job. The Bureau argued correctly that women found themselves segregated into job ghettos. In 1936, for example, well over one-quarter of employed married women worked as maids.[22] The Bureau noted that most men would not deign to work at the types of jobs some married women so desperately sought to keep. Clearly, economic problems did not stem from married women stealing jobs.[23]

The Bureau analysis overemphasized the theme that only dire necessity drove married women out of their homes. In so doing, it maintained the same approach to women workers illustrated by the *Bulletins* published through the 1920s. Women who worked had to do so. They did not work for pin money. Under such circumstances, discrimination by companies and unions deserved censure. Bureau members, for instance, masterminded a successful telegram campaign opposing the C and O Railroad's decision to furlough married women. After receiving a barrage of messages from Bureau allies in such organizations as the YWCA and the WTUL, J. J. Bernet, president of the line, capitulated and rescinded the order.[24] Still, as it had during the 1920s, the agency hastened to reiterate its support for traditional roles for women: "The Women's Bureau is not trying to convert homemakers into wage earners," assured Mary Robinson, longtime Information Division director for the Bureau.[25] In a speech Robinson wrote for delivery by Secretary of Labor Frances Perkins, she continued the theme: "In fact we should be glad to see many [married women] released from their present monotonous factory or office jobs through the husband's earning of an income adequate for support of the family."[26] Mary Anderson told a meeting of the National Association of Manufacturers, "[Woman's] place is everywhere, but her most important place is in the home."[27] She noted the "reassuring" fact that the 1930 census showed 23 million housewives who were not in gainful employment.[28] The agency message was that in a stable economy, one which provided a minimum wage as a floor below which their husbands' wages could not fall, most married women would wish to stay home. As a Bureau radio script titled "Crying Tommy" phrased the argument: "Altogether too many Tommies are crying for their mothers just now in this country of ours."[29]

The Bureau's continued focus on low-wage factory work obscured shifts in the female labor force. Recent works by historians and sociologists incorporate Census and Labor Department statistics from the 1930s, which certainly would have been available to the Women's Bureau, and conclude that substantial numbers of married women from middle-class families were in the paid work force. During the Depression, an annual wage of $1,500 a year put a family in the middle class. Many families were able to maintain this standard of living only by putting additional members in the work force. Unlike the nineteenth century, when the great majority of these additional family members were teenage and adult children, by the 1930s wives were more likely than their children to occupy the position of supplemental wage earner. Of families with income between $1,600 and $2,500 some 35 percent pooled the income of more than one wage earner. Between 1930 and 1940, the number of married women at work increased by almost 50 percent, while the number of married women increased only 15 percent. By 1940, married women constituted almost one-third of the female labor force.[30]

The Women's Bureau was right. Most wives did not work. Of those who did, most worked out of necessity. Still, a middle-class minority worked not for the bare minimum of food and clothing but because of a changing definition of economic need and rising consumer aspirations. A wife's income might help the family keep up payments, for instance, on the radio and refrigerator.[31]

The Bureau members, Outsiders as Insiders, probably would have received even less Congressional or Labor Department support if they had presented the more complex reality of women's work patterns. Governing a nation ready to blame working women for some of the ills of the Depression, politicians in Congress and high-level administrators in the Executive Branch gave aid to women workers with great reluctance. Lacking the clout that a constituency of well-organized, united women workers might have provided, the Women's Bureau could not threaten, but rather had to cajole, seeking to shame superiors with stories of hungry women. Hungry women by the millions did exist in the 1930s, but theirs were not the only faces of women workers.

Still, the decade signaled hard times for women workers, who, even as professionals, earned one-half of a man's wages for comparable work. Job opportunities declined even in traditional female fields, and tens of thousands kept receiving some kind of paycheck by accepting demotions or less-skilled work. Teachers who became maids, typists, or salesgirls were not uncommon. Women did find work during the Depression. In 1940, the number of women working was 25 percent higher than it had been in 1930 at the depth of the Depression. By comparison, only 11 percent more men had found jobs by 1940, when the economy began to recover. Nevertheless, vast numbers of those seeking jobs failed in their searches. Perhaps as many as 25 percent of all women normally employed were without work. Though unemployment figures were not well kept, probably over 2 million women workers lost their jobs.[32]

Federal reaction to the plight of these millions of out-of-work women was an act of willed suspension of disbelief. Few of the new alphabet agencies became allies of the Women's Bureau. In fact, ambivalence and hostility characterized relations. The Works Progress Administration provides a case in point. The administrators of the WPA, after 1935 the major source of public work relief in the country, did not see working women, even if unemployed, as a notable constituency.

The director of the WPA Women's Division concentrated on the establishment of programs to occupy destitute women in traditionally feminine chores—primarily sewing, housework, mattress making, and washing. Its own surveys convinced the WPA that the majority of women involved in its projects were not "unemployment problems but . . . relief problems caused by other factors than lack of employment." Only a minority of women responding to an investigation of the sewing projects reported that they were looking for work, and of that group, two-fifths were fifty years of age or over.[33] A closer look, then, at the WPA Women's Division reveals not a project that could be called a federal reaction to the problems of female workers, but rather a project that existed as an arm in an octopus of other efforts with the primary purpose of family relief.

Mary Robinson regularly attended WPA conferences and planning sessions not only to indicate Bureau interest but also to "keep a critical eye."[34] She questioned the effectiveness of the WPA household workers' training program. Housework would only become an attractive job, she argued, when employers paid decent wages and provided acceptable working conditions. For this to happen, houseworkers themselves must receive respect. The fact that, in contrast to a general WPA policy of paying for training work, the women in the household workers' program received no wages while completing their course indicated, Robinson argued, undue acceptance of an exploitative situation.[35] The Women's Bureau Information Division director asked for investigation of charges that black women in WPA women's sewing rooms had to help pay for fuel to heat the workrooms when white women did not.[36] When Frank March, a Works Division director, justified the household workers' program as a project that "(1) will make housework more attractive as a field of work for women, and (2) will better the situation from the standpoint of housewives,"[37] Robinson questioned, "whether emphasis was not on 2 instead of 1."[38]

Initially the Bureau waxed enthusiastic about the proposed wage and hour codes of the National Recovery Administration (NRA). In 1933, the Bureau Information Division prepared a series of radio scripts discussing New Deal programs. In one episode, a Women's

Bureau agent sits alone in her hotel room, compiling her notes from the factory interviews she has conducted during the day. Suddenly the door flies open and Meta, the hotel maid, rushes in laughing and dancing. She hugs the startled Bureau investigator and joyfully shouts, "The NRA, the NRA. . . . It means I'll have a whole day off each week, and I haven't had a whole day off for three whole years. Then I'm going to get a dollar more wages a week."[39] But when NRA Administrator Hugh Johnson proposed unequal NRA wage-code differentials for men and women, the Bureau protested.[40] Spokeswoman Robinson was interviewed on station WJSV in Washington, D.C., and advised listeners to report unequal codes and code violations to the Bureau.[41] She summarized the Bureau's skepticism saying, "Remember like the mills of the gods the NRA grinds slowly—even so, it does not grind surely, and we do not see the millennium on the horizon."[42]

In a clearly nonmillennial decade, the Women's Bureau remained the only federal agency solely concerned with working women. While the Bureau maintained its wary interest in the programs of major agencies like the NRA and the WPA, it focused its attention elsewhere, on the few New Deal programs involving the interests of working women.

Two such programs, the Federal Emergency Relief Administration and the National Youth Administration's summer camps for unemployed women, set forth the limits of federal efforts and provide a second in-depth illustration of federal response to women workers during the 1930s. The government-sanctioned worker camps illustrate again the importance and the limits of the alliances formed during the previous decade between government woman-worker experts and private women's organizations.

The woman-worker summer school movement, part of the larger Workers' Education Movement, antedated the Depression. A coalition of trade unionists, college educators, and Progressive reformers, Workers' Education sought to establish a national network of schools where workers could supplement their meager formal education by studying English, mathematics, history, and economics. By 1925, forty-one AFL unions provided financial support for one- or two-month summer schools usually located at colleges out of regular session for the summer. Interested colleges, reform groups, and women's clubs often provided the classrooms and sponsored worker students. Scholarships from these sources provided only minimal living expenses, and employers often refused to grant leaves of absence. Thus, many summer school participants had to quit their jobs to attend, then had to search for other jobs when they returned home.[43]

By 1928, four schools had been established specifically for women workers: the Bryn Mawr Summer School at Bryn Mawr College, the Barnard School at Barnard College, New York City, the Wisconsin School at the University of Wisconsin, Madison, and the Southern Summer School, which began at Sweetbriar College, and held sessions at Arden, Asheville, and Burnsville, North Carolina. Most of the schools had ceased to function by the early 1940s. The Bryn Mawr School moved to West Park, New York, and changed its name to the Hudson Shore Labor School. The Barnard School merged in 1934 with a WPA worker education project in New York City. The Wisconsin Legislature eliminated funds for the School for Workers from the budget for the University in 1939. The Southern School met for a time at the Normal and Teachers College in Asheville, North Carolina, and then it, too, died.[44]

During the two decades of their existence, most schools for women workers emphasized the study of economics. The coordinating organization for the schools, the Affiliated Schools for Workers, issued an explanation of the purposes of worker education, stating that "The basic course in a workers' education curriculum is always the economics course. Some of the questions that are discussed in this course include: 'Why is there so much unemployment when there is such a great need for the goods and services that the workers who are unemployed could produce? Why is it so difficult to get enough in the weekly pay envelope to provide for the bare necessities?'"[45]

The schools established to ask these challenging, probing questions were small. Numbers of students varied, but no school was large enough to accept more than 100 women. The mere fact that a woman went to a summer school meant that she was not average. Recruiters for the schools looked for industrial workers who were potential leaders. During the 1920s, the average summer school student, except for those from the South, was likely to be foreign born, single, about twenty-five years old, a woman who had usually taken her first paid job by age sixteen. Though still a group of young, single, experienced workers, the women who came to the summer schools in the 1930s were usually native born, reflecting the decline in immigration in the previous decade. Women who came during the 1930s were also usually unemployed. During the early years, attendance at night classes at the YMCA often led to a scholarship. By the 1930s, women workers came because of their memberships in trade unions. Not surprisingly, since unions recruited for and supported the schools, the average student was an industrial worker, in a union or hoping to help organize one. Of course, the average woman worker in the 1930s still was a domestic servant, not a pattern cutter or a power machine operator. The summer school class rosters, in sum, included bright, young, single women—usually industrial workers—lacking formal education but eager to grapple with complex social and economic questions. Although only in her mid-twenties, the average summer school student was a woman with ten years of work experience. Despite this status as a seasoned worker, she rarely had the chance to settle into a regular job. The work history of one student profiled as typical in data collected by the Affiliated Schools and published by the United States Department of Labor included work as a waitress and telephone operator, a job filling orders for a seed company, another filling boxes with face powder, work as a box stitcher in a rubber mill, and work as a machine operator in a ladies' garment shop. At the time she quit to attend the Bryn Mawr school, she was a cook.[46]

The summer sessions lasted only six to eight weeks, but encouraged by teaching staffs that included radical labor leaders and Socialist Party functionaries as well as politically moderate members of regular college faculties concerned with exploitation of female labor, many students asked hard questions and expressed unhappiness with aspects of the American economic system.

During those weeks, students at most schools prepared mimeographed pamphlets, "workers' magazines," in which envy and resentment of the regular college girls who stayed on campus to act as tutors sometimes surfaced. They were "daughters of the rich" who "walk so easy and . . . don't smell at all. . . . But who makes your cleanliness, your sweetness, possible?"[47] An industrial system that made them economic pawns also received student condemnation. Mae Kelley, a student at the Hudson Shore School, wrote, "A man I know recently said, if we holler loud enough some one is bound to hear us. . . . Hear our cry for equal rights." Her classmate, Marjorie Solomon, added, "We've seen you duck with 'owners need incentives to produce.' You forgot workers need the same."[48]

Some Bryn Mawr alumnae protested that the summer school was too radical. One wrote, "Can Bryn Mawr be condemned for asking the school to move on where it could study as little and picket as much as it wanted?" Participation by three faculty members in a 1934 strike against a New Jersey packing company precipitated a final confrontation between school and Board.[49]

Throughout the 1920s, the Women's Bureau gave the woman-worker schools enthusiastic support. As the Depression posed greater problems for women workers, the Women's Bureau increased its involvement with the summer schools. Both the director and her staff frequently lectured at the summer schools, gave speeches at opening and closing convocations, and provided Department of Labor and Bureau publications to be used as classroom texts in economic courses. More importantly, class members acted as conscious collaborators by writing Bureau studies assessing the Depression's impact on women workers. Both their warm relationship with the summer schools and their always limited budgets encouraged Women's Bureau agents to examine the job and personal histories of workers at the schools as case studies. Helped with funding from the Affiliated Schools for Women Workers, the Bureau produced a series of reports describing those women who attended the summer schools.[50]

The Women's Bureau published, almost in its entirety, a study written by the Bryn Mawr Summer School class of 1932 as "Women Workers in the Third Year of the Depression," *Bulletin #103*.[51] The 109 women who attended summer classes at Bryn Mawr in 1932 decided to undertake a study of their own experience from 1929 to 1932 as a first step in understanding the impact of the Depression. The Bryn Mawr students compiled information about weekly and yearly earnings losses, connections between trade-union membership and unemployment, and the effects of unemployment on their standards of living. The individual essays they inserted poignantly illustrated the charts and statistics. They told stories of thwarted marriages, travels from city to city in search of menial work, desperation when they could no longer pay the rent or care for dependent relatives.

Bulletin #103 included a chapter of quotations from women workers, overwhelming in their collective impact:

> I was planning to get married, but I could not quite pick up the courage enough to take this step with no security and maybe bring children into the world only to starve.
>
> . . .
>
> I had moved in with my brother, also a victim of unemployment. . . . We had to cut out dental work and changing eye glasses.
>
> . . .
>
> I can no longer support my mother, who has no income.[52]

These statements alone provided indication that many of the women workers did not come to the Depression era summer schools just to try to improve their grammar. The average summer school student faced low wages, unemployment, strikes, and lockouts. She, the Women's Bureau argued:

> wants to know more about working conditions and difficulties. What are the causes of these economic evils which constantly confront her? Why do they exist? Can they be avoided? It is to discover the answers to those questions that she comes to the summer school.[53]

The few hundred workers able to attend one of the summer schools were not the only women seeking to learn the causes of economic evils confronting them. While controversy swirled around the private woman-worker schools, President Franklin Roosevelt received urgent telegrams from relief administrators scattered around the country. A January 5, 1934, cable from Oregon read:

> WOMEN HUNGRY AND DESPERATE   WAITING IN LINE FOR WORK AS YET DENIED THEM NOT ELIGIBLE

AS CWA PROJECTS SAME TERMS AS MEN STOP MEN
BUILD ROADS BUILDINGS BRIDGES WOMEN BUILD
CLOTHES HOMES HEALTH AND BABIES STOP PLEASE
DO NOT LET THIS BE DELAYED EVEN ONE UNNEC-
ESSARY DAY.[54]

Hilda Smith, director of the Federal Emergency Relief Administration (FERA) Workers' Education Project had been lobbying for
adult education schools as one solution to the problems of unemployed women since October 1933. Her special interest in workers'
schools for women was not surprising. As director of the Bryn
Mawr Summer School for workers, she went to Washington in the
summer of 1933 in hopes of securing federal funds to aid the woman-
worker schools. Rather than receiving an immediate promise of
assistance for her schools, she received a job offer to develop a
program of federal adult education under FERA on the summer
school model. By the fall of 1933, Hilda Smith had begun a plan
for organizing government-sponsored summer schools for unemployed women. She circulated letters to state school officials
and state relief administrators, outlining the policies she believed
such summer schools should follow. Among other criteria, she
argued that the teaching should emphasize economic and social
problems related to the experience of the worker, that the right of
workers to organize and bargain collectively had to be recognized, and
that classes should be organized as "democratic groups, with the teacher as a leader and one of the group, not as an authority."[55] Unemployed
women, she stated, were generally very poorly educated about economic matters. Education—as well as food, shelter, and clothing—was
a genuine relief need if women workers were to be "socially responsible" citizens able to cope with a severe economic crisis.[56]

Contemporaries credited Eleanor Roosevelt with maintaining
pressure for a national hearing on possible federal action to aid
desperate out-of-work women. Mary Anderson felt that the First
Lady "could no longer bear to see and listen to the misery of this
army of employable but jobless women."[57] Mrs. Roosevelt hosted
a White House Conference on the needs of unemployed women on
April 30, 1934. Seventy-five educators, trade unionists, and state
federal government officials met to consider specific proposals for

government-funded aid projects. By the end of the afternoon, Hilda Smith's plan for summer schools had received conference approval.[58] Following the conference, Harry Hopkins, administrator of FERA, wrote to state relief administrators, saying that limited funds were available for resident schools and camps for women and asking the states to send word at once if they intended to apply for funds. Twenty-six states and the District of Columbia replied, and during the summer of 1934, twenty-eight schools provided food, shelter, and education for 1,800 unemployed women. By the end of 1935, seventy schools had employed 750 teachers with 50,000 students. FERA grants provided salaries for staff, maintenance for the students, and upkeep for buildings. State and private funds were used for equipment, renting buildings, and organization expenses. States rented or borrowed college campuses, YWCA or Girl Scout camps, and, in a few instances, large private homes to establish the schools. In four cases, women on FERA scholarships attended existing women-worker schools at Wisconsin, Oberlin, and Southern, and at Bryn Mawr Summer Schools.[59]

After 1935, the National Youth Administration (NYA) operated a smaller program of schools and camps. By 1937, when the program was discontinued, over 8,000 unemployed women had taken part in two- to four-month programs emphasizing English grammar, domestic training, health education, and economics. One NYA camp took unemployed women workers over age thirty-five, but the average student was a young woman, under twenty-one, younger than her counterparts in the established woman-worker schools. An attempt to establish an interracial camp in Colorado failed when Colorado relief officials reported that they were unable to locate "a single Negro girl" to attend. The system put into operation was segregated, with a camp for unemployed black women workers held annually in Maryland.[60] As part of the NYA, the camp program had to be conducted as a work project. The students spent from two to four hours a day in work such as making hospital bandages, Braille books for the blind, or binding together government pamphlets.[61]

Hilda Smith kept a diary as she toured twelve schools during the summer of 1934. "To see a group of girls assemble on the first night of any school," she said, "was to receive an immediate and tragic impression of the results of unemployment." She wrote of emaciated women overwhelmed at the sight of a simple supper, of women who told her that they had contemplated suicide, of women bewildered in their attempts to understand what was happening in their own lives.[62]

Planning for the schools and camps could never be long range since funding decisions rarely were made more than a few months prior to scheduled beginning dates for classes. With the sole exception of the school director, the staff candidate list had to come from state relief rolls. Thousands of teachers faced unemployment throughout the nation, yet the limited time allowed for staff selection sometimes made it impossible to seek out the best qualified teachers among those on relief. In truth, as Hilda Smith herself admitted, some incompetent people worked for the programs. Given its emergency nature, the woman-worker school program defined the word "teacher" in a very broad way. Many nonprofessional teachers became involved: lawyers, musicians, nurses, artists, journalists, and others taught classes. The final report of the Workers' Education Project argued that "a democratic attitude in the classroom, a knowledge of subject matter, a friendly approach to the worker students and a desire to learn with them were considered more important factors in selecting the new teachers than any formal status or professional degree."[63] After receiving a maximum figure of $6,000 for sixty students from the federal government, each camp or school was on its own. State and private contributions varied, and no uniform accounting system for the program existed. Some directors spoke of inadequate money for enough food or proper medical care, and of a lack of money for emergencies. Others experienced no such financial crises.

Because of the haste in which the programs emerged, many of the teachers and students arrived confused about the purposes of the schools. Often unemployed women wrongly felt that the schools would train them and place them in jobs. The unidentified worker who wrote complaining about her continued unemployment was echoing a commonly expressed student misunderstanding: "I attended the F.E.R.A. school with the idea that the school being a government school would mean a lot in securing a job. The school was a good idea but if you can't get a job after you return the government school can't mean very much."[64]

Only some 20 percent of the women workers secured jobs

at the end of the school term, as a result of skills or information acquired. Although most of the schools taught typing, sewing, and cooking courses, the stated purpose of the schools was not to secure placement for students. Hilda Smith acknowledged that a haze of confusion surrounded the objective at most schools and argued that the project was most important for its relief aspects. Over one-half of the young women coming to the summer programs were in severe need of medical or dental treatment. Most were noticeably underweight due to a simple lack of proper food. Approximately one-half of the students who required medical care received it; over 75 percent gained weight. In one Oklahoma school, students did sewing for a hospital in exchange for surgical care for any woman in the program who needed it.[65] Most students had a chance to improve their understanding of the basics of English grammar. In common with the earlier private worker schools, students would often practice that grammar writing angry essays on economics or on labor history subjects.

Not surprisingly, given the political climate and the nature of the programs, by 1937 controversy doomed both the government schools for women workers and the private network of schools. The National Advisory Committee for the schools, which included representatives from the Women's Bureau, the NYA, the WPA, the Office of Education, the American Red Cross, and others, reported conflicts, even shouting matches, between local school boards and both affiliated and NYA schools.[66] Some schools borrowed or rented buildings on college or high school campuses. Others used Girl Scout or YWCA camps. Frequently representatives from the loaning institutions stayed to observe. Hilda Smith surely could not have forgotten her disputes with the Bryn Mawr trustees when she outlined problems encountered by some of the schools and argued that frequently members of institutions loaning buildings "watched suspiciously every slightest action of the girls in the [NYA-FERA] schools."[67] Students at the NYA schools, as had their sisters at the already established workers' schools, used a variety of free "textbooks," prominently *Bulletins* from the Women's Bureau, on aspects of women's employment in the labor force as well as pamphlets from the Affiliated Schools and educational departments of industrial unions. Trustees and board members of several of the institutions loaned for the summer again echoed the Bryn Mawr troubles by challenging teaching methods and assignments and by arguing that too many controversial ideas were receiving government subsidy.[68]

In 1936, Pearle Hutson, who claimed to be a former teacher at the camp for unemployed women at Smyrna, Georgia, wrote a Red-baiting article for the Seattle Post *Intelligencer* falsely charging that the camps meant to turn women workers into cadres of Communist infiltrators bent on destroying the American free enterprise system. Why else, she argued, would the government seek such an isolated spot, an unused YWCA camp in the hill country of Georgia?[69] Hutson's charge that, as a music teacher, she received student requests to play the *Internationale* was at least more plausible.

With such incendiary reports filtering into the newspapers, the NYA went before Congress for a review of its budget in 1937. Despite protest, Congress abruptly canceled the program for schools for unemployed women in July 1937 on stated grounds that the schools had proved too expensive, even though no one disputed that the costs per student were less than those incurred by the Civilian Conservation Corps (CCC).

Of course, many of the worker schools had encouraged young women to think searchingly about their economic position. Some teachers and students openly supported leftist politics, and supporters of the schools in and out of government believed that the American economic system did not treat women workers fairly. However, neither the private nor government schools could accurately be labeled subversive. During extremely lean years for women workers, they provided an environment in which women workers could study English, labor history, and economics. Clearly, both in and out of class, some worker students planned union organizing campaigns or criticized their bosses. No school, not even the ones run directly by federal agencies after 1934, promoted "my country, right or wrong" patriotism. The freewheeling, critical climate soon alienated private donors and politicians. The schools engaged in running battles with both, but lost funding and offers to use facilities and campuses. Male union leaders, already under pressure, retreated and withdrew what small support they had offered. They had little to fear from an angry membership. Over 92 percent of all unionized workers during the Depression were men. Women workers, weak constituents both of union bosses and politicians in the 1920s, remained weak and unorganized, burdened by both family and work obligations, poorly equipped to back lobbyists for their interests. Each year the government schools were in operation, Congress appropriated funds for them on a last-minute basis, dooming the projects to haphazard planning and confusion.

Even WPA officials expressed doubts about programs for unemployed women, echoes of an already established, wary hostility between the WPA and the Women's Bureau. The schools suffered, along with such programs as the WPA sewing rooms, from a general lack of support among federal relief officials for women's work projects. Ellen Woodward, director of the Women's Work Division, wrote a speech for a regional conference of WPA officials held in 1935. Delivered by an aide when Woodward was unable to attend, the speech argued that work assignments to women were unfair. Woodward had written: "In Pennsylvania one out of every four certified [for work] men and only one out of forty certified women are working." She continued, "If you men, either regional engineers or assistant engineers fail to interpret the policies concerning women's work, then we have no one to do it for us."[70] After the speech, a "family discussion," encouraged by several women's work division officials, aired complaints. Women's work officials from Kansas and Nebraska charged that women's projects were the first to be shut down. "It is a lot easier to shut down a women's project when money runs short in the middle of the month . . . whereas if you shut down a road project your equipment seems to be always bothering."[71] Miss Ownings, Ellen Woodward's delegated spokesperson, confronted Frank March and asked, "How in the world can we expect an engineer to be passionately interested in women's work projects? I suddenly found that I wasn't passionately interested in the rural electrification survey, so how could we expect you to be interested in our work?" March responded tellingly, "Frankly our hearts don't palpitate over the sewing rooms."[72]

The hearts of high-level administrators did not palpitate over the women workers' schools either. Both public and private schools faced problems of financial insecurity, haphazard planning, and confused teachers and students. At the very least, however, several thousand women workers had an opportunity for a few months of rest, friendship, education, medical care, and sometimes vocational training.[73] Supporters of the schools argued that these women worker-students deserved this chance and challenged a status quo that seemed to ignore the fact that women, too, faced hunger, sickness, unemployment, and wished to understand the economic system in which they participated. That challenge was a moderate one, restricted by small budgets and Congressional and public opposition.

Hilda Smith continued to lobby unsuccessfully for a resumption of the summer school program through 1940. In a May 1940 letter to Eleanor Roosevelt, she commented, "The C.C.C. camps with their millions of dollars for wages, educational work, travel and supervision constantly remind me of what we might do for women from these same families. As so often the case, the boys get the breaks, the girls are neglected."[74] Her letter provided an appropriate epitaph. During these years, unemployed women and working women got few breaks. Lobbyists for their interests were neglected.

Militant feminists argued that women would not be neglected once they gained absolute legal equality, but federal policy toward women workers remained steadfast in support of protective and special legal treatment of women workers. The protective labor law debate provides the third case study of federal reaction to women workers during the Depression. Naturally, those who favored protective labor legislation made enemies among the supporters of the Equal Rights Amendment. Alice Paul, a militant suffragist whose Congressional Union had renamed itself the Woman's Party after the Nineteenth Amendment victory, began a crusade in the 1920s for another constitutional amendment abolishing all legal distinctions between men and women.

In 1923, the Woman's Party persuaded a friendly congressman to propose for the first time an Equal Rights Amendment to the Constitution. So the debate comparing protective labor legislation to a federal Equal Rights Amendment neither began nor ended during the New Deal. Forty years passed before federal policy in support of sex-specific labor protections changed, and during these forty years, 1923-1963, congressmen continued to debate, on an annual basis, yet another resolution demanding an Equal Rights Amendment. Nevertheless, the economic crisis facing millions of women in the 1930s gave a sense of added urgency to those, in government and out, concerned with finding tools they could use to make the American legal structure benefit women. Frieda Miller, the labor economist who succeeded Mary Anderson and who during the 1930s was an official with the New York State Department of Labor advocating laws limiting night work and physical stress for women, argued years later that "you never give up a tool that is useful in furthering your purpose until you have a better one to substitute for it."[75] Women's Bureau agents and other federal experts on women's work advocated protective labor legislation as that tool. Not until the 1960s did they find a substitute for it in equal pay legislation, Affirmative Action and, after decades of opposition, the Equal Rights Amendment itself.

Moderates, led by the Women's Bureau, asked, "Would an E.R.A provide equal rights only for a professional elite?" "Would it properly protect women's marriage and child-support rights?" Until the 1960s, many analysts of women workers, including those in the Department of Labor, argued that women were emotionally and physically unique and needed protective legislation. Militant feminists demanded immediate abolition of all legal distinctions between male and female citizens' rights and duties.

Different judgments about the utility of legal change provide a key to understanding both the debate and federal policy. Interestingly, both federal bureaucrats and Woman's Party members used the problems of working-class women workers to justify either their caution or their optimism. Educated middle-class women advocated or opposed the Equal Rights Amendment (ERA) as either a boon or a harm to an economic class of women to which they did not belong. In each case, the female elite that debated the value of the ERA argued that either victory or defeat would benefit all women, but especially working women.

Although the National Federation of Business and Professional Women endorsed the ERA in 1937, most major women's organizations united behind the Women's Bureau in opposition. That coalition did not disintegrate until the 1960s. Approval of the proposed amendment by both the Democratic Party and Republican Party platforms in 1940 and 1944 and its endorsement by the General Federation of Women's Clubs proved to be war-year apostasy. Enthusiasm for the Amendment among moderates wavered, and decisions debated and made in the 1930s held for another decade.

Those decisions involved agreements among moderates led by the professional experts of the Women's Bureau to campaign—not for an Equal Rights Amendment but rather for night-work prohibitions, the eight-hour day, the six-day week, weight-lifting limits, and special facilities within factories that employed women. Women, they argued, were still too poorly paid, poorly educated, and unorganized to gain fair treatment in the work place, even should they get complete constitutional equality. Women should not be legally equal to men unless they were socially equal. The analysts in the Women's Bureau paid lip service, not insult, to traditional societal norms, which decreed that even single women bear much heavier domestic burdens, implying as they did so that social equality might neither be possible nor desirable. As long as society acquiesced in low pay scales for women and demanded that working women shoulder most home duties, society should also provide protective labor legislation. Eventually, adherents argued, the benefits of night work and hour restrictions, requirements about safety and weight-lifting limits, could also be extended to male workers. No one should have to work excessively long hours under unsafe conditions. Even after the validation by the Supreme Court of the Fair Labor Standards Act in 1941, establishing the legality of principles of wage and hour regulation for men as well as women, the Women's Bureau continued to urge protective labor legislation. Large numbers of women workers, it argued, were not covered by the Fair Labor Standards Act. Women still properly fulfilled different social roles. Despite the minimum wage and the eight-hour day, women workers still needed extra guardianship. Opposing these arguments, members of the Woman's Party declared that without full legal equality, guaranteed by constitutional amendment, social equality would forever remain elusive.

By 1930, opponents and proponents of the Equal Rights Amendment had had seven years to take each other's measure. Woman's Party members had already disrupted two Women's Bureau conferences on women in industry, one held in 1923, the other held in 1926. In 1926, a session on night work for women erupted chaotically as Gail Laughlin and other Woman's Party delegates rose to their feet, shouting, waving placards, overturning tables, and, according to one startled observer, engaging in at least one fist-fight.[76] The Depression intensified the need to find solutions to the dilemmas faced by working women. It also intensified the ERA-Protective Labor Law controversy, by now a battle between bitter rivals. Mary Anderson called the Woman's Party leader "hysterical.''[77] Alice Paul, in turn, described the Women's Bureau as an "enemy camp" full of bureaucrats "sitting there with their nice big governmental salaries and all *BREATHING* incompetence.''[78]

"The Effects of Labor Legislation," Women's Bureau *Bulletin #65,* published in 1928, but not widely circulated until 1931, was one of the longest and most extensively researched of all Bureau *Bulletins.* It concluded that labor laws did not constitute a major handicap to women's economic advance and that any Equal Rights Amendment would most surely have disastrous consequences for working and nonworking women alike.[79]

Bulletin #65, the most important Bureau publication issued between 1920 and 1940, was a better illustration of the agency's continued advocacy of Progressive rhetoric about women's proper roles within society than it was the unbiased and exhaustive study the Bureau claimed it to be. *Bulletin #65* argued that only a minority of women suffered from restrictions such as night work or prohibitions on contact with noxious chemicals since "naturally" most women had an aversion to jobs of these types. The argument, like others presented in the document, offered not proof but theory about social values. In effect, *Bulletin #65* argued that society and not protective labor laws determined what jobs women should and should not hold. The Bureau's own voluminous files, documenting hundreds of unsuccessful applications by women to join unions or to get employment where work emphasized dangerous or physically taxing tasks, refuted its claim that the laws did not sway or justify employer and union restrictions against women workers.[80]

Bulletin #65 was only one concrete illustration of the controversy. The domestic debate pitting an Equal Rights Amendment against protective legislation included a search for international allies. Doris Stevens, like Paul a former militant suffragist, directed the Party's international campaign. In 1928, the sixth Conference of Pan-American Republics met at Havana, Cuba, and Stevens, in charge of a delegation of women from some Latin American republics as well as from the United States, arrived to lobby for the negotiation of a statement that supported legal equality of the sexes. She and her supporters marched through the streets, held rallies, and aggressively cornered individual delegates in hotel lobbies, restaurants, and meeting rooms. Although the conference refused to ratify a resolution supporting equal rights for women, Doris

Stevens won a partial victory: The conference voted to establish an Inter-American Commission of Women to study the problems of women in the Western Hemisphere. Secretary of State Frank Kellogg sent Doris Stevens as unofficial United States member to the Commission.[81]

The Seventh Pan-American Conference, held in Montevideo in 1933, passed a resolution urging equal rights for all women in the Americas. The resolution, Stevens hoped, would be a World Equal Rights Treaty to be ratified by the League of Nations. However, Stevens had no official role at the Montevideo conference. President Franklin Roosevelt had appointed social worker and protective legislation advocate Sophonisba Breckenridge rather than Stevens as the first official United States delegate to the conference, and Mary Anderson, an old friend, had written her:

> I was so happy when you were appointed. . . . And I know that you must have had a hectic time here because as you know I know the ladies that you met down there. . . . Doris Stevens is back, and she is going to be here in Washington, and up on the Hill to lobby. We will hear much of them, and may have to counter-act some of their work.[82]

Anderson took plans for a counterattack seriously. She contacted influential women in the Democratic Party in an attempt to minimize the influence of the Woman's Party at the next Pan-American conference to be held in Lima, in December 1938. Mrs. Buston Musser, National Democratic Committeewoman from Utah, wrote Molly Dewson, head of the Women's Division of the Democratic Party, that she worried about the party's "tremendous and powerful propaganda in Latin America." She urged that Dewson, a confidante of both Eleanor and Franklin Roosevelt, warn the president about Doris Stevens.[83] In 1939, under pressure from an obviously hostile administration, Doris Stevens resigned her position as head of the Inter-American Commission of Women. Secretary of State Cordell Hull, in an act beautifully symbolic of the rivalry, then appointed former Women's Bureau member, Mary Winslow, to fill Stevens' seat.

The Inter-American Commission of Women was not the only international forum for the dispute between American organizations that differed on the Equal Rights Amendment. In 1935, the General Assembly of the League of Nations debated the question of the general status of women. In 1933, the International Conference of American States, held in Montevideo, had debated an Equal-Rights-for-Women resolution. The resolution failed, despite the strenuous lobbying efforts of Doris Stevens. However, several of the Latin American member countries that had voted in its favor requested that the League consider the topic of equal rights for women.

The League dealt with this request by calling upon the International Labor Organization (ILO), one of its branches, to investigate the effects of an equal rights treaty upon labor legislation throughout the world. In turn, the Governing Board of the ILO asked members of its Advisory Committee on Women Workers to coordinate studies of the economic status of women. Mary Anderson agreed to organize a committee to prepare the United States report. In the process, she and other members of the Women's Bureau became involved in an effort she would later describe as "completely unsuccessful."[84]

As Anderson met with the women economists, historians, and business, government, and labor leaders she had recruited, the group gradually decided not to confine itself to a specific statement on the economic status of American women. Instead, they decided to draft a "Women's Charter" with the objective that the women of the United States and Europe could cooperate with the women of India, Asia, Africa, and Latin America. All could benefit from such an international declaration of women's rights. The American originators of the Charter idea, all of whom supported protective labor legislation in the United States, saw not only a way to get an international statement attacking exploitation of women but also a way to receive world support for their continuing battle with the Woman's Party over the Equal Rights Amendment.[85]

After several months of meetings, the Women's Charter Committee presented a proposed draft of their document:

> Women shall have full political and civil rights; full opportunity for education, full opportunity for work according to their individual abilities, with safeguards against physically harmful conditions of employment and economic exploitation. Where special exploitation of women workers exists, such as unhealth-

ful working conditions or long hours of work which result in physical exhaustion and denial of the right to leisure, such conditions shall be corrected through social and labor legislation which the world's experience shows to be necessary.[86]

Mary Anderson did not wish the Charter to be labeled a federal government proposal. However, she and Mary Pidgeon, of the Women's Bureau Research Division, sat on the Charter planning committee. Moreover, the Women's Bureau had already offered to act as the United States coordinating center to collect material and to edit a comprehensive report for the ILO on the economic status of women in the United States.

Anderson, Mary Pidgeon, and Mary Robinson traveled widely, giving speeches to promote it, and for a year, the idea of a Women's Charter sparked widespread interest. But Charter Committee minutes reveal that only Women's Bureau representatives expressed real dedication to the Charter idea. The movement lost momentum in a flurry of resolutions pledging careful study.[87]

The Woman's Party vehemently denounced the Charter as yet another Bureau ploy to support its vested interest in protective labor legislation. Party members denounced the Charter draft as the "Secret Mary Anderson Charter."[88] Woman's Party members in Washington visited their congressmen, charging that the Women's Bureau wished to put the stamp of United States governmental approval on a program of ill-reasoned international advice.[89] Worried, Mary Anderson tried to prod friendly organizations to action.[90]

Instead, the Charter Committee engaged in an embarrassing public wrangle. A feature article in the January 7, 1937, *New York World Telegram* titled, "Sponsor Spurns Charter for Women," heralded historian Mary Beard's disaffection with the project. In a series of letters to Mary Anderson, Mary Beard, a nominal member of the Woman's Party, had criticized the wording of the Charter. The Charter, she commented in November 1936, was a "very hard thing to get tight. . . . It still contains what seem to me to be contradictions, and it ends with a very vague idea of necessity."[91] When Mary Beard's name appeared on a newspaper list of Charter sponsors, she publicly objected. Torn between the arguments for protection and the arguments for absolute equality, Beard issued a statement saying she belonged to "neither camp." She

agreed with members of the Woman's Party that protective legislation for women "embodies the objectionable idea of dependence."
But on the other hand, "liberty to compete on equal terms with
men implies satisfaction with the fight over the crumbs which fall
from Dives' table."[92]

Mary Van Kleeck, former Department of Labor colleague with
Mary Anderson and Charter committee member, wrote to Beard
that she was "deeply shocked" by the newspaper article.[93] Mary
Beard stood her ground. She had, she argued, merely attended one
Women's Charter planning session, and had left that meeting convinced that the group understood that she had attended as an un-
committed individual.[94]

In the aftermath of this committee furor, Secretary of Labor
Frances Perkins persuaded a reluctant Grace Abbott to present the
Women's Charter at the international meetings of the ILO in 1937.
The chief of the Children's Bureau, already a delegate to the 1937
meetings, felt that the evident lack of unity among members of
the United States Committee weakened the usefulness of any statement the Charter might make. She introduced a resolution para-
phrasing the Charter, but only as a member of the United States
delegation, not as the spokeswoman of a united group of the
world's women. The assembled delegates to the ILO conference
passed the resolution, which stated that women should have full
opportunity to work and should receive pay without discrimination because of sex, that women as well as men should be guaranteed
freedom of association by governments and should be protected
by social and labor legislation "which the world's experience has
shown to be effective in abolishing special exploitation of women
workers."[95] The disunity even among members of the committee
guaranteed that little international attention would be paid to this
statement favoring protective labor legislation.

The Women's Charter imbroglio illustrates an interesting irony
about federal efforts promoted during this decade of crisis by the
experts in the Women's Bureau and their allies outside government and within other New Deal agencies. The Bureau won an
international endorsement of its Charter; it lobbied for and helped
to win repeal of federal legislation curbing the right of married
women to work; the federal summer camps for unemployed women
did become a reality; protective legislation and not the Equal Rights

Amendment received legislative approval. But the victories were limited ones, tinged with an edge of defeat and hampered by public opposition, infighting among women's groups, and Congressional unwillingness to champion women workers.

During New Deal years, which other historians identify as providing expanded opportunities for women officials in politics and government, programs directly responding to women workers received short shrift.[96] President Franklin Roosevelt's record for appointing women professionals to important federal posts set precedents and was not matched until the 1960s. The Roosevelt Administration's response to women in the work force, however, broke little new ground. Most officials analyzing the issue of women's labor force participation repeated Progressive rhetoric. Women workers toiled from economic necessity. They deserved the chance to work, but they also deserved special protection. The fact is that few of the Roosevelt women appointees championed women workers as a special cause. Roosevelt named women officials to be United States ambassador to Norway, United States ambassador to Denmark, secretary of labor, assistant treasurer of the United States, Civil Service commissioner, and director of the United States Mint.[97] These and other jobs were not tokens, and these women toiled not solely from economic necessity. During a decade when millions of women workers lost their jobs and cries echoed in state after state for women to go back home and leave the jobs to men, these women, highly visible, may have felt that the issue of women in the work force was too volatile. Moreover, these women did not defy Progressive attitudes about women's work. Most of them were born in the 1870s and 1880s and had come of age during the Progressive era fighting not just for suffrage but also for protective labor legislation and government maternal health care. They personalized the Progressive legacy in the New Deal and helped programs such as a government-mandated minimum wage and government unemployment insurance finally become law. For many, the passage of a bill such as Social Security had been a goal for thirty or forty years. Few demanded a dramatically different government policy toward women workers, however. None came. Moreover, many of Roosevelt's women appointees still clustered on the outer circles of power, as administrators or lobbyists for social welfare programs. No woman, not even Eleanor Roosevelt, belonged to Roosevelt's most intimate group of political advisors. In such a climate, as Hilda Smith complained, it was not surprising that "the boys get the breaks."

NOTES

1. Mary Anderson, Third Race Betterment Conference, Battle Creek, Michigan, January 2, 1928, "Speech File #341-S-61," Bx. 69, Records of the Women's Bureau (R.G. 86), National Archives, Washington, D.C. (hereafter cited as WB, NA).

2. The White House directed all such letters to the Women's Bureau, as did other federal agencies. For complete file, see "Correspondence—Individuals, 1930-1939." The files are alphabetized by state and divided into two-year periods, WB, NA; the Women's Bureau sent copies of many letters to the Secretary of Labor, excerpts of which are quoted here; see "Women," "Secretary Perkins' General Subject File, 1933-1940," Records of the secretaries of labor (R.G. 174), NA (hereafter cited as Labor, NA). The secretary's file of personal letters also contains many originals, copies of which were sent to the Women's Bureau.

3. Mary Anderson, memorandum to Elizabeth Christman, "Work to be Done," dated 1932, "Organizations File: N.W.T.U.L.," WB, NA.

4. See "The Effects of the Depression on Wage Earners' Families," Women's Bureau *Bulletin #108* (Washington, D.C.: Government Printing Office, 1935); "Women Unemployed Seeking Relief in 1933," Women's Bureau *Bulletin #139* (Washington, D.C.: Government Printing Office, 1935); Mary Anderson, "What the New Deal Has Done for Women-in-Industry," address before National Biennial Nursing Convention, April 24, 1934, "Speech File #342-S-129," WB, NA; Mary Robinson, "Depression Lessons for Women," speech draft (typescript), "Speech File, June, 1933," WB, NA; Mary Winslow, draft of remarks on female employment, symposium at Institute of Public Affairs, University of Virginia, Charlottesville, "Round Table on Unemployment," July 11, 1932, "Speech File #341-S-114"; Jean Brown, article prepared for Secretary Perkins to send to Women's Study Club of Winston-Salem, NC, "The New Economics," November 16, 1933, "Article File #341-S-332," WB, NA; Mary Anderson, "A Share the Work Plan," memorandum (typescript) to Elizabeth Christman, December 1932, "Article File (unnumbered)," WB, NA.

5. Louis Scharf's *To Work and To Wed: Female Employment, Feminism and the Great Depression* (Westport, Conn.: Greenwood Press, 1980) provides a useful overview of employment patterns for women, both single and married, during the 1930s.

6. The Bureau report on Section 213 can be found in U.S. Congress.

House. Congressional Record. 75th Cong., 1st Sess., v. 81, Part 6, pp. 6934-6945, June 8, 1937 (hereafter cited as Bureau/CR).

7. The Bureau kept a file of court cases dealing with this question. Especially useful are its summaries of the following: Indiana: *Kostanzer et al. v. State*, ex. rel. *Ramsay* 187 337 (1933); Louisiana: *State* ex. rel. Kundert v. Jefferson Parish School Board, 184 SC 555 (1938); Missouri: Staryhorn v. Bladgett Consolidated School District No. 35 of Scott County, 86 SW (2d) 37 (1936). See "Married Women's Files," Bx. 831-832 WB, NA; the Bureau "Speech File #341-S," contains hundreds of speeches, organized chronologically and within years, by subject (for 1931-1935), which illustrate championship of married women. Illustrative of Bureau advocacy are the following studies: "Short Talks About Working Women," Women's Bureau *Bulletin #59* (Washington, D.C.: Government Printing Office, 1927); "The Woman Wage Earner—Her Situation Today," Women's Bureau *Bulletin #172* (Washington, D.C.: Government Printing Office, 1939); "Household Employment in Chicago," Women's Bureau *Bulletin #106* (Washington, D.C.: Government Printing Office, 1933); "Piecework in the Silk Dress Industry," Women's Bureau *Bulletin #141* (Washington, D.C.: Government Printing Office, 1936); "Hours, Earnings, and Employment in Cotton Mills," Women's Bureau *Bulletin #111* (Washington, D.C.: Government Printing Office, 1933).

8. Mary Anderson, speech before the Arlington Soroptimist Club, March 28, 1940, "Discriminations Against Women," "Mimeograph File," WB, NA.

9. Results of the poll summarized in "Working Wives and Other's Bread," *The Literary Digest* (May 15, 1937), pp. 25-26.

10. Mary Anderson, "Statement of Women's Democratic Rights," May 1939, "Mimeograph File," WB, NA.

11. *Ibid.*

12. Mary Anderson, copy of reply to Roger Babson, January 17, 1939, "Organization File—Business and Professional Women," Bx. 841, WB, NA.

13. Press release, January 28, 1931, "Press Release File #341-A-227," WB, NA.

14. Mary Anderson, "Wives Are People," article draft, May 17, 1939, "Article File #341-A-437," WB, NA.

15. See for example: "The Family Status of Breadwinning Women," Women's Bureau *Bulletin #23* (Washington, D.C.: Government Printing Office, 1922); "The Share of Wage-Earning Women in Family Support," Women's Bureau *Bulletin #30* (Washington, D.C.: Government Printing Office, 1923).

16. Mary Robinson, "The Place of Women in Industry," is illustrative of the series, July 6, 1925, all under "Radio Script Files #342-RR," WB, NA.

17. *Ibid.*

18. Mary Robinson, "The Home and Family Problems," speech draft, "Speech File #341-S-96," WB, NA.

19. Babson was a broker, columnist, stock analyst, the originator of *Babson's Reports* and the Babsoncharts. Roger Babson, *Actions and Reactions, An Autobiography* (New York: Harpers, 1949); *Washington Post,* January 17, 1939.

20. Mary Anderson reply to Roger Babson, January 17, 1939.

21. The Bureau continued to print studies emphasizing the heavy role married women played in family support in the 1930s. See "The Employed Woman Homemaker in the U.S.: Her Responsibility for Family Support," Women's Bureau *Bulletin #148* (Washington, D.C.: Government Printing Office, 1936); "Employed Women and Family Support," Women's Bureau *Bulletin* #168 (Washington, D.C.: Government Printing Office, 1939).

22. Mary Anderson, "Married Women in Industry," speech before meeting of the NWTUL, New York, May 8, 1929, "Speech File #341-S-76," WB, NA.

23. *Ibid.*

24. See "Summary of Women's Bureau Action on Proposals to Dismiss Married Women—Case I-C. and C. RR" (copies and summaries of telegrams), memorandum (typescript), March 1933, "Married Women's File," WB, NA.

25. Mary Robinson, "The Family Problems of Women Workers," speech delivered at Merchantville, N.J., October 15, 1930, "Speech File #341-S-96," WB, NA.

26. "Drafts of speech on female opportunity for the use of Secretary Perkins" (typescript notes), July 1933, "Article File #341-A-32a," WB, NA.

27. Mary Anderson, New York, October 5, 1926, "Speech File #341-S-51," WB, NA.

28. Mary Anderson, speech before the annual meeting of the American Home Economics Association, Atlanta, Georgia, June 20, 1932, "Speech File #341-S-110," WB, NA.

29. "Radio File #341-A-67," 1933, WB, NA.

30. See Ruth Mikman, "Women's Work and the Economic Crisis: Some Lessons From the Great Depression," *The Review of Radical Political Economics,* v. 8, no. 1. Spring 1976, pp. 73-97; Winifred Wandersee, "The Economics of Middle Income Family Life: Working Women During the Great Depression," *Journal of American History,* 65 (June 1978), pp. 66-74; Winifred Wandersee, *Women's Work and Family Values, 1920-1940* (Cambridge, Mass.: Harvard University Press, 1981); Susan Ware, *Beyond Suffrage—Women in the New Deal* (Cambridge, Mass.: Harvard University Press, 1981); Lois Scharf, *To Work and To Wed,* pp. 38-107. Scharf's treatment of the Women's Bureau oversimplifies the Bureau's position of married women's work.

31. This is a major argument made by Winifred Wandersee, "The Economics of Middle Income Family Life," pp. 60-65.

32. Figures found in Michael Gordon, ed., *The American Family in Social-Historical Perspective* (New York: 1973); see also Frank Stricker, "Cookbooks and Law Books: The Hidden History of Career Women in Twentieth Century America," *Journal of Social History,* 10 (Fall 1976), pp. 1-19.

33. Mary Robinson, memorandum (handwritten), April 8, 1938, "Correspondence File—Organizations" (marked, "to be attached to letter," letter missing), WB, NA; memorandum: "Survey of Women," Works Progress Administration, Division of Social Research, April 6, 1937, typescript, in Sewing Projects File, Records of the Works Progress Administration (R.G. 69), National Archives, Washington, D.C. (hereafter cited as WPA, NA).

34. "Minutes of Meeting on Household Training Project," May 15, 1937, WPA, NA; Mary Robinson to Anna Marie Driscoll, May 15, 1937, "Household Training Project File," WPA, NA.

35. *Ibid.*

36. Mary Robinson to Anna Marie Driscoll, May 15, 1937; Mary Jean Simpson (technical advisor on sewing projects) to Ann Garrity, assistant director, Women and Professional Division, November 28, 1936, "Household Training Project File," Bx. 9, WPA, NA.

37. Frank March to the Honorable Ellison Smith, April 5, 1938, "Household Training Project File," Bx. 9, WPA, NA.

38. Mary Robinson, memorandum (handwritten), April 8, 1938, "Correspondence File—Organizations" (marked, "to be attached to letter," letter missing) WB, NA.

39. The script continues with Meta saying, "May the Lord bless and keep you " "The Women's Bureau agent, who, though not personally responsible, nevertheless stood to Meta as Uncle Sam's representative and so appeared to her in the guise of a fairy godmother whose wand had waved a bright spot into the dull routine of Meta's job." Radio Script File, #342-S-125, WB, NA.

40. A series of Bureau protests to Secretary Perkins resulted in a letter from the secretary to Administrator Hugh Johnson. Mary Anderson to Frances Perkins, memorandum: "Unequal Wage Codes," October 14, 1933, October 20, 1933, Secretary of Labor File, Bx. 1280, WB, NA. Perkins wrote to Johnson, "I deplore the growing tendency of the codes to set up a differential in rates based on sex, and I particularly object to the wording which will give the false appearance of fairness." Perkins to Johnson, Secretary Perkins' General File, 1933-1940 (R.G. 174), Perkins, NA.

41. Mary Robinson, interview transcript, for a "Close Up of Women Workers Under the NRA, station WJSV, Washington, D.C., Radio Script File (unnumbered), June ?, 1933," WB, NA.

42. Mary Robinson, radio talk, "Remember the Forgotten Woman," December 22, 1933, Radio Script File, #341-S-125, WB, NA.

43. Libby Corngold, a student at the 1927 Bryn Mawr Summer School, described "A typical employer's reaction" as her contribution to the 1927 student magazine of essays:

> *Employee:* Mr. M., I would like to ask you to give me a leave of absence of two months, which I would like to spend attending school.
>
> *Employer:* A leave of absence? In the time when the season has started? What kind of school is this?
>
> *Employee:* Bryn Mawr Summer School.
>
> *Employer:* Oh. So you want to attend a school which teaches workers how best to fight the bosses.
>
> *Employee:* Not at all. This school's aim is to enable workers to think more clearly on problems they are confronted with.
>
> *Employer:* What for do you want education? Can't you stitch coats without having any? And to become a professor—it is too late, anyhow.
>
> *Employee:* Mr. M., I do not see any difference between a professor and a worker.
>
> *Employer:* I can't understand what you talk about. Workers educated . . . workers professors; you are crazy.

Copies of the Bryn Mawr mimeographed student magazines can be found in Hilda Smith Papers, Bx. 3-4, Schlesinger Library (hereafter cited as SL).

44. See Florence Schneider, *Patterns of Workers' Education: The Story of the Bryn Mawr Summer School* (Washington, D.C.: American Council on Public Affairs, 1941); Spencer Miller, "Summer School for Workers," *American Federationist,* 32 (July 1925): pp. 569-571; Orlie Pell, "A Workers' School for the Office Workers," *American Federationist,* 42 (June 1935): pp. 622-624; Hilda Smith, "Bryn Mawr Summer School of 1927," *American Federationist,* 43 (October 1927): pp. 1217-1223; Hilda Smith, "The Bryn Mawr Summer School of 1928," *American Federationist,* 34 (October 1928): pp. 1498-1500; Hilda Smith, "The Bryn Mawr Summer School of 1929," *American Federationist,* 36 (September 1929): pp. 1107-1110; John Troxell, "Wisconsin's Summer School for Working Women," *American Federationist,* 32 (October 1925): pp. 943-945; Andra Hourwich and Gladys Palmer, eds., *I Am a Woman Worker: A Scrapbook of Autobiographies from the Summer Schools for Women Workers* (New York:

The Affiliated Schools for Workers, Inc., 1936) (reprint, Arno Press, 1974); Lillian Herstein, "The Significance of the Southern Summer School for Women Workers," *The American Teacher* (January 1931): pp. 54-57; "Schools at Bryn Mawr" (editorial), *The American Teacher* (February 1931).

45. "Information Regarding Workers' Education and the Affiliated Schools," typed report, dated March 16, 1937, Records of the Works Projects Administration and Its Predecessors (R.G. 69), Subject Series 1937, National Archives, Washington, D.C., WPA, NA.

46. *Ibid.* See also "The Industrial Experience of Women Workers at the Summer Schools," Women's Bureau *Bulletin #89* (Washington, D.C., Government Printing Office, 1939), pp. 3-12.

47. *Shop and School,* 1936 (Hudson Shore). Most of the Hudson Shore pamphlets are labeled "Shop and School." After 1936, Bryn Mawr Summer School had relocated to West Park, New York, but sometimes the name, "Bryn Mawr" still appears on student pamphlets. "Workers' Magazine" was a term used at the Bryn Mawr School. The pamphlets for the Bryn Mawr and the Hudson Shore Labor Schools can be found in the Hilda Smith Papers, Ex. 3-4, SL. Also included in the Hilda Smith Papers, FDR Lib. (and to a small extent, SL) is correspondence between Bryn Mawr and Hudson Shore students and students at the other women's working schools in the South and Wisconsin.

48. Shop and School, "The Awakening," 1936 (Hudson Shore/Bryn Mawr), Hilda Smith Papers, Bx. 3, SL.

49. Virginia Schieffelin to the editor of the New York *Herald Tribune,* June 7, 1935: clipping in Mary Van Kleeck Papers, Bx. 6, Sophia Smith Collection, Smith College (hereafter cited as SS). The Van Kleeck Papers provide a wealth of documentation about the dispute between the Bryn Mawr Summer School and the college's board of directors, esp. Ex. 6, SS.

50. "Job Histories of Women Workers at the Summer Schools, 1931-34 and 1938," Women's Bureau, *Bulletin #174* (Washington, D.C.: Government Printing Office, 1939); "Changing Jobs," Women's Bureau, *Bulletin #54* (Washington, D.C.: Government Printing Office, 1926); "The Industrial Experience of Women Workers at the Summer Schools, 1928-1930," Women's Bureau, *Bulletin #89* (Washington, D.C.: Government Printing Office, 1931); "Women Workers in the Third Year of the Depression," Women's Bureau, *Bulletin #103* (Washington, D.C.: Government Printing Office, 1933).

51. The preface to the workers' study read, in part, "Many reports on unemployment have been written during the past three years. Few of them have shown in any detail the changed living conditions forced upon the workers who had lost their jobs, in spite of the fact that the human cost

of the breakdown of the economic apparatus is measured in the effect on standards of living." The Women's Bureau went on to state that only rarely did workers ever receive any opportunity to analyze their own condition.

52. *Bulletin #103,* pp. 10-11.

53. *Bulletin #174,* p. 6.

54. Mrs. W. W. Gabriel (Oregon director of Women's Work) to Franklin Roosevelt. "Confirmation Copy" telegram. January 5, 1934, Perkins' General File, BX 81, Labor, NA.

55. "The Workers' Education Project of the FERA and the Workers' Service Program of the WPA, 1933-1943" (typescript), May 1956, p. 3, Bx. 3, Hilda Smith Papers, SL (hereafter cited as Smith, 1956 Report).

56. "Report on Resident Schools and Camps for Unemployed Women," Office of the Specialist in Workers' Education, Federal Emergency Relief Administration (typescript), April 1935, p. 8, Bx. 3, Hilda Smith Papers, SL (hereafter cited as Smith, 1935 Report).

57. Mary Anderson to Secretary Perkins, memorandum: "Women's CCC Camps," December 4, 1936, "Secretary of Labor File," Bx. 1280, WB, NA. Roosevelt asked Anderson to keep her informed of activities of all government agencies with regard to unemployed women. See memorandum, December 13, 1935, also Roosevelt to Anderson, January 1, 1935, Eleanor Roosevelt Papers, Series 70, Bx. 641, Franklin D. Roosevelt Presidential Library (hereafter cited as FDR Lib).

58. Smith, 1935 Report, p. 10.

59. *Ibid.* Plan Report Summary, unpaged.

60. Ethel Clark, field representative, Workers' Education, to Helen Hermann, September 15, 1935, Hilda Smith Papers, SL; Hilda Smith to Eleanor Roosevelt, May 17, 1934, Hilda Smith Papers, SL.

61. Dorothea de Schweinitz to Mary Anderson, "Educational Camps for Unemployed Young Women," memorandum, December 2, 1936, "Secretary's File" Bx. 1280, WB, NA.

62. Smith, 1935 Report, pp. 4-13.

63. Smith, 1956 Report, p. 5.

64. Smith, 1935 Report, pp. 18-23.

65. *Ibid.,* p. 27.

66. Other representatives included the Rural Electrification Administration and the Bureau of Home Economics. See Report to the Secretary from Mary Anderson, December 4, 1936, Bx. 1280, "Secretary's File," WB, NA.

67. Smith, 1935 Report, p. 24.

68. Smith, 1956 Report, pp. 4-7.

69. February 23, 1936.

70. "Mountain States Regional Conference," transcript, typed, Tuesday

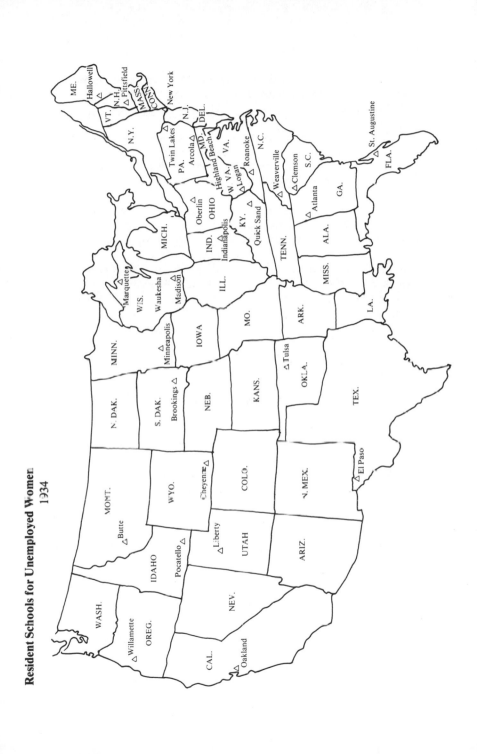

Resident Schools for Unemployed Women
1934

Afternoon Session, April 25, 1935, Series 375, Records of the Women's Work Division, pp. 16-17, WPA, NA.

71. *Ibid.,* p. 23.

72. *Ibid.,* p. 25.

73. See map. Some of the 1934 schools shown here reopened under the NYA program in 1936. This map, from the Smith, 1935 Report, shows a representative geographic distribution of the schools for one year.

74. Hilda Smith to Eleanor Roosevelt, May 15, 1940, Hilda Smith Papers, SL.

75. Frieda Miller, "The National Economic Scene as It Concerns Women," speech before the Idaho Conference on the Status of Women and Children, Boise, Idaho, August 28, 1950 (typescript), Frieda Miller Papers, Folder 204, SL.

76. Mary Anderson to Mary Van Kleeck, Mary Van Kleeck Papers, December 15, 1922, Bx. 63, SS. A strikingly different Woman's Party interpretation of the Conference can be found in the Jane Norman Smith Papers, esp. Folders 145-148, SL; the Doris Stevens Papers, Bx. 23, SL; and the Alma Lutz Papers, Bx. 1, SL. For a transcript of the conference proceedings see Women's Bureau "Summary of the Proceedings of the Second Women's Industrial Conference," January 1926 (typescript), "Domestic Conference File," WB, NA.

77. Mary Anderson, *Woman at Work,* p. 168; Mary Anderson, "Should There Be Labor Laws for Women—Yes," *Good Housekeeping,* 21 (September 1935).

78. The Alice Paul Oral History, typescript—Regional Oral History Office, Bancroft Library, University of California, Berkeley, 1976 (interviewer, Amelia Fry) (hereafter cited as Alice Paul Oral History).

79. Women's Bureau field agents collected data in eleven states and included statistics on some 660,000 women workers.

80. Sheila Rothman, *Woman's Proper Place: A History of Changing Ideals and Practices* (New York: Basic Books, 1978), pp. 155-167, provides an interesting analysis of protective labor legislation, in which she labels *Bulletin #65* an "odd" document—its own internal evidence damning some of its conclusions.

81. For a hostile account of the Pan-American Conferences, see Stanley Lemons, *The Woman Citizen,* pp. 197-198. For sympathetic accounts of the Woman's Party efforts see Doris Stevens, "Feminist History Was Made at Havana," *Independent Woman,* March 3, 1928, p. 29; Inez Haynes Irwin, *Angels and Amazons* (New York: 1933), pp. 424-427. The Doris Stevens Papers contain material that outlines the role played by the Woman's Party in the Inter-American Commission of Women. The Papers contain a set of press releases issued while Stevens was on the Commission;

also Stevens' set of workbooks showing discrimination against women in each of the Latin American republics, in which Woman's Party members are listed as researchers. See especially v. 1-39, "Inter-American Commission of Women," Report to the Seventh International Conference of American States, Doris Stevens Papers, SL.

82. Anderson to Breckenridge, January 26, 1934, "Correspondence—International File," Bx. 829, WB, NA.

83. Mrs. Buston Musser to Mary Dewson, Mary Dewson Papers, March 3, 1938, Bx. 9, FDR Lib.: see also Dewson Papers, Bx. 9, FDR Lib. for additional letters between Democratic National Committeewomen on the subject.

84. "The Women's Charter," memorandum, June 10, 1938, Bx. 123, WB, NA; Anderson, *Woman at Work*, p. 210.

85. The advisory group continued to be informal, so the roster of committee "members" fluctuated. Women who attended at least one Charter planning session included the historian Mary Beard; Frieda Miller, at the time with the New York State Department of Labor; Frances Cummings, National Business and Professional Women; Mary Van Kleeck, former director of the Women's Bureau and head of the Industrial Division of the Russell Sage Foundation; Rose Schneiderman, president, and Elizabeth Christman, treasurer, of the WTUL; Helen Atwater, American Home Economics Association; Anne Hartwell Johnstone and Edith Cook of the League of Women Voters; Josephine Doggett, General Federation of Women's Clubs; Elize Eastman and Elsie Harper of the YWCA; Lucy Mason, National Consumers' League; Elizabeth May, American Association of University Women; Agnes Regan, National Council of Catholic Women; Federal Judge Florence Allen agreed to provide informal legal advice; Mary Anderson, Mary Pidgeon, and Louise Stitt of the Women's Bureau attended, though Anderson did not want them to say that they represented the Women's Bureau. See "Minutes of Conference Group to Consider the Women's Charter: November 12, 1936," WB, NA.

86. Printed pamphlet, 1936, "The Women's Charter, What and Why," "Women's Charter—International Conferences File," WB, NA.

87. Mary Anderson, "The Significance of the Women's Charter," speech before the American Jewish Congress, New York City, March 30, 1937, "Speech File (unnumbered)," WB, NA; Mary Robinson, in 1935, prepared a draft of a speech intended for radio delivery, analyzing the political condition of women in Latin America, Europe, and the Soviet Union since World War I, "A Balance Sheet for Feminism," "Speech File #341-A-370" (speech draft, typescript, 2), WB, NA.

88. See Jane N. Smith to Alice Paul, March 7, 1937, Jane Norman Smith Papers, Folder 227, SL.

89. "Report of the Temporary Committee of Organization—Prepared for Submission at Meeting in Washington, D.C., January 30, 1937," Bx. 81, WB, NA. The Women's Charter Committee spent much time at this 1937 strategy session discussing the Woman's Party attacks.

90. Anderson to Lucy Mason, Records of the National Consumers' League, Bx. C-16, December 10, 1936, LC.

91. Beard to Anderson, November 8, 1936, "Women's Charter—International Conferences File," WB, NA.

92. *The New York World Telegram,* January 7, 1937.

93. Mary Van Kleeck to Beard, January 8, 1937, copy, "Women's Charter—International Conferences File," WB, NA.

94. Mary Beard to Mary Van Kleeck, January 13, 1937, copy, "Women's Charter Files," WB, NA.

95. Anderson, *Woman at Work,* p. 213.

96. Susan Ware, *Beyond Suffrage;* Joseph Lash, *Eleanor and Franklin* (New York: 1971).

97. For a group biography of women officials in the New Deal, see Susan Ware, *Beyond Suffrage,* Appendix B.

The Reaction to Rosie the Riveter: War Policy and the Woman Worker

5

Overnight, Pearl Harbor changed the Depression caricature of women workers as evil job stealers. By mid-1944, nineteen million women earned wages; of every three members of the labor force, one was a woman. A new caricature made the woman worker an angel, loyally staffing the home front arsenals of democracy. Magazines, movie newsreels, popular songs, and public leaders all praised her. Rosie the Riveter was a national heroine.

Despite these outpourings of sentiment and enthusiasm on the part of government officials, a clear federal plan to assimilate women into home front labor pools never materialized. Once again, federal response to a crisis deeply affecting working women was haphazardly managed by competing agencies and characterized by a lack of vision. Two major topics—government planning and supervision of female war work, and the activities of the Women's Advisory Committee to the War Manpower Commission—illustrate the weaknesses of federal war policy toward female workers.

No official plans for integrating women into the work force existed in 1941, though for years Women's Bureau agents had warned that a major war would require expert coordination of the services of millions of women workers. Of course, the Women's Bureau remembered its birth as a planning agency of World War I. From the 1920s, Bureau members had prepared war contingency plans "in case history repeats itself."[1]

In 1917, the lure of higher pay attracted women from low-wage work in textile mills and left those industries understaffed. Consequently, during the first stages of American involvement, American soldiers lacked necessary woolen clothing.[2] Determined to prepare for smoother transitions in case of future wars, the Women's Bureau studied records of the War Production Board, analyzed the shifts in numbers of men and women employed, and prepared a series of reports on the need for female labor in future emergencies, which it sent annually to the War College. In 1932, War Department officials ceased soliciting these Bureau summaries, but Mary Anderson remained confident that the War Department would count on both women and her agency extensively in any major future conflict.[3]

By 1938, as war threatened both in Europe and Asia, Women's Bureau agents shifted their investigations from an emphasis on factory studies to studies projecting which industries would most need women if the United States became involved in war. In 1939, the Bureau brought together representatives from unions and national women's organizations to discuss ways to facilitate a massive entrance of women into war work.[4] A shooting war appeared imminent in 1941, and Mary Anderson toured the country giving speeches emphasizing the large role women would have to play in the war effort. In one speech, the Women's Bureau director proclaimed, "It now becomes our time to be the powerhouse from which ideals spread throughout the world. Our national powerhouse is dependent upon woman power as well as man power."[5]

Allied battle plans certainly required that the United States become an industrial powerhouse, fueled to a significant degree by the labor of women. During the war, the size of the female labor force more than doubled. Many of these women workers differed strikingly from earlier counterparts. Many of the newcomers were married and over thirty-five. By the end of the war, working wives had achieved a turnabout: They were almost a majority among all women at work.[6] War work, moreover, caused dislocations and readjustments for thousands of women already at work. In 1941, defense demands withdrew vital materials from certain production areas and temporarily threw women out of work all over the country. War work shifts, for instance, pushed 11,000 women out of jobs in Pennsylvania textile mills, 16,000 from hosiery works when silk stockings gave way to parachutes, and, 41,000 from auto plants when assembly lines shut down to retool. Even in areas that became centers of war production such as Detroit, women faced temporary unemployment because most did not have the seniority rating necessary to hold them in the jobs that continued during conversion to war production.[7] Most of these women reentered the labor force, but thousands had to move to areas where new war industries demanded the services of women.

Again, the Women's Bureau made efforts to coordinate federal policy toward women workers in time of crisis. Again, most members of the Women's Bureau worked bone-wearying hours, but they saw their agency encounter official apathy. The Women's Bureau had little role in the development of federal policy, such as it was, and none in enforcement.

Bertha Nienburg, in a bitter but persuasive summation of Bureau war activities, charged that government attempts to involve women in the war resulted in "human waste and waste in production."[8] A good way to adapt to changed wartime needs, argued the assistant Women's Bureau director, would have been to provide funding to strengthen old agencies while using their experienced staffs as an "administrative base". "The head of the old agency may not be receptive but it is better to remove the head than to start a new agency."[9] That was not done. Instead, dozens of new alphabet agencies sprang up amid confusion and inefficiency. In a report written during the war, the Bureau of the Budget claimed that there had been little reason to think that women workers would be necessary in a full-scale mobilization for war and admitted that the need for women workers had been "unanticipated."[10] Since 1939, Mary Anderson had been writing a yearly newsletter hypothesizing the kinds of work that would have to be done by women in the event of a major war. The Bureau of the Budget as well as dozens of other agencies had been on her mailing lists.

Apparently these warnings were not read. Certainly the Women's Bureau was not strengthened in preparation for war. In fact, its formerly close advisory ties with the War Department had disintegrated during the 1930s, as rumors floated about Bureau involvement with worker education and other "radical" programs. By the onset of the war, Women's Bureau agents had difficulty gaining access to war plants.[11] More frustrating than administrative inefficiency or War Department hindrance, however, was high-level administrative unwillingness to commit time or energy to serious consideration of problems involving women. Nienburg correctly concluded, "The actual number of women who have been employed by the government during this wartime on women's problems has been very few."[12]

The optimism with which Bureau officials had first viewed their possible roles in directing the mobilization of women for war soon vanished. During the prewar years, with millions still clamoring for jobs, federal officials did not worry about labor shortages for either sex. As late as 1941, unemployment had remained high.[13] The vast requirements of World War II punctured the myth of endless labor supplies but found the federal government unprepared.

During the first year of the war, a series of new agencies, the National Defense Advisory Commission (NDAC), the Office of Production Management (OPM), and the War Production Board (WPB), grappled with the problems of retooling industry, redirecting transportation lines, reorienting financial priorities, and recruiting labor. The fact that Sidney Hillman, of the Amalgamated Clothing Workers, chaired the Labor Division of each of these boards gave Mary Anderson initial cause for optimism. She and Hillman were friends. She went to him first in June 1940, when the creation of the NDAC signaled the beginning of defense efforts. Hillman promised both to use the services of the Women's Bureau and to appoint a woman advisor. He soon reneged. Disappointed, Anderson approached Hillman early in 1941 in his new role as chairperson of the Labor Supply Committee of the OPM, insistent that the committee must begin to consider in detail the part women should play in war production. Although Anderson testified before a 1941 Senate Appropriations Committee that the Women's Bureau had received the official backing of not only the OPM but also the War and Navy Departments, she discovered the OPM to be utterly uninterested in the issue of women workers and failed in her lobbying attempts to gain extra funding from the War and Navy Departments.[14] Privately, she acknowledged that her hands were tied.[15] In April 1942, yet another agency, the War Manpower Commission (WMC) assumed direction of labor supply problems. Like its predecessors, the WMC established a labor advisory committee, the Management Labor Policy Committee (MLPC), which, like its predecessors, was little interested in questions of female labor supply.

With no agency designated to coordinate planning for female worker mobilization, thousands of women found jobs by word of mouth. Tens of thousands drove to isolated defense towns in distant states to discover half-completed dormitories, no child care, and hostile male co-workers. Never officially designated the agency that should plan for women war workers, the Women's Bureau sought to undertake the task anyway and acted as an information conduit to other government commissions and agencies, and advisor to unions and employers. It repeated its peacetime New Deal role in wartime.

Bureau relations with new war work agencies were often tense, echoing the strained nature of interagency relations during the 1930s. Many government officials greeted Bureau estimates of potential numbers of necessary women war workers with condescension, arguing that unemployed men in the nation would provide a large enough pool of war production. In fact, officials in November 1941, limited the number of occupations for which the government could train women. The Women's Bureau estimated that war needs would require not only the services of girls trained for unusual jobs but also the services of more mature married women. It advised making contingency plans for national coordination of child care centers despite its long-standing opposition to publicly supported care.[16]

This Bureau recommendation won modest implementation. The Lanham Act, passed in 1942, enabled federal officials to establish day care centers for the children of women war workers. But the program was a badly organized one, with an emphasis on temporary emergency care and cost sharing with local communities. Areas wishing to apply for federal day care funds had to provide suitable sites, personnel, and equipment as well as half the necessary monies. With no real national coordination, the Lanham program fell far short of meeting wartime needs. A Bureau survey published in 1946 estimated that fewer than 10 percent of women war workers with children had made use of federally sponsored day care.[17] The day-care program was a good illustration of general federal reaction to Rosie the Riveter. Haphazard planning and agency infighting prevailed.

Bureau members charged repeatedly that various federal government programs were inefficient largely because Bureau officials found themselves called upon to advise and train people to do jobs that the Bureau felt, given proper funding, were rightly within its domain. Bureau members, asked to participate in their own diminution, made no secret of their anger. Tensions rose even within the Department of Labor when Secretary of Labor Frances Perkins attempted to channel more money into the newly established Bureau of Labor Standards, sparking rumors that she planned to eliminate the Women's Bureau. The Bureau's long-standing feud with Clara Beyer erupted when Beyer, newly appointed as assistant director of the Bureau of Labor Standards, established regional offices and asked Anderson if Labor Standards people could accompany Women's Bureau agents on factory visits. The Women's Bureau director said she replied: "We can only get into the plants ourselves because we have experienced people; we're not only going in there, we're being called in, and we can't take your inexperienced people with us."[18]

In 1942, the Bureau had begun its own survey of shipyards that employed large numbers of women, but lack of funding prevented immediate printing.[19] Anderson charged that the woman hired by the Maritime Commission came to the Bureau for its unpublished information and schedules about shipyards and then used them as her own.[20] When the Navy Department hired the former dean of Washington University to survey conditions for women, she came to Mary Anderson and confessed that she had never been in a plant before. The Women's Bureau director snipped:

> I said, "What are you going to do?" and she said, "I am going to visit the plants and suggest standards." I said, "I would like you to have our standards." She said, "Well, I don't know." She didn't refuse it, of course, but she didn't care much about the idea, so I didn't hand her anything. She said, "Oh, I will know better later on. I am going to Philadelphia, and after I have been in one plant I will know more about it. I have never been in any yet." I wanted to say to her, "Well, do you know what to look for?" She stayed three weeks and quit.[21]

Clearly, Bureau agents with territory to protect could be expected to make such complaints. More objective analysis, however, corroborates many of their charges. Sara Southall was typical of the outside consultants hired by other government agencies. A personnel executive of the International Harvester Company, Southall provided advice for the United States Employment Service (USES) from 1942 to 1943. However, she continued her duties with International Harvester and, pressed for time, asked the Women's Bureau Research Department to give her access to its draft reports and to help her edit her memoranda to the USES.[22]

This Rube Goldberg consultation system helped to guarantee that few Bureau recommendations would be followed point by point. Bureau work with the National Housing Authority provides an example. The Bureau reminded the Housing Authority that small communities where war plants were rising would not accept women workers easily and urged that plans for barracks-type dormitories to house women in newly built rural defense plants be modified to include kitchens and washing facilities.[23] Few were.

As the war wore on, Bureau members worried that many women were showing signs of work strain. Opal Gooden reported: "All the troubles noted in our community surveys are beginning to take a heavy toll in fatigue, loneliness, and illness. [Women] are living on their nerves."[24] Bureau agents, who seem to have been living on nerves themselves, attempted to couple counseling with research studies. In their roles as consultants to both management and unions, the Bureau agents occupied a precarious position as invited critics. Bureau observers charged that in many war plants women did men's jobs and received women's wages. The title of the job might be changed in order to pay women a different wage than men, but a title change did not change the nature of the work. A woman who operated a speed lathe by day would, under this system, receive a lower wage than her male counterpart who operated the same lathe on the night shift.[25] Some women who worked as supervisors received laborers' pay. May Bagwell, investigating war work on the Pennsylvania Central Railroad, asked the company personnel director about women she had observed directing the work of groups of pipefitters, machinists, and icers for air-conditioned cars. He answered, a disbelieving Bagwell reported, "That this could not be the arrangement, as no women could be gang leaders under their agreement with the union."[26]

Bagwell's comments illustrated the fact that the Bureau's previous problems with management and male union leadership did not end when the war began.

The Women's Bureau sought to aid employers, especially those in heavy industries, who had before the war managed traditionally male work forces. Bureau agents like Ethel Erickson kept seven-day workweeks, traveling throughout the country to discuss with employers the proper kinds of seating, the particular health hazards posed to women by such chemicals as lead oxide, the effect of pneumatic tools and arc welding on women's health, or the necessary clothing regulations for women doing heavy physical work. Bureau field agents formally divided the task of securing technical advice and expertise in the requirements of a particular war industry.[27] When in 1942, War Department officials suddenly ordered the ordnance depots to employ work forces composed of at least two-thirds women, Erickson, a self-taught ordnance expert, traveled to every major defense site to offer counsel during the necessary adjustment period. She and other Women's Bureau agents sympathized with the problems that employers faced in hiring and transferring women to defense industry. Erickson, for instance, agreed with the objections of foremen and employers in ordnance depots that many older women could not adequately perform their assigned tasks. She reported, "They have been slow, not adjusted well, done considerable complaining, and, as I have watched them work, I have felt that the complaints of the foremen have been justified." Erickson, however, supported Bureau statements that argued that the blame did not lie, necessarily, with the women workers themselves but with ill-advised hiring practices and poor training.[28]

Moreover, Bureau agents argued that women workers needed not only training but also respect. Women, performing a vital service for the war effort, did not deserve to be made the butt of jokes. Bureau members attacked stories that made women appear to be cute and frivolous. Mary Anderson began a speech to a California personnel association by relaying a joke she had read earlier in a newspaper, in which an irate superintendent in a factory making soldiers' caps called together his women workers and chastised them saying, "It has come to my attention that some of you girls are sewing your telephone numbers in bands." "This kind of thing doesn't help the war effort," scolded the Women's Bureau chief.[29]

Respect, and with it equal pay, was not forthcoming. Both unions and management accepted unequal wage structures. Elizabeth Christman, another Bureau investigator, tried to represent women's interests at union contract negotiations. In 1942, for instance, the Bureau sent her out to the Delco Plant in Akron, Ohio, to plead women's interests with the United Auto Workers (UAW). Christman persuaded a contingent from the UAW to see Mary Anderson. Anderson described the encounter as one where she appealed "to their selfishness for their own preservation" when she lobbied for equal pay. Anderson argued that if women did the same work, with equal skill, for lower wages, employers naturally desiring to hire labor at the cheapest possible price would fire men and replace them with women.[30]

The Bureau's continued advocacy of special conditions and special legislation for women workers weakened its advocacy of equal pay. The Bureau campaigned for women's dressing rooms furnished with cots, lunchrooms, weight-lifting limits of thirty-five pounds, prohibitions on work requiring overhead stacking, and restrictions on work with lead, benzene, and mercury. Employers justified paying women workers less because of the expenses involved in setting up separate restrooms or new equipment, even if these costs were far less than the money saved through lower female salaries for substantially the same work done by male workers. Unions justified including what came to be called successor clauses in their contracts, which argued that at war's end employers would have the right to disregard strict seniority if, during the war emergency, they had been forced to hire workers who were not entirely "suitable" and required special treatment. Although several states suspended numerous protective requirements during the war to allow women to take over from men, especially in heavy industry, they needed only to lift the suspensions after the war to justify widespread removals of women.[31]

By war's end, agents of the Women's Bureau had tangled not only with employers and male unionists, but, interestingly, also with women leaders in unions, who wanted more help in their campaigns to prevent postwar layoffs. During the war, female membership in some traditionally male unions had increased enormously. For instance, some 350,000 women belonged to the UAW, a union where historian Sheila Tobias claims "real alienation" developed between the UAW Women's Bureau and the federal Women's Bureau.[32]

Of course, the Women's Bureau agents, without a strong base of support either inside or outside the bureaucracy, were not equipped to do vigorous battle to help prevent layoffs and firings of women in heavy industry. As the war effort began to make Allied victory seem imminent, the Women's Bureau did attempt to help plan for a postwar transition. From December 1944 to January 1947, it organized a series of conferences designed to develop a "reconversion blueprint" for women workers.[33] Union representatives and leaders of national women's organizations met to consider ways to handle the postwar employment problems of women. Women's employment, the participants in the 1944 conference resolved, must be considered not only a woman problem but also one "of human welfare, which includes women's status in the wage-earning world, their home and family responsibilities, and their relation to the national economy."[34]

The resolution emphasized a familiar Bureau theme—that the vast majority of women workers had to earn a living, and more often than not, had to help support others. During 1944 and 1945, Bureau agents gathered firsthand accounts of women's wage-earning responsibilities when they interviewed 13,000 women workers in ten war production areas. Fully 75 percent of the women questioned expressed the intention of remaining in the postwar labor market. Eighty-four in every 100 said they had to support themselves and contribute to the support of others. In keeping with long-established arguments, the Bureau emphasized that only eight in every 100 wanted postwar employment primarily because they liked to work.[35]

The Bureau did not foresee major problems for women willing to take any kind of work but accurately predicted that the bulk of postwar openings for women would be in clerical work and in consumer goods, trade, or service industries. This would, for many war workers, mean a return to low wages and undesirable working conditions. Still, the Bureau was quick to emphasize, as it had for two decades, that women had certain "natural" abilities that would ideally suit them to clerical and service work. Bureau publications that investigated the subject of postwar transition spotlighted opportunities for women in department stores, offices, and light industries such as plastics and electrical parts. Rather than challenging stereotypes about women workers, these publications repeated them, noting that women workers often had better finger dexterity, patience with repetitive tasks, and willingness to work in groups and follow directions.[36]

Though Frieda Miller warned, "For women who helped to build the nation's vast arsenal of democracy [a return to poor working conditions] is not enough," she offered no concrete solutions.[37] In a keynote address to a January 1947 conference on postwar employment problems, Bureau Director Miller demanded that employers end "blind employment prejudice."[38]

Such a suggestion, without enforcement authority, was a whistle in the wind, a fact that perhaps even Frieda Miller tacitly acknowledged when she ended the same speech by saying:

> In the final analysis working women realize that they must turn to other women for the help they need in the attainment of their post-war objectives. To be sure, understanding and fairness are needed in other quarters from employers, city planners, and key individuals in every locality of the nation. For the real impetus to their post-war drive, however, they must look to other women.[39]

Bureau members were themselves, of course, other women, but other women who often chafed at the haphazard planning and supervision of women war workers, which their superiors tolerated. They were also other women torn between demands for equal pay and equal opportunity for women workers and rhetorical commitments to traditional views of the family and women's roles. They were Outsiders as Insiders, fence sitters. Their wartime complaints usually met silence.

In a rare victory, however, Bureau complaints about a lack of female representation on the War Manpower Commission did stimulate chairperson Paul McNutt to appoint a Women's Advisory Committee (WAC) in 1942. The history of the WAC provides a second illustration of the slapdash nature of the wartime federal response to Rosie the Riveter. This victory, like so many others, was to be a diminished one. McNutt did appoint the Committee but gave his thirteen women advisors practically nothing to do. Pleading union opposition, he even denied them voting privileges on his Labor Advisory Committee to the War Manpower Commission. By war's end, a bitterly disappointed Women's Bureau concluded that the WAC had spent the war on the sidelines.

By 1945, one member of the Women's Advisory Committee had resigned to protest McNutt's treatment. Others rarely attended meetings.[40] The staff of the WAC were volunteers, paid only for their travel expenses to monthly meetings in Washington. They were necessarily either financially independent or funded by their organizations. All were white; most were well-educated club and professional women; of thirteen committee members, only two came from unions. Margaret Hickey, chairperson of the committee and its most active member, was a lawyer and business executive. Many represented organizations long active in support of the Women's Bureau. All publicly supported ideas about women's role in the war emergency that were compatible with Bureau positions. In fact, many confined themselves to quoting Bureau documents.[41]

Members of the WAC did attempt to act as genuine advisors, but they failed to persuade Paul McNutt to authorize a meaningful budget, office space, or assignments for the Committee. The Committee issued dozens of policy statements, but in most instances these policy statements disappeared into the files of the War Manpower Commission. In only one instance did the WAC receive permission to direct a program: cooperation with women's organizations on recruitment campaigns to persuade women to enter war service. Even here, the WAC became a servant—in this instance, subordinate to the budgets and wishes of dozens of different women's groups, from the League of Women Voters to the General Federation of Women's Clubs. Dependent on a variety of patrons each seeking recognition for its organization, and without an independent advertising budget, the WACs recruitment program became mired in confusion and misguided enthusiasm. During the summer and fall of 1942, in Missouri, Indiana, Ohio, and several other Midwestern states, hundreds of women appeared in small farm towns ready to work in land armies before any agricultural employment shortages existed in these areas. No similarly spectacular instances of bad timing plagued other recruitment campaigns, but haste and poor communication weakened the effort. Although not fully responsible for the many deficiencies of the recruitment effort, the WAC bore most of the blame. This unhappy experience injected additional tension into an already hostile atmosphere. Continued Committee suggestions brought before McNutt and the Labor Advisory Committee for the recruitment, training, and employment of women met a deaf ear. Only once again did McNutt actively solicit Committee help. In May 1943, he used the WAC as a vehicle to protest the Kaiser Corporation's receipt of $1.5 million from the Maritime Commission to set up child-care centers. The WAC had earlier endorsed the Lanham program, in which communities, not individual employers, were to provide partial funding and establish programs for child care. The Maritime Commission informed McNutt that the allocation of funds would not be annulled. However, the Kaiser Corporation assured the War Manpower Commission that the project would be handled through community facilities. The WAC continued to monitor the Kaiser child-care program and in April 1944 reported with ironic satisfaction that the Kaiser day-care centers were underutilized to such an extent that the company was accepting children of working fathers. Although criticizing the choice of poor locations for a few centers and citing some cases of mismanagement, the WAC realized that ultimately the facilities failed because the public still associated them with charity, but the WMC authorized no effort by Committee members to convince women workers at Kaiser and elsewhere that there was no shame in using day care.

The WAC failed not solely because of a part-time volunteer staff, an inadequate budget, and a hostile superior. Working women themselves were not well enough organized to demand an effective voice on the War Manpower Commission, and the public stereotyped the woman worker, caricaturing her rather than accepting her as a permanent part of the labor pool. Government agencies, even the Women's Bureau, expressed contradictory aims. The woman worker herself felt role conflicts, and she expressed confusion. The WAC, like the Kaiser child-care centers, stood idle, and the Committee's members, without the power of organized, coordinated women's interest groups to back them up, were ineffective lobbyists, as were the agents of the Women's Bureau who had hoped to use the WAC as a mouthpiece.[42]

NOTES

1. Bertha Nienburg, "War History Statement, May 26, 1945, Office of the Secretary, Information Division, World War II Administrative Histories of Programs Series II, Drafts, Bx. 10, Nienburg to Secretary of Labor Perkins, Records of the Secretary of Labor (R.G. 174), The National

Archives, Washington, D.C. (hereafter cited as Nienburg War History).

2. *Ibid.*

3. *Ibid.* See also "Administrative War History of the Department of Labor," Secretary Schwellenbach's "General Subject File," 1945-1957, Records of the Secretaries of Labor (R.G. 174), NA (hereafter cited as Admin. War History).

4. The plans for the conference are summarized in memoranda found in Records of the League of Women Voters, Series II, Bx. 433, Library of Congress, Washington, D.C. (hereafter cited as LC).

5. Mary Anderson, "Women in Democracy Today," speech before AAUW meeting in Asheville, N.C., March 26, 1941, "Speech File #341-S-221," Records of the Women's Bureau (R.G. 86), National Archives, Washington, D.C. (hereafter cited as WB, NA).

6. Many recent publications discuss the role of women workers during World War II. See Karen Anderson, *Wartime Women: Sex Roles, Family Relations, and the Status of Women During World War II* (Westport, Conn.: Greenwood Press, 1981); Jan Ellen Trey, "Women in the War Economy, World War II," *The Review of Radical Political Economics* (July 1972), pp. 40-57; Alan Clive, "Women Workers in World War II: Michigan as a Test Case," *Labor History* 20 (1979), pp. 44-72; Marc Miller, "Working Women and World War II," *New England Quarterly* 53 (1980), pp. 42-61; Mary M. Schweitzer, "World War II and Female Labor Force Participation Rates," *Journal of Economic History* 40 (1980), pp. 89-97.

7. Nienburg War History, 2; also Report of Senator O'Mahoney on the Work of the Women's Bureau. U.S. Congress. Senate. Congressional Record, 77th Cong., 1st Sess., v. 87, Part 8, p. 8189, October 23, 1941.

8. Nienburg War History, p. 16.

9. *Ibid.*

10. Bureau of the Budget, *The United States at War,* Historical Reports on War Administration, 1 (Washington, D.C.: Government Printing Office, 1946).

11. Nienburg War History, p. 17.

12. *Ibid.*

13. See "Changes in War Employment During the War," Special War *Bulletin #20* (Washington, D.C.: Government Printing Office, 1944): There were still 5.5 million unemployed in 1941.

14. U.S. Congress. House. Committee on Appropriations: Department of Labor—Subcommittee Hearings, House of Representatives, 77th Cong., 2nd Sess., 1942.

15. Mary Anderson, Draft War History (hereafter cited as Anderson War History), Mary Anderson Papers, Folder 3, Schlesinger Library (hereafter cited as SL); Mary Anderson to Elizabeth Christman, June 14, 1941 (confidential), "Regional Field Offices Files," WB, NA.

16. Nienburg War History, pp. 5-10; Anderson War History, pp. 4-7; In fact, during the 1920s the Bureau had once floated the idea of government pensions for widowed mothers to enable them to stay out of the labor force, though, of course, it defended the right of married women to work out of economic necessity. See Women's Bureau *Bulletin #13*, "What Industry Means to Women Workers" (Washington, D.C.: Government Printing Office, 1923); Women's Bureau *Bulletin #41*, "Family Status of Breadwinning Women" (Washington, D.C.: Government Printing Office, 1925).

17. Women's Bureau *Bulletin #209*, "Women Workers in Ten War Production Areas and their Postwar Employment Plans" (Washington, D.C.: Government Printing Office, 1946), pp. 50-56; see also Karen Anderson, *Wartime Women*, pp. 122-153, for an excellent summary of the problems with the Lanham program.

18. Anderson War History, p. 18. In return, Beyer, in a 1976 interview with the author criticized Anderson as an earthy but naive woman, implying her to be too concerned with protecting her own turf; Clara Beyer, interview with author, January 12, 1976, Washington, D.C.

19. Eventually published in 1944: Women's Bureau *Bulletin #192-6*, "Employing in Shipyards" (Washington, D.C.: Government Printing Office, 1944).

20. Anderson War History, p. 14.

21. *Ibid.*

22. Personal memorandum, April, 1943, typescript in Records of the Women's Advisory Committee of the War Manpower Commission (R.G. 211), National Archives, Washington, D.C. (hereafter cited as WAC, NA).

23. Nienburg War History, pp. 8-12; see also Frieda Miller, "Draft for Schenectady Speech," Frieda Miller Papers, October 19, 1942, Folder 196, SL.

24. Opal Gooden to Mary Cannon, June 4, 1943, "International File—Correspondence," Bx. 913, WB, NA.

25. Ethel Erickson, Field Report (confidential) December 18, 1942, Buick Motor Aircraft Engine Co., Melrose Park, Chicago, "Regional Field Offices File," WB, NA.

26. May Bagwell to Mary Anderson, memorandum, August 21, 1943, "Field Offices File," WB, NA.

27. The Bureau schedule files for its wartime bulletins, "Schedule Files— Bulletins 189-211," include everything from architectural blueprints of factories to medical reports on the ability of women to lift heavy metal cores, WB, NA.

28. "Excerpts from Miss Manning's Notes to Field Agents," Opal Gooden to Mary Cannon, 28 April 1943, International Files, Bx. 913, WB, NA.

29. Mary Anderson speech, "Women on the Labor Front," Speech File #342-S-251," WB, NA.

30. Anderson War History, p. 8.

31. UAW Policy Established by Convention Resolution Relative to Women Workers' Rights, 1942-1968, UAW, Women's Bureau, Detroit, Michigan; Sheila Tobias and Lisa Anderson argue that the employment gains made by women during the war were almost guaranteed to be temporary, given the ambivalence of government, unions, management, and even organized women's groups. *What Really Happened to Rosie the Riveter: Demobilization and the Female Labor Force, 1944-1947* (New York: MSS Modular Publications, 1974).

32. Tobias and Anderson, *What Really Happened to Rosie the Riveter*, pp. 31-33.

33. See *Special Bulletin #18*, "A Preview as to Women Workers in Transition"; also Conference Proceedings, "Conference Files, 1944-48," Bx. 1596, WB, NA.

34. *Resolutions: Adopted at a Conference (December 5, 1944) of the Women's Bureau with Officials of 30 National Organizations* (typescript), Frieda Miller Papers, Folder 199, SL.

35. Women's Bureau *Bulletin #209*, "Women Workers in Ten Production Areas"; *Special Bulletin #18*, "A Preview as to Women Workers in Transition."

36. See Women's Bureau Special War *Bulletin #18*, "A Preview as to Women Workers in Transition from War to Peace (Washington, D.C.: Government Printing Office, 1944); Women's Bureau *Bulletin #216*, "Women Workers After VJ Day" (Washington, D.C.: Government Printing Office, 1947).

37. Frieda Miller, address before 21st Woman's Patriotic Conference on National Defense at Hotel Statler, Washington, D.C., January 25, 1947 (typescript), Frieda Miller Papers, Folder 199, SL.

38. *Ibid.*

39. *Ibid.*

40. First Draft (typescript), "Comparisons of American and British Recruitment Campaigns for Women," 1944, WB, NA; the quoted statement also appeared in *Bulletin #244*, "Womanpower Committees During World War II: United States and British Experience" (Washington, D.C., Government Printing Office, 1953); for evidence of the "sidelines" position, see also "Womanpower" An Appraisal by the Women's Advisory Committee, War Manpower Commission (typescript), April 30, 1944; transcript, "Interview with Margaret Hickey," September 1, 1943; memorandum, Entry #139, To Paul McNutt from Glenn Brockway, "Policies Governing Conduct of Women's Enrollment Campaigns as Part of the Program for Accelerating the Employment of Women," January 9, 1943; transcript, "Statement of the Women's Advisory Committee of the War

Manpower Commission with Respect to Cut-Backs Affecting Women in Industry," March 1, 1944; all in WAC, NA.

41. A list of WAC members included Eleanor Park of New York City, assistant to the manager of Industrial Relations, Union Carbide and Carbon Corporation (active alternate); Blanche Ralston of Coahoma, Mississippi, former regional director of the Professional and Services Division of the Work Projects Administration; Ruth Allen, University of Texas, San Antonio, Texas (did not serve full term of office); Mrs. Harris T. Baldwin of Washington, D.C., former vice president of the League of Women Voters; Dorothy J. Bellanca of New York City, vice president of the Amalgamated Clothing Workers of America; Bess Bloodworth of New York City, vice president and a director of the National Women's Trade Union League (active alternate); Saidie Orr Dunbar, of Portland, Oregon, executive secretary of the Oregon Tuberculosis Association and past president of the General Federation of Women's Clubs; Gladys Talbott Edwards of Denver, Colorado, director of education for the National Farmers Union; Dr. Esther Cole Franklin, associate in social studies, American Association of University Women, Washington, D.C. (did not serve full term of office); Beatrice Blackmar Gould of Philadelphia, Pennsylvania, co-editor of the *Ladies' Home Journal*; Margaret A. Hickcy of St. Louis, Missouri, lawyer and business executive; Mrs. Lowell Fletcher Hobart of Cincinnati, Ohio, past national president of the American Legion Auxiliary; Jenny Matyas of San Francisco, California, vice president of the International Ladies' Garment Workers' Union. Names given in minutes of Women's Advisory Committee (typescript), January 17, 1945, in records, WAC, NA.

42. See "Womanpower" An Appraisal by the Women's Advisory Committee, War Manpower Commission (typescript), April 30, 1944; transcript, "Interview with Margaret Hickey," September 1, 1943; transcript, "Statement of the Women's Advisory Committee of the War Manpower Commission with Respect to Cut-Backs Affecting Women in Industry," March 1, 1944; all in WAC, NA; Women's Bureau *Bulletin #244*, "Womanpower Committees During World War II: United States and British Experience."

In the Shadow of
Good Neighbor:
Purposes of International
Programs for Women Workers

6

The New Deal, of course, spanned both the years of Depression and the war emergency. The experts on women's work in such places as the Women's Bureau, the NYA, the FERA, and the Women's Advisory Committee naturally concentrated on domestic issues. For them to do otherwise during a time when American women workers faced a succession of crises would have been surprising and reprehensible. Nonetheless, the era was not one of change in work roles for American women alone.

Clearly, industrialization and growth in the white-collar sector altered employment patterns most noticeably for North American and West European women, but Asia, Africa, and Latin America did not go unaffected. The federal government, primarily through the Department of Labor and the Women's Bureau, expressed interest in the status of women workers in foreign countries.

Secretary of Labor Frances Perkins, soon after taking office in 1933, proclaimed, "It is only through the hearty cooperation of women throughout the world that peace and economic opportunity can be obtained."[1] The Women's Bureau had certainly sought to cooperate in international ventures since its inception during World War I as an agency whose first assignment was a pamphlet explaining British female recruitment campaigns. Federal participation in the activities of international women's organizations and Women's Bureau consultations with counterparts in other governments provided an American presence without providing any kind of powerful American commitment to the cause of international labor. An examination of these federal involvements illustrates in another way the complicated network, which even extended internationally, connecting the Women's Bureau and its sponsors within certain women's organizations. It also illustrates the interesting diplomatic uses of the woman-worker issue. The Women's Bureau not only provided a symbol of American interest in international social and labor issues, it tried to use its international contacts and alliances to gain support for its positions and to bolster a fragile status at home. The Women's Bureau participation in President Roosevelt's Good Neighbor programs for Latin America was the most important international effort initiated by the agency between 1920 and 1963. Examination of this Latin American program, as well as Bureau involvement with the International Labor Organization, provides a study of objectives, tactics, and consequences of Bureau efforts to make, in a small way, its mandate to "investigate the condition of working women" an international one.

Bureau international efforts did not focus solely on Latin America during the New Deal era. Hints of the low-key role designated for it to play appeared in the 1920s. Women's Bureau members' aggressive attempts to expand their assignments and gain international allies for their domestic disputes with the Woman's Party also foreshadowed their larger New Deal role.

Ironically, while the United States Senate debated and refused the Treaty of Versailles, the International Labor Organization, mandated by that controversial treaty, first convened in Washington, D.C. The United States, of course, did not join the League of Nations and delayed joining the ILO until 1934, but Women's Bureau cooperation with the ILO between 1920 and 1934 provided a vehicle for the Bureau's promotion of protective labor legislation and for attempts to lobby its own government to expand its support of international treaties and regulations governing female labor.

The ILO kept an office in Washington in order to maintain contact with various United States government departments. The United States government did not object to the presence of the ILO office and welcomed ILO documents and reports, but, until the Roosevelt Administration, did not reciprocate by allowing Americans to act as technical advisors. Throughout the 1920s, Albert Thomas, head of the ILO Washington office, and Harold Butler, director of the ILO, waged a campaign to persuade United States officials that United States participation in the ILO would not mean, even indirectly, that it had joined the League. Even though technically they were two separate organizations, the ILO and the League of Nations were linked in the public and official mind. Given the government's reluctance to identify itself with the League, its interest in the ILO was symbolized by the restrained activities of such agencies as the Women's Bureau.[2]

In the 1920s, as a battle began at home with the Woman's Party over protective labor laws, Women's Bureau agents sought reinforcements. Bureau members Anne Larrabee and Isadore Spring traveled to Europe in May 1926 to solicit technical advice about night-work laws from the Geneva office of the ILO. Martha Mundt, a coordinator of the ILO Advisory Committee on Women, welcomed the two women and wrote to Mary Anderson that she would be only "too delighted" to review and support the Women's Bureau's proposed protective labor recommendations.[3]

In 1931, Anderson persuaded Secretary of Labor William Doak to ask Secretary of State Henry L. Stimson to grant her a special passport to sit as an unofficial American observer at the ILO annual conference in Geneva.[4] Stimson agreed, and Anderson was already en route to Europe when the Department of State reversed its decision. Some members of the Women's Trade Union League felt that the Woman's Party, which opposed United States participation in the ILO because of ILO support for protective labor legislation for women, had influenced the State Department's retraction.[5] Anderson agreed that she "could not have gone into Geneva without the Woman's Party raising cain" but felt that the Party "rode in on a band wagon" of government fears of any apparent involvement with international labor.[6]

A year later, however, in 1932, the Department of State offered no objections when Harold Butler asked Anderson to become a member of the Advisory Committee on Women's Work of the ILO.[7] After checking with the Department of State and the secretary of labor, she accepted the post on October 12, 1932.[8] Though Anderson's advisory committee membership did not oblige the United States formally to join the ILO, the change of administration brought two advocates of the ILO to high office—Franklin Roosevelt and Frances Perkins.

In November 1930, when Roosevelt was governor and Perkins

industrial commissioner, New York State had sponsored an area-wide Governors' Conference to consider questions of unemployment insurance, public works projects, and relief measures for the millions of unemployed. Harold Butler, learning of the conference, had written offering ILO assistance. Roosevelt and Perkins accepted the offer of technical advice and maintained contact with Butler.[9] Secretary of State Cordell Hull personally asked individual members of the Senate Committee on Foreign Relations to support a resolution favoring United States membership in the ILO.[10] Roosevelt encountered no Department of State or Congressional opposition when he named Anderson to lead a delegation of unofficial American observers to the 1933 annual ILO conferences. The Roosevelt Administration, by such appointments, gradually involved the United States in the activities of the ILO. By August 1934, Roosevelt had accepted the ILO offer of membership.

Clara Beyer of the Bureau of Labor Standards argued that most women officials in the Department of Labor felt that ILO solutions to problems encountered by female wage earners were "ridiculous." Women's issues were the first to be bumped when crowded agendas threatened extended sessions. Nevertheless, they publicly supported the ILO, which at least gave lip service to protective labor law and fair pay for women, and which joined them in opposing the Woman's Party.[11] Alice Paul damned the ILO as a group of "impossible men" and demanded that the United States withdraw. Mary Anderson, a woman with better contacts, not only rebutted Paul's statements but also managed to persuade the Advisory Committee on Women's Work of the ILO to deny the Woman's Party a hearing.[12] "They do not speak for industrial women," she explained to Labor Secretary Frances Perkins.[13]

Most of the American women that the ILO Governing Board did judge to be qualified to speak for industrial women were female officials of the United States Department of Labor. Heeding the advice that Mary Anderson had first given Woodrow Wilson in 1919, President Roosevelt appointed at least one woman member to each American delegation to the ILO annual conferences. A list of woman delegates from 1934 to 1946 included former Women's Bureau Director Mary Van Kleeck and future Women's Bureau Director Frieda Miller. Bureau members Mary Winslow and Mary Robinson, Clara Beyer of the Bureau of Labor Standards, and

Katherine Lenroot, Grace Abbott, and Patricia McConnell, all of the Children's Bureau, were appointed delegates. Secretary of Labor Perkins frequently represented the United States as a delegate. In fact, only a few women not affiliated with the Department of Labor received appointments.[14]

Official attendance at sessions of the ILO soon became subordinate, however, to Bureau participation in another New Deal effort to revise American foreign policy: the Good Neighbor program for Latin America. By the mid-1930s several developments in Latin America posed a challenge to United States economic and political dominance. The Depression proved to be a watershed both for Latin America and for inter-American relations. Not only did the economic crisis lead to a series of political collapses, but it also highlighted an ironic phenomenon that had been developing since World War I. Despite the initial promise of economic stimulus, increases in foreign, primarily North American, investments acted after 1920 as a drain on capital. The "Depression Nationalism" displayed by such countries as Mexico and Argentina sought to check this flow of excess profits abroad. In many countries, authoritarian governments replaced elected legislatures. These political changes did not necessarily imply a defeat for democratic procedures, in many cases already nonexistent in parliaments where foreign investors had allied with powerful interest groups. However, governmental changes sometimes brought altered tax structures or the imposition of property ownership laws, which revealed the real percentages of capital leaving the country because of foreign investments. The prospect of a belligerent Latin America, possibly influenced by German Fascism and seeking to expropriate or discourage United States investments, concerned the Roosevelt Administration. The resultant Good Neighbor policy was certainly not a simple North American statement of friendly intentions. Rather it was a complicated set of attempts to ensure that Latin American economic development would continue under closer United States supervision.[15]

Changes in Latin America due to industrialization particularly concerned those United States policy makers responsible for Good Neighbor. Industrialization, especially textile manufacture, acted in the years between World War I and World War II as an impetus that changed the life-styles of thousands of Latin American women who for the first time earned wages. Since Latin America remained through the 1930s and 1940s predominantly agricultural, traditional patterns of life did not really alter for most women. A few signs of change, however, did surface. The Mexican Federal Labor Law of 1931 provided for equal pay for equal work, regardless of sex, pregnancy care for working women, and day care centers. In 1932, Colombia's Law 28 allowed married women for the first time to manage their own economic affairs. Juan Peron, as he ascended to power in Argentina, encouraged Argentine women to participate in the paid work force. By 1940, Brazil, Uruguay, and Peru had granted women the vote. By 1950, Chile, Colombia, Argentina, Panama, and Venezuela had followed suit.[16]

The Women's Bureau attempted to respond to questions posed by this changing status of Latin American women. The Good Neighbor program used the talents of many government bureaucrats not members of the Women's Bureau. In fact, Good Neighbor quickly became a loosely organized collection of many small projects incorporating the personnel and abilities of existing agencies. In 1938, shortly after the Mexican expropriation of the oil industry, Assistant Secretary of State Nelson Rockefeller assumed leadership of a State Department-directed committee meant to act as the coordinating agency of the Good Neighbor program. This Interdepartmental Committee on Cooperation with the American Republics included representatives from the Department of Agriculture; the Civil Aeronautics Board; the Department of Commerce; the Export-Import Bank; the Federal Communications Commission; the Public Health Service; the Departments of the Interior, Justice, and Labor; the Library of Congress and Smithsonian Institution; the United States Tariff Commission; the Treasury Department; and the Department of State.[17]

The Women's Bureau's contribution to this Medusa structure need not be analyzed as a representative example of a Good Neighbor program. The Bureau, funded to investigate the problems of women workers, collected different kinds of supporters and opponents and was not an organization interchangeable in its bureaucratic style with the Export-Import Bank or the Civil Aeronautics Board.

The Bureau's prior involvements with international labor projects and the composition and interests of its personnel mark it as a unique element of Good Neighbor diplomacy, not a typical case study of methods and programs used to implement President Roosevelt's policies in Latin America. Its participation in Good Neighbor illustrates federal attitudes about the parameters of problems raised by female workers.

The Women's Bureau and the Department of State played an interesting game of influence and persuasion. Women's Bureau agents seized the initiative to persuade the Department of State to allow their participation. Their lobbying helped to coax initially reluctant Department of State officials to approve Bureau projects to send American agents abroad and provide funds for training Latin American women government aides in the United States. But the Department of State limited the scope of the fact-finding missions that Women's Bureau agents conducted in Latin America and limited the freedom with which Bureau members discussed their conclusions about Latin American labor conditions.

The reactions of Women's Bureau agents involved in Good Neighbor activities betray complicated, mixed emotions about the worth of the program. Bureau agents clearly saw the ulterior motivation or ideology of the Washington policy makers responsible for Good Neighbor. These motives demanded federal support for an expanding American trade system. Yet Women's Bureau members sincerely believed that closer cultural and economic ties could benefit Latin America. In that sense, they espoused the larger purpose of Roosevelt's hemispheric diplomacy. After several years of tours, however, the director of the Women's Bureau Latin American projects, Mary Cannon, privately denounced United States paternalism and talked about the dangers of economic imperialism. She warned that developing economic trends might not necessarily improve the position of Latin American workers, women or men. She worried about the resentments she heard throughout her travels expressed toward a diplomacy whose overriding objectives were those of economic and political supervision and not social uplift.

Yet Mary Anderson sought to make the Women's Bureau an active participant in Good Neighbor by proposing programs aimed at providing closer formal and informal links between groups in the Americas interested in the problem of working women. Women's Bureau agents were not victims or dupes of a system that required them to broker in persuasion and not in power, but they were often odd bedfellows, situationally compelled to make statements that were compromises or modifications of private beliefs. Their international Latin American programs further illustrate this complex status. In fact, the Women's Bureau had begun these hemispheric contacts prior to the formal establishment of Nelson Rockefeller's committee. Through earlier work with the International Labor Organization and with many international women's groups, Mary Anderson had met Latin American women government officials and club leaders. Her Bureau, independently of the Interdepartmental Committee, established an Inter-American Division and had the good luck to hire Mary Cannon. An executive with the international YWCA and a trained economist who spoke fluent Spanish and Portuguese, Cannon had spent years in Argentina supervising the YWCA's programs in Latin America.[18]

Under her direction, the Women's Bureau sought to receive a definite assignment from the Interdepartmental Committee. Cannon proposed that the Committee provide funds to send a representative from the Women's Bureau on inspection tours through Latin America and enable Latin American women to come to the United States to work for a period of months as interns of the Women's Bureau.[19]

In effect, the Women's Bureau simply proposed to become an information conduit. Nevertheless, the Department of State and the Interdepartmental Committee did not embrace the offer.[20] In fact, Department of State officials rigorously debated the worth of the proposed projects and finally allocated the Bureau only a few thousand dollars a year.[21]

Charles Thomson and William Schurz of the Division of Cultural Affairs of the Department of State worked as aides to Nelson Rockefeller in coordinating the work of the Interdepartmental Committee. During 1942, both argued that Women's Bureau plans for trips to Latin America had no direct bearing on the war effort and should, therefore, be curtailed. However, M. L. Leap, their superior and senior divisional analyst for the Division of Cultural Affairs, replied to one memorandum from Thomson and Schurz that, "If the Interdepartmental Committee were to submit every project to the same such scrutiny it exercised over Women's Bureau requests, it would be necessary to eliminate most of the program."[22]

Despite such arguments, both Schurz and Thomson seemingly remained unconvinced of the worth of Women's Bureau activities abroad. By 1943, stories of the dispute had circulated through Congressional circles. Congresswoman Frances Bolton, Democrat from

Ohio, who sat on the House Committee on Foreign Relations, went over to the Department of State to "stir them all up" over what she regarded as unfair treatment of the Women's Bureau. Mary Anderson, in a letter thanking Bolton for her efforts, revealed the details of a July 1943 visit she and Mary Cannon had made to the Department of State to confront Thomson and Schurz, who, after lengthy wrangling, agreed to pay Cannon's travel expenses. Although the men began by explaining that wartime conditions imposed severe transportation problems, especially for women, they eventually confided, according to Anderson, that they were "old fashioned" enough to think that women should be in their homes. Moreover, Schurz continued, "There is a feeling your Bureau is interested in getting women out of the home, an attitude which is not welcome in South America." Thomson added that the program of the Women's Bureau "impinges on social change and is apt to incite emotion." Anderson exploded, protesting that the Women's Bureau had not pushed Mary Cannon or anyone else out of her home, but rather that many women in every country had to work outside the home not only to have a home but also to keep their families from starvation. Mary Cannon, furious, extracted from both officials admissions that they had never received any comments from her Latin American hosts that her work had "incited emotion."[23]

Twice, when the Department of State did transmit funds to the Department of Labor, the letter of transfer to the secretary of labor included special instructions to members of the Women's Bureau. One letter from G. Howland Shaw, assistant secretary of state, to Anderson and Perkins read: "It is especially desired that representatives of the Women's Bureau engage in no activities which might be construed as an effort on the part of the United States Government to influence, directly or indirectly, policies in social and labor fields."[24]

Given such attitudes, the Department of State and the Interdepartmental Committee's willingness to fund any Women's Bureau projects at all was another of the diminished victories that characterize the history of the Women's Bureau. Once again the Bureau's network of allies in national women's organizations helped achieve it. Under Secretary of State Sumner Welles, addressing a meeting of the Interdepartmental Committee in 1942, urged its members to remember that Congress had funded the Committee specifically to "develop the cultural aspects of our international relations with Latin America."[25] He continued: "We have the task of learning . . . the traditions and customs of our neighbors in the other American Republics and of making it possible for them to see our way of life."[26]

The activities of women, of course, formed a part of the matrix of Latin American "tradition and customs." If the Interdepartmental Committee did not choose to emphasize that fact, other groups in the United States certainly did. Women's organizations, led by the League of Women Voters, bombarded Department of State cultural affairs officials with detailed suggestions.[27]

Charles Thomson, the Department of State intermediary in this matter, countered that American women's groups should coordinate their plans with the United States' representative to the Inter-American Commission of Women. He promised that the Department of State would then "naturally wish to be guided" by the judgment of the Inter-American representative. The woman whose advice the Department of State pledged to seek was Mary Winslow, former member of the Women's Bureau and one of Mary Anderson's closest friends.[28] Thomson, Schurz, and other Department of State officials probably realized that the expenditure of a few thousand dollars to fund Women's Bureau requests would stop a flood of letters from the League, the General Federation of Women's Clubs, the Women's Trade Union League, and the National Federation of Business and Professional Women.

Moreover, occupants of Latin American desks raised questions about the political implications of woman suffrage in Latin America. Mary Cannon, however, did not receive Department of State orders to travel through South America compiling reports on the political activities of newly enfranchised Latin American women. Officially, she acted as consultant to Latin American departments of labor, helping to draft labor legislation for women, inspecting factories, and offering advice about the establishment of women's bureaus. Unofficially, she realized, "This Good Neighbor policy had an ulterior motive. . . . We wanted to know what they [Latin Americans] were thinking. . . . We wanted them on our side."[29] Unofficially, of course, the Women's Bureau had its own ulterior motives as well. It wished to build a network of Latin American female labor officials on its side. "Our [international] contacts may help come appropriations time" read an unsigned penciled addition to a long Bureau outline of plans for trips in 1943.[30]

Cannon traveled to Uruguay, Chile, and Argentina in 1941, and to Brazil, Paraguay, Peru, and Ecuador in 1943.[31] She returned to Argentina in 1945 and spent two months in Mexico in 1948, drafting proposals for the regulation of Mexican piece-goods industries.[32] The United States embassies in these countries issued statements praising her work and sent official reports back to the secretary of state noting her "exemplary knowledge of Spanish," her "understanding of the Latin temperament," her "natural tact."[33] Some of the embassy enthusiasm for Mary Cannon's missions appeared genuine. Several officials, however, privately expressed their reluctance to support the visits of the Women's Bureau representative. The United States legation in Uruguay telegraphed the Department of State that "no good" would come from the visit. The United States ambassador to Peru told Cannon that he felt the trip was not an "especially suitable venture."[34]

Such doubts were difficult to support if the expressed aims of Good Neighbor were taken literally. The stated purpose of the work of the Interdepartmental Committee was to promote understanding between the United States and Latin American countries and to attack the false cultural stereotypes harbored by both sides. By that definition, Mary Cannon's visits to Latin America were indeed "suitable." Perhaps because Cannon spoke fluent Spanish and Portuguese, perhaps because she presented the novel spectacle of a single woman touring alone to represent the United States, her speeches drew large crowds.[35] In these speeches and in numerous radio addresses, she emphasized ideas that Bureau agents had repeated for decades to domestic audiences: American movies presented fantasy American career women, not real women. Few American women, and certainly very few working women, lived in huge houses or had several automobiles. Most American women who worked did so for the same reasons Latin American women worked—to help support their families.

However, like her embassy escorts, Mary Cannon's public reactions to her missions to Latin America were very different from those she expressed privately. Publicly, she painted a pleased and hopeful picture of conditions for women. In her speeches to American audiences, she left the impression that she had toured freely, that she had inspected places of work without much fanfare or preparation, and that she had met and talked with women workers as well as women government officials and upper-class Ladies Bountiful. In truth, United States embassy and Latin American labor officials planned Cannon's agenda and supervised her rounds of factory inspections and speeches. Members of the host country's department of labor usually accompanied her to appointments.[36] Since Cannon usually spoke to the organizations that formed a network of support for the Women's Bureau, she not surprisingly chose to describe her activities with what appears to be a certain amount of calculated romanticism. Moreover, given the chilly climate between the Department of State and the Women's Bureau, perhaps she felt it wise not to inject any public note of criticism about projects funded by the former.

Cannon emphasized to audiences at home that Latin American women were "following in the steps of their U.S. sisters." More women were rejecting domestic work to go to the factories; more women were continuing their academic or vocational training. Girls in school, Cannon reported, did not have to endure so many male jibes and insults. Middle-class families no longer felt shame when daughters worked outside the home. Daughters no longer went to clerking and office jobs wearing mantillas so that neighbors would think they were going to mass.[37] The women of Latin America looked to the United States as "an exponent of democracy— not just political democracy but democracy in every phase of life."[38] Her message buttressed the Good Neighbor argument that United States economic, social, and political institutions formed the best available model for Latin American development.

Home in America, Cannon told middle-class club women, whose lobbying had helped the Women's Bureau secure funding for her trips, that the Latin American groups that might be labeled their counterparts "were alert, intelligent, and eager to accomplish something for women."[39]

In reality, upper-class women's groups affiliated with the Catholic Church had supplied most of the pressure exerted in Latin America to better conditions for working women.[40] Cannon's meetings with trade union groups had a religious flavor. During her July 1941 trip to Argentina, she reported: "Saturday: I went to an 8:30 mass with Srta. Ezcurra and her union of seamstresses."[41]

Cannon spent time on each trip and in each country visiting the projects that upper-class women's groups had organized to benefit women workers. She visited dining rooms where low-cost meals were served and toured night schools where working-class women learned to make lace.[42] Back in the United States, Cannon described these visits as a "thrilling experience."[43]

Privately, she was less breathlessly enthusiastic. She declared the lack of union organization for women and found that even the approved factories to which she had access were often filthy and dangerous.[44] A confidential report on a cotton mill in Brazil described an "air of indifference and apathy" and described machines tended by barefooted women and children dressed in threadbare clothing.[45] Indeed, Cannon expressed concern not only about factory conditions but also about the structure of the program in which she participated. While in Argentina in 1941, she wrote a letter to Women's Bureau Assistant Director Bertha Nienburg, arguing that:

> It might be well to interrupt the string of official visitors for a few months and think of some other ways to get our good intentions over. . . . There is a very real fear among some people that the United States is entering into a policy of economic and commercial imperialism, and that all these missions coming down are part of that policy. It has even been said of me in one instance that I know of.[46]

"Frenzied interest in Inter-American solidarity" was a phenomenon concentrated in the United States, she continued.[47] If the United States Department of State really intended to support a program of genuine cooperation and wanted to promote communication among the women of the Americas, it should appoint some women as consuls in major Latin American cities.[48] Before any real inter-American cooperation could be possible, the United States would have to "remember that Latin American countries are not markets for exploitation, but nations of people."[49] Rather than "sending second rate pianists down," the United States should emphasize programs where funds would be available so that Latin Americans could visit and study in the United States.[50]

Cannon's suggestion was not a repudiation of the general Good Neighbor aim to draw Latin American leaders into an American orbit. Indeed, one such effort, which Cannon coordinated, the

Bureau-sponsored Latin-American Women Intern program, understandably received more enthusiastic Department of State support.
In 1940, Mary Winslow, back from a tour of Latin America as a
representative of the Inter-American Commission of Women,
criticized the type of scholarship programs the United States government had already extended to individual Latin American women:
"We bring young students. They are impressionable and. . . .
[They find] the United States much better than their backward
countries and spend all their time trying to get back."[51] Instead,
Winslow argued, the United States government should extend
scholarship aid to mature women, "not so likely to become mal-
adjusted to situations in their own countries."[52]

The Women's Bureau intern program, initiated in 1944 and
continued through 1949, followed Winslow's advice. The four or
five Latin Americans who came to the United States yearly for
periods of from three to six months were officials in the labor departments of their home countries.[53]

Mary Cannon, whose trips to South America had given her
opportunities to meet her female counterparts in the labor departments of host countries, directed the internships. The program,
like her inspection tours, received separate funding channeled
through the Department of State. In addition, national women's
organizations furnished traveling interns with bed and board.

Applicants whom Cannon knew personally received preference.
Clearly, she wished to bolster her carefully built system of contacts in the Bureau's favor. As the Bureau agent argued to the
Interdepartmental Committee, she could plan realistic training
programs for interns from countries that she had visited, where
personal relationships helped her and other members of the Bureau
to grasp the industrial and administrative problems facing the
labor departments to which the women interns would return.[54]

As a member of the selection committee of the Interdepartmental
Committee of Cooperation, Cannon proved a persuasive lobbyist
for candidates she favored. Sometimes she even collaborated in
schemes to place a woman in a department of labor so that she
could be a potential candidate. For instance, she advised Dr. Paul
Migone of the Argentine Ministry of Foreign Relations to use his
contacts in the Argentine Department of Labor to help place Christina
Gorsch, an Argentine representative of the ILO whom Cannon

knew. Within a month, Srta. Gorsch received the proper "opening wedge," an appointment on one of the wage-fixing committees for homework regulations of the Argentine Department of Labor.[55] Cannon advised Jandrya Rodriguez of the Mothers and Children Division of the Department of Labor, Brazil, to "study English as hard as you can. I am going to do everything I possibly can to offer the internship directly to you. . . . Please don't say anything about this to anyone, or we might spoil it for both of us."[56]

As Cannon's advice indicates, selected interns had to speak and write English. However, the selection system that Cannon engineered tried to award internships nine months in advance so that women with no English or with faulty English would not be automatically eliminated from consideration, and, if chosen, would have time to prepare before coming to the United States.[57] An ability to read and speak English was vital. The Women's Bureau provided no translators. The interns sometimes traveled alone when making field investigation trips; they submitted written reports to the Women's Bureau in English.

Upon their arrival in the United States, the interns first spent several weeks in Washington, D.C. Provided with desks in the Women's Bureau, the women studied the organization of the Bureau and spent time observing the work done by each division. The trainees then left the Capitol to spend the major portion of their time in two or more state departments of labor. Women's Bureau coordinators attempted to choose states with types of female employment similar, if possible, to work done in the trainee's home country.

Interns usually received a warm welcome back home in Latin America and resumed their government positions.[58] Most kept in touch with the Women's Bureau, exchanging publications and labor statistics, but Mary Cannon worried that the Bureau's alliance with the Department of State might alienate Latin American government and labor officials. She was right in fearing that her Department of State connections would repel Latin American labor leaders and some Latin American government officials who saw the Good Neighbor and Inter-American Cooperation programs of the 1930s and 1940s as a repetition of earlier American manipulation of the Pan American Federation of Labor. Many Latin American labor officials had decided that the Pan American Federation of Labor was simply a tool of the United States Department of State.[59]

If the Bureau had received independent Congressional funding, its agents might have escaped the stigma of being operatives for the Department of State. Yet even if Congress and the Department of Labor had supported the Women's Bureau international efforts handsomely and enabled the agency independently to send dozens of representatives abroad and offer substantial scholarships for foreign interns to come to the United States, it is questionable whether the status of working women in Latin America would have changed noticeably. Of course, it is unlikely that anyone in the Women's Bureau or anyone connected with Good Neighbor in a policy-making position was naive enough to sincerely expect any such major transformation.

Bureau members, certainly did not present their programs as a panacea to Latin American working women. It is hard to imagine how they would have received any outside support at all, had they done so. As they saw it, the Good Neighbor program gave them an opportunity to provide a symbol of American interest in the common problems facing Latin and North American employed women, and, perhaps, a chance to gain international reinforcement for controversial and poorly funded Bureau efforts at home.

During years of crisis and transition at home, these federal woman-worker experts sought to widen their contacts. Unable to persuade the AFL at home to establish a women's bureau, they were able to persuade the governments of several Latin American countries to establish women's bureaus. By the early 1950s, when the last of the interns had returned home, the Women's Bureau had broadened its influence among women government officials in Latin America. But its domestic influence among union leaders, employers, and administrative supervisors remained small. Government policy toward women workers began to change, but a diminished and reorganized Women's Bureau no longer sought to direct and co-ordinate those changes, no longer sought in every way possible to expand its circle of supporters.

NOTES

1. The message was widely reprinted in overseas newspapers, including one South American newspaper, *El Legionario,* Peru. For full text and copies of the article see Records of the Secretary of Labor (R.G. 174),

Secretary Perkins' General Subject File, 1933-1940, National Archives, Washington, D.C. (hereafter cited as Labor, NA).

2. Daniel Moynihan, *The United States and the International Labor Organization,* thesis presented to the Fletcher School of Law and Diplomacy, 1960 (microfilm).

3. Martha Mundt to Mary Anderson, letter undated, but stamped "received in WB Offices, May 28, 1926," Mary Anderson Papers, Folder 20, Schlesinger Library (hereafter cited as SL).

4. Doak to Stimson (copy), Anderson Papers, April 3, 1931, Folder 22, SL.

5. In reply to such charges, Mary Anderson wrote a letter to Mary Winslow stating, "The Secretary [of State] assured me that the Woman's Party had nothing to do with my being withdrawn, that they just rode in on the band wagon, and I think that was so, because I think it happened before they knew about it." Anderson to Winslow, Anderson Papers, August 22, 1931, Folder 22, SL.

6. *Ibid.*

7. Copy of the letter asking Anderson to become a member of the Advisory Committee: Anderson Papers, October 10, 1932, Folder 23, SL.

8. Anderson to Harold Butler, Anderson Papers, October 12, 1932, Folder 23, SL.

9. For an account of the relationship Roosevelt and Perkins, as New York State officials, maintained with the ILO, see Moynihan, *The United States and the International Labor Organization.*

10. Perkins' lobbying efforts are detailed in George Martin, *Madam Secretary: Frances Perkins, A Biography of America's First Woman Cabinet Member* (Boston: Houghton Mifflin, 1976), pp. 427-428.

11. Clara Beyer, interview with author, January 19, 1976, Washington, D.C.

12. Memorandum: Mary Anderson to Perkins, quoting Alice Paul from *Equal Rights,* March 14, 1936, March, 1936, Bx. 1280, WB, NA.

13. *Ibid.*

14. Among them Hilda Smith, of the WPA; Florence Thorn of the AFL; Linna Bresette, Catholic Charities; and Mrs. E. Beresford Fox of the YWCA. See list compiled by the American Embassy, London: Dispatch #781, Embassy Report #148, "Subject: Women and the I.L.O.," February 5, 1946 (copy included), Bx. 1699, WB, NA.

15. David Green, *The Containment of Latin America: A History of the Myths and Realities of the Good Neighbor Policy* (Chicago: Quadrangle, 1971); James Petras and Maurice Zeitlin, eds., *Latin America: Reform or Revolution?* (New York: Fawcett, 1968); J. Lloyd Mecham, *The United States and Inter-American Security* (Austin: University of Texas Press,

1961); Lloyd Gardner, *Economic Aspects of New Deal Diplomacy* (Madison: University of Wisconsin Press, 1964).

16. For a discussion of female wage-earning patterns in South America see Ann M. Pescatello, *Power and Pawn: The Female in Iberian Families, Societies, and Cultures* (Westport, Conn.: Greenwood Press, 1976), pp. 184-193; Gino Germani, *Estructura social de la Argentina* (Buenos Aires: 1955); Murray Gendell and Guillermo Rossell, *The Economic Activity of Women in Latin America* (Washington, D.C.: Government Printing Office, 1967); Blanca Stabile, ''The Working Woman in the Argentine Economy,'' *International Labor Review,* 85 (1962), p. 122.

17. Interdepartmental Committee on Cooperation with the American Republics: ''Minutes of the Meetings, August 12, 1942,'' 832.4055/8; i.e., Records of the Department of State, R.G. 59, National Archives, Washington, D.C. (hereafter cited as DS/NA).

18. Mary Cannon, interview with author, January 15, 1976, Washington, D.C.; see also biographical resume, ''Inter-American Division File,'' WB, NA.

19. ''Women's Bureau: Description of Projects, Summary,'' memorandum to Interdepartmental Committee on Cooperation with the American Republics, September, 1942 (copy), Bx. 912, WB, NA.

20. See memorandum to William Schurz from Mary Anderson, Subject: ''Allocation of Funds to the Women's Bureau,'' September 17, 1943, ''Inter-American Division Files,'' WB, NA; Secretary Perkins' General Subject File, 1941-1945, ''Interdepartmental Committee on Cooperation with the American Republics: Summary Budgets,'' Labor, NA; Nelson Rockefeller to Mary Anderson, October 14, 1941, Bx. 914, WB, NA.

21. The amounts were: $10,000: 1942, $5,675: 1943, $7,810: 1944; letter to G. Holland Shaw, assistant secretary of state to Anderson and Secretary Perkins, August 7, 1942 (copy), ''Inter-American Division Files,'' WB, NA; Shaw to Perkins, July 2, 1943 (copy), ''Inter-American Division Files,'' WB, NA.

22. Leap to Schurz and Thomson, September 14, 1942, FS/832.4055/8, DS/NA.

23. Anderson wrote a letter discussing the meeting to assistant director of the Women's Bureau, Bertha Nienburg, Mary Anderson Papers, July 16, 1943, Folder 38, SL; see also Anderson to Bolton, July 23, 1943, Bx. 914, WB, NA. Opal Gooden corroborated Anderson's account in a three-page undated memorandum: Bx. 1382, WB, NA; Anderson to Bolton, July 23, 1943, Bx. 914, WB, NA.

24. August 7, 1942, Bx. 912, WB, NA.

25. Interdepartmental Committee on Cooperation with the American Republics: ''Minutes of the Meetings, August 12, 1942,'' 832.4055/8, DS/NA.

26. *Ibid.*

27. See memorandum, "Subject: Conversation between Mr. Charles Thomson and Mrs. Herbert Stabler, October 23, 1941," 811.431/137, DS/NA.

28. Winslow ghosted Anderson's autobiography, *Woman at Work*. She and Anderson were co-workers and confidantes for forty years. Ethel Erickson, interview with author, January 6, 1976, Washington, D.C.

29. Cannon interview.

30. See Report on Trip Itineraries (typescript, edited with notes), "Inter-American Division Files," WB, NA.

31. For complete dates of itineraries see "Inter-American Division Files," WB, NA.

32. For complete dates of itineraries see "Inter-American Division Files," WB, NA.

33. See Ambassador William Dawson, Montevideo, Uruguay, September 10, 1941, Report to the Secretary of State on the Visit of Mary Cannon of the Women's Bureau, 140/030, DS/NA; Ambassador Wesley Frost, April 9, 1943, Report to the Secretary of State: Subject, Visit to Paraguay of Miss Mary Cannon, 102.9/030, DS/NA.

34. M. Leap called Bertha Nienburg to read her the telegram so that she could take action to let Mary Cannon know of the Embassy's reluctant attitude before her arrival in the country. Nienburg wrote to Cannon. Nienburg to Cannon, June 24, 1941, Bx. 911, WB, NA.

35. Cannon interview; Josefina Marpons, "The North American Woman Asks For Her Place as a Patriotic Citizen," *El Hogar,* January 21, 1942. See a translated copy of the Hogar feature story in "Inter-American Division Files," WB, NA.

36. Report for the Inter-American Division, Preliminary Survey: Reports Received from Cannon, "Inter-American Division Files," March, 1943, WB, NA.

37. Cannon, Fort Worth speech to General Federation, "Inter-American Division Files," WB, NA.

38. Mary Cannon, speech draft (to be used for a lecture tour through California, summer 1943), "Inter-American Division Files," WB, NA.

39. Cannon, speech draft (to be used for a lecture tour through California, summer, 1943). Most of the speech drafts are typescripts, unpaginated. WB, NA.

40. Some of the women's groups, which Cannon herself acknowledged to be dominated by socially elite women, included Legion Pro Education Popular (Ecuador), Consejo Nacional de Mujeres (Paraguay, Chile), Damas Protectors del Obrero (Ecuador, Argentina), Accion Catolica (Mexico, Paraguay), Union Cultural Femenina (Peru), Uniao Social Femina (Brazil). See Mary Cannon to John Daly, Press Division, Office, coordinator of Inter-American Affairs.

41. Mary Cannon to Mary Anderson (from Buenos Aires), July 28, 1941, Bx. 914, WB, NA.

42. The Consejo Nacional de Mujeres in Santiago, Chile, invited Cannon to have lunch in a dining room where the club served some forty to eighty employed women daily. The particular night class mentioned was conducted by the Legion Pro Education Popular of Ecuador; Cannon to John Daly, Press Division, Office, coordinator of Inter-American Affairs.

43. Cannon, Fort Worth speech to General Federation, WB, NA.

44. Cannon interview; "Confidential: Brief Summary of Reports on Brazil," August, 1943; "Confidential: Report on Assignment in Mexico," December 21, 1948.

45. "Confidential: Brief Summary of Reports on Brazil," August, 1943, WB, NA.

46. Cannon to Bertha Nienburg (from Cordoba, Argentina), June 28, 1941, "Inter-American Division Files," WB, NA.

47. Mary Cannon to Mary Anderson (from Buenos Aires), April 28, 1941, Bx. 914, WB, NA.

48. Cannon to Nienburg (Cordoba, Argentina), June 28, 1941.

49. Mary Cannon attributed the statement to a young lawyer who asked her to bring back a message to the people of the United States, "Press Release," "Inter-American Division Files," (undated, probably August 1943), WB, NA.

50. Cannon to Nienburg (Cordoba, Argentina), June 28, 1941.

51. Mary Winslow, Mary Winslow Papers, memorandum, August 10, 1940, Bx. 2, SL.

52. *Ibid.*

53. See Report (typescript): "Prospectus: Internships in the Women's Bureau. U.S. Department of Labor," 1943, "Inter-American Division Files," WB, NA.

54. Mary Cannon and Opal Gooden to Inez Johnston, Interdepartmental Committee on Cooperation with the American Republics, October 23, 1944 (copy), "Inter-American Division Files," WB, NA.

55. Cannon to Mary Anderson (from Santiago, Chile), September 21, 1941.

56. Cannon to Rodriguez, September 6, 1943, "Inter-American Division Files," WB, NA.

57. Cannon and Gooden to Inez Johnston, October 23, 1944.

58. Francisco Trujillo Guerria to Secretary of Labor Frances Perkins, February 6, 1945 (copy), "Inter-American Division Files," WB, NA.

59. Sinclair Snow, *The Pan American Federation of Labor* (Durham, NC: Duke University Press, 1964).

Seedtime for Change: The Emergence of a New Federal Policy Toward Female Work in Postwar America

7

World War II ended, and Bureau agents returned from travels abroad and travels throughout the country to investigate war work. As they had warned, women workers did not stampede back to their kitchens. Rosie no longer riveted, but she did find a part-time filing job in a downtown office. Rather than a time that marked a return to traditional patterns of women's work, the postwar decade was a seedtime for dramatic change. Federal bureaucrats inched toward the major changes in policy announced in the 1960s. The increased entrance of older women, married women, and middle-class women into the labor force proved not to be a war-emergency anomaly but a new fact of American economic life. The baby boom was also an undeniable fact of economic life in the 1950s. A watershed, however, had been passed. Wives with children also brought home paychecks. The middle-class family of male breadwinner and female cakewinner had existed for a small minority before World War II. Motivated by postwar inflation and rising consumer expectations, more and more middle-class families combined the incomes of two spouses.[1] The woman worker no longer matched the stereotypes of poverty and youth used in 1920 by Progressives to justify the formation of a national Women's Bureau.

Two topics, reorganization in the Department of Labor, and the Kennedy Commission on the Status of Women, help illuminate the nature of government reaction to women in the work force during this time of transition, 1947-1963. The Department of Labor, reeling from cuts mandated by the "Meat-Axe" Congress of 1947, reorganized. The changes, which had begun during the troubled tenure of Secretary of Labor Frances Perkins, destroyed the independence and significance of the Women's Bureau, though it continued to exist in name. In a sense, the Women's Bureau network proved hardier than the agency itself. The Women's Bureau was moribund by the mid-1950s as a source of policy advice about working women. Its members and former members, however, led by Women's Bureau Director and Assistant Secretary of Labor Esther Peterson, strongly influenced President John Kennedy's Commission on the Status of Women, which met from 1961 to 1963 and formed a capstone to forty years of federal policy on women workers.

Secretary of Labor Frances Perkins, the first female Cabinet appointee, unwittingly spurred a series of Department of Labor disputes with Congress that left the Department a defeated skeleton by 1947. Perkins, a Maine blue blood, Holyoke graduate, and former industrial commissioner of New York state, presented a startling contrast to the cigar-chomping figures of her predecessors William Wilson, James Davis, and William Doak. Union leaders vehemently opposed the nomination of a woman. William Green of the AFL had warned, "Labor can never become reconciled to her selection."[2] Some refused to speak with Perkins even after her Senate confirmation as secretary of labor. No love was lost between Perkins and many of the Department of Labor employees she encountered during her first months in office either. Reviewing her career as Secretary of Labor in 1941, she caustically remarked that the Department of Labor in 1933 was: "in shocking condition. . . . The offices were dirty, files and papers were missing. There was an internal spy system, and everyone was scared of everyone else. . . . I had made up my mind not to discharge employees just because they were Republicans, but I found I had to discharge many of them because they were incompetent."[3] Perkins, who made a point of excusing the Women's Bureau from her litanies of horror, was right. Her predecessors had tolerated corruption and waste and were the appointees of presidents not terribly concerned that the secretaries of labor be top-caliber administrators.[4] The Women's Bureau, a small ghetto of sixty to seventy female bureaucrats, had, before Perkins, received little secretarial attention. Its members had more professional dealings with the League of Women Voters or the National Women's Trade Union League than they did with fellow bureaucrats in the Department of Labor. In fact, until the New Deal, the Bureau offices were separate from the rest of the Department of Labor. Only a fire, which destroyed the floor of its building on F Street, forced the Bureau into new quarters in the same building with other Department of Labor agencies.

In 1933, Women's Bureau agents finally had a superior as secretary of labor who was equally dedicated, competent, and genuinely concerned about women workers. Despite that fact, both the Bureau and the Department of Labor suffered under Perkins' management. Perkins never recovered politically from a clash in 1934 with congressmen concerned that she was soft on Communism. The 1934 California longshoremen's strike was one of the most bitter and bloody of the first Roosevelt Administration. In San Francisco, thousands of workers in other trades had struck in sympathy, and charges spread that the longshoremen were Communists with plans for a national general strike. Congress inundated the Department of Labor with demands that one of the strike leaders, Harry Bridges, an Australian, be immediately deported as an undesirable alien. The longshoremen's strike soon collapsed, and a Department of Labor investigation determined that Bridges was in the country legally. The Federal Bureau of Investigation, however, continued to search for evidence that he was a Communist, and in 1937 unearthed witnesses willing to testify to seeing Bridges at Communist Party meetings. Instead of immediately beginning deportation proceedings, however, Secretary of Labor Perkins postponed the Bridges hearing, awaiting a Supreme Court decision on mandatory deportation of aliens who had once been Communist Party members. The postponement was perfectly proper, but it unleashed a storm of attacks on Perkins and the Department of Labor. Congressman Martin Dies of Texas, head of the Special Committee on UnAmerican Activities, accused her of willfully harboring Communists. Whisper campaigns intimated that either Perkins or her teen-aged daughter, Susan, had secretly married Harry Bridges. Congressman J. Parnell Thomas, a member of the Dies Committee, introduced a resolution demanding that Secretary Perkins be impeached.

In 1938, the Supreme Court ruled that the Immigration Service could not deport an alien simply because of a prior connection with the Communist Party. In 1939, the Immigration Service, acting on this ruling and finding no proof that Bridges was a Communist at the time of his arrest, refused to deport him. Moreover, the House Judiciary Committee unanimously concluded that the Dies Committee charges did not warrant impeachment proceedings against Frances Perkins.[5] This legal vindication, however, did not persuade Secretary Perkins' opponents to cease attempts to prove that the Department of Labor was a subversive force within the government structure.

Caught in a web of lies and bitter confrontations, Frances Perkins lost one administrative battle after another. A woman who had carved a reputation as a skilled manipulator on the New York Industrial Commission, she failed to get the Social Security Administration in the Department of Labor, despite the fact that she was a prominent crusader for Social Security among high-level New Dealers. The United States Employment Service transferred out of the Department of Labor. The Treasury Department acted as new home for the United States Housing Corporation, and the Department of Justice began to supervise the Immigration Service. Unlike Secretary Wilson, who had acted as war labor administrator during World War I, Perkins played no major administrative role in World War II mobilization. War agencies during World War II bypassed the Department of Labor. In a time of mushrooming growth of the federal bureaucracy, Congress cut appropriations for the Department of Labor.[6]

Understandably, Perkins felt herself to be in an armed camp without a gun. She cultivated a hypersensitivity to charges that she favored any special groups or issues. Above all, she feared identification as a special champion of women. Clara Beyer, whom Perkins appointed to be assistant director of the Bureau of Labor Standards, recalled Perkins saying to her on more than one occasion: "I can't have too many women. They are all watching to see how many women I appoint." Beyer excused Perkins' failure to appoint her as director of the Bureau of Labor Standards, "even though she told me I was far and away the best candidate for the position."[7]

Mary Anderson and the women of the Women's Bureau were not so forgiving. When Perkins sought to consolidate the Women's and Children's Bureaus in 1933, Anderson threatened, "Any action you might take to change the status of the Women's Bureau at this time would subject the Department of Labor to a tremendous amount of criticism from women throughout the country."[8] The secretary backed down, but Mary Anderson continued to be wary. The Bureau director stage-managed a letter-writing campaign in 1934, in which allies in organizations like the Women's Trade Union League, the National Consumer's League, and the YWCA bombarded Perkins with letters praising the work of the Women's Bureau.[9]

Her conflict with the secretary of labor became regular fodder for Mary Anderson's private correspondence. She claimed, unfairly, that Perkins intentionally humiliated the Women's Bureau during Congressional appropriations hearings.[10] The two independent, work-obsessed, strong-willed women, both cursed with a confrontational style, battled each other for a decade until both resigned from the Department of Labor at the end of World War II.

There is no doubt that Frances Perkins' lack of special attention to women workers aroused the ire of Mary Anderson. The feud between the two, however, bore little of the blame for the reality that Frances Perkins left a crumbling Department of Labor. National union leaders continued to dislike their patrician female Cabinet secretary. Feuds with Congress undermined Perkins' ability to run her department.

The autonomy and future of both the Department of Labor and the Women's Bureau within that department appeared in question in the late 1940s and early 1950s. Both survived, though in a reduced and altered form. Under Lewis Schwellenbach, a weak administrator, trapped in the middle of a major postwar strike wave, the Department of Labor reached its nadir. The 80th "Meat-Axe" Congress effectively reduced the department to a skeleton and gave it a miniscule budget. The Women's Bureau, the Bureau of Labor Standards, a stripped Bureau of Labor Statistics, the Wages and Hours Division, and the Public Contracts Division were all that was left of the Department of Labor. In March 1947, House Appropriation subcommittees met and cut over 44 percent from the Department of Labor budget. The Women's Bureau, however, remained intact. Some Appropriation Committee members, when interviewed, acknowledged the influence exercised by the strong defense of the Women's Bureau mounted by women's organizations and other long-time supporters.[11]

Maurice Tobin, brought in by President Truman in 1948, sought to revive an emaciated department. Some of the agencies removed by Congress, such as the Conciliation Service, remained independent. Tobin did succeed in restoring a much larger budget, the United States Employment Service, the Bureau of Employees' Compensation, and the Compensations Appeals Board.[12] Ironically, he also revived an intradepartmental investigation begun by Perkins in 1944, challenging the need for an independent Women's Bureau. In 1945, new Women's Bureau Director Frieda Miller submitted a twenty-four page answer to Secretary Perkins' query, "Why should the Women's Bureau continue to exist as a separate agency of the Department of Labor, reporting directly to the administrative head of the Department?" After summarizing the Bureau's work, she concluded:

> The Washington office and the regional offices of the Bureau together constitute a small but highly trained and experienced organization strategically integrated to assist and to promote the welfare of employed women throughout the United States. It is the only agency which through years of knowledge can give direct service to employers, employees and all organizations requiring help.[13]

She went on to argue that consolidation with the Division of Labor Standards would be "particularly ill-advised and destructive."[14]

That "particularly ill-advised" move did not take place in 1945. New Labor Secretary James Mitchell enacted it in 1954. In a reshuffling that promoted the Women's Bureau director to be assistant to the Secretary of Labor for Women's Affairs, the Women's Bureau was not abolished. Instead, Mitchell reassigned employees of the Women's Bureau working on subjects relating to work in other Bureaus to teams with people performing the related work, regardless of Bureau affiliation. The dispersed employees were to remain part of the Women's Bureau, but their immediate supervisors might no longer be members of the Bureau.[15] Under Secretary of Labor Millard Cass, interviewed in 1970, argued that both this reorganization and Secretary of Labor Arthur Goldberg's decision in 1960 to promote Esther Peterson stemmed from a desire to elevate top-ranking women in the Department of Labor. Goldberg created for Peterson the post of Assistant Secretary for Labor Standards by merging the Bureau of Labor Standards, the Bureau of Employees' Compensation, the Employees' Compensation Appeals Board and the Women's Bureau.[16] Perhaps Goldberg knew of the vigorous lobbying in defense of the Women's Bureau in 1934 and 1945. In any event, according to Cass, he took care to touch bases with members of Congress, especially those on the Senate Civil Service Committee, telling them that the reorganization was meant as a promotion, meant to recognize the role women played both in government and in the American economy.

Although the secretary billed the changes as promotions and increased government recognition of women's economic role, some labeled the Bureau a less effective agency, an agency with different goals and a more narrow constituency. Mary Anderson clearly revealed her biases in a letter written in 1959 to Mary Van Kleeck:

> I just want to say one little word about the Women's Bureau. It does nothing for women in industry. What little is done is for Business and Professional women. I know Mrs. Leopold quite well and like her as a person, but I think she ought to stay on her job and do some work for the women.[17]

Old timers like Mary Anderson correctly perceived the diminished importance of the Women's Bureau. They regretted it. Nevertheless, Under Secretary Cass was right. The reorganization and eclipse of the Women's Bureau prophesied a greater, not a lesser, involvement with working women. The transformation to a federal government that spawned the 1964 Civil Rights Act, Affirmative Action, the Equal Employment Opportunity Commission (EEOC), and other programs with enforcement powers and budgets never granted the Women's Bureau was not immediate. The government did not encourage married or older women to flood into the labor force. In 1960, Under Secretary of Labor James O'Connel, speaking at a conference held to celebrate the fortieth anniversary of the Women's Bureau, summarized what he described as the Department of Labor's traditions with regard to women workers:

> Women account for 53% of the Soviet Union's total labor force. Their predominance in some economic sectors seems startling. 85% of the work force in the health fields is female,

66% in education . . . 75% of all doctors are women. Perhaps we ought to applaud the USSR and emulate their accomplishment. I don't think so. What they have accomplished is based upon a system of day care, even week care of children. When a woman comes to be viewed first as a source of manpower, second as a mother, then I think we are losing much that supposedly separates us from the Communist world. The highest calling of a woman's sex is the home.[18]

Whatever their highest calling and whatever their ages or marital status, American women increasingly left the home in the 1950s to work either full or part time. Their presence, national prosperity, and, finally, a climate of social protest that began with the Civil Rights movement of the 1950s spurred major changes in the pattern of federal reactions to women workers.

Hints of changes to come during the Kennedy years and after occurred in the 1950s. One was an increased emphasis on equal pay legislation. In fact, calls for equal pay for equal work came to characterize the merged and reorganized Women's Bureau of the 1950s as much as calls for night-work laws seemed to characterize the Women's Bureau of the previous decades. The Bureau hosted several conferences on equal pay and issued special publications devoted to the subject. Of course, the Bureau's support for federal equal pay legislation was not new. A Bureau report on the 1952 "National Conference on Equal Pay" correctly noted that, "the Women's Bureau has earnestly worked for the adoption of the practice over the years."[19] Still, the soft-pedaling of protective legislation after 1956 made it possible for the restructured Bureau to demand equal pay for women with more ideological consistency since, without protective legislation, women workers were at least theoretically more likely to find work where conditions could be labeled comparable to those for men.

Another sign of change was a dramatically altered focus for the investigations of the Women's Bureau. For decades, Bureau agents had reported about the work of factory laborers, maids, and seamstresses on piecework. Suddenly, Alice Leopold, an Eisenhower appointee who replaced Frieda Miller, Mary Anderson's friend and hand-picked successor, redirected the Bureau's mission. Leopold argued that "it no longer makes sense to think of women as a separate segment of the work force, or as Under Secretary Arthur Larson recently put it, 'to herd them into categories.''"[20] By the late 1950s, Bureau publications began to reflect the new emphasis Leopold placed on work opportunities for middle-class, well-educated women in business and the professions. *Bulletin* titles like "Careers for Women in the Physical Sciences," "Employment Opportunities for Women Mathematicians," "First Jobs of College Women," "Employment Opportunities for Women in Legal Work," and "College Women Go to Work," contrasted starkly with the library of previously published *Bulletins,* which had more commonly investigated the routines of women workers in canneries, tobacco warehouses, or laundries.[21]

But befitting a time of transition, Women's Bureau officials coupled their radical reorientation of investigations and their campaign for equal pay with assurances that they truly respected traditional roles for women. Alice Leopold assured Secretary Mitchell that a Women's Bureau-sponsored "Conference on Effective Uses of Womanpower" did not slight the useful role of housewives:

> On consulting the transcript of speeches I find nowhere any remarks from representatives of the Labor Department which would imply that we desired to urge married women to leave their homes. On a personal note you know how strongly I believe in the influence and prime importance of religion, the family and the home.[22]

Despite such rhetoric and the official equivocation that stood behind it, policy toward women workers had begun to shift. Department of Labor participation in the deliberations of the United Nations Commission on the Status of Women provided another hint of changes to come. Like the women delegates and advisors to the ILO, the eighteen United Nations Commission members could command media attention but no real power. They were, however, far more forthright in asserting women's right to independence, free choice of jobs, and legal equality. Woman as independent person, not essential cog in the wheel of family and society, emerged as a theme. Year after year, Commission members issued press releases urging that restraints on paid work and types of education available to women be lifted. The emphasis on protective legislation that had characterized ILO Women's Advisory Committee meetings was absent.

Frequently meeting in Washington in Department of Labor conference rooms, Commission members pledged "to eradicate discrimination against women in the political, economic, social, civic and educational fields, thus giving women equal rights with men." In a sense, the United Nations Commission on the Status of Women foreshadowed by some six years the changes in official policy toward women taken by the United States federal government after 1963. In 1959, for instance, the Women's Bureau hosted a "Conference on the Status of Women around the World," immediately following the thirteenth annual session of the United Nations Commission. The Commission members traveled from New York to Washington and while at the Department of Labor fielded questions from reporters and fellow conference delegates about their "feminism." Rather than deny the label, Commission chairperson Minerva Bernardino of the Dominican Republic answered, "In this new society in which we live women are persons and as such should be treated that way. We are working for this within the United Nations."[23]

In its official report on "Woman Power Recruitment" campaigns during World War II, the Women's Bureau concluded, "In the climate of war crisis it was easy for men in the administration to evade the pressures or dismiss the requests of action as unnecessarily feminist."[24] Two decades later, government administrators found pressures for change less easy to evade. President John Kennedy entered office on the eve of a decade of social activism, a decade in which women in a resurgent women's movement would demand to be treated, to paraphrase Chairperson Bernardino, as persons deserving equal political rights and economic independence.

The Kennedy Administration was one whose rhetoric championed social activism and crusades against injustice. It was also one willing to examine the consequences of an altered demographic reality for women workers. In 1920, there were 8.25 million working women. By 1960, that number had almost tripled, swelled especially since World War II with married, middle-aged and middle-class women. President Kennedy received pressure from female trade unionists, the United States Department of Labor, and prominent women leaders to formally consider women's status in America.

Further, he expressed interest in government "white papers" issued by the Bureaus of the Census and Labor Standards, discussing the rise of the two-income, middle-class family and projecting even further economic and social change for American women. Esther Peterson, Kennedy's appointee as the new director of the Women's Bureau, differed from her predecessor, Alice Leopold, and strongly urged the creation of a commission.[25] So did a woman with even more political clout among Democrats. Eleanor Roosevelt chastised John Kennedy for naming too few women to significant government posts and seconded Peterson's recommendation to set up a commission.[26] Thus motivated, John Kennedy, in December 1961, established his President's Commission on the Status of Women, with Eleanor Roosevelt as chairperson. The twenty-six members of the Commission received orders to submit a written report to the president by 1963, evaluating the economic and social status of American women.

Committees appointed by the Commission investigated a diverse range of topics, not all of which addressed female employment. In an interesting way, however, despite the pains the commissioners took to define their work as a complete review of women's status in America, the separate committees on education, taxes, civil and political rights, as well as committees on labor law and employment, focused on women at work.

Leaders of women's organizations, women trade unionists, and women educators participated. The presidents of the National Council of Jewish Women and the National Council of Catholic Women, the National Council of Negro Women, and an official of the National Council of Churches sat on the Commission. So did a female executive of the Electrical and Machine Workers, American Federation of Labor and Congress of Industrial Organizations (AFL-CIO), and the president of Radcliffe College. The Women's Bureau staff was deeply involved with the Commission. Esther Peterson, bureau director from 1961 to 1963, sat on the Commission, and Women's Bureau members provided its Washington research staff. Twelve Bureau members, including former director, Frieda Miller, and future director, Mary Keyserling, served as members of specialized committees appointed by the Commission. But the President's Commission, unlike the Bureau, was not exclusively female. If the Commission included prominent women, it also included powerful men. Members of Congress, union leaders, businessmen, and five Cabinet members joined the Commission. There is no question that the members of the Kennedy Commission, as a group, were able to tap resources and gain attention more easily than the Women's Bureau.

Most of the twenty-six members of the Kennedy Commission were prominent persons whose careers were not primarily identified with problems encountered by working women. The Executive Order that established the Commission required only that the body be composed of persons "with a competency in the area of public affairs and women's activities." Robert Kennedy, Orville Freeman, Luther Hodges, Arthur Goldberg, George Aiken, and many others who sat on the Commission had larger and more diverse constituencies than did the staff of the Women's Bureau.[27]

According to Felix Frankfurter, "Commissions are admirable means for taking the nation to school."[28] Presidents since Theodore Roosevelt have appointed commissions of well-known, respected individuals when they wished to generate publicity and advocate solutions for a particular problem. Despite the great growth of the federal government in the twentieth century, the number of commissions appointed during any given year has always been relatively small. President Kennedy, for instance, appointed only twelve during his years in office.

The Kennedy Commission on the Status of Women heralded the beginning of a noticeably different posture toward working women while not yet breaking with past policy. Contemporary analysis correctly forecast that the Commission marked both an end and a beginning. The Interdepartmental Committee established in 1963 to continue the work of the Commission argued, "No year since the passage of the Nineteenth Amendment in 1920 can be compared to the period October 1963 to October 1964 in terms of new opportunities offered to women."[29] The famous anthropologist, Margaret Mead, hired by editors at Scribners to study the Commission's publications, concluded, "Like a solid, protective wall, the Commission's Report divides the past with its limitations and difficulties, from a future in which it may be expected that these hindrances will be overcome."[30] Certainly, the Commission never concluded that American women should leave the home to work. It did, however, affirm the worth of paid work.[31] A report made to the Committee on Social Insurance and Taxes even suggested that work within the house could be given more social status by allowing housewives to build up equity in the Social Security system as if they were earning outside wages. The idea did not gain the approval of the entire Commission, but it indicated the strength of the belief held by many commissioners that women had a right to the rewards of work for pay regardless of their marital status. *American Women,* the Commission's final report, labeled inequality before the law and in job opportunity as the two principal handicaps suffered by women. While the Commission opposed the ERA as a solution to problems of legal inequality, it did urge a series of court tests based on equal protection guarantees of the Fifth and Fourteenth Amendments of laws and practices that discriminated against women. Its recommendations for the problems of job inequality were far more specific: The Federal Fair Labor Standards Act should be extended to cover areas such as hotels, restaurants, and laundries, where large numbers of women labored without its benefits. Women workers should be paid maternity leave or comparable insurance benefits. States should follow the federal example and adopt equal pay legislation for women. Discriminatory educational, union, and employer practices that restricted female access to promotions and higher paid jobs should be eliminated through stricter laws. Legislation, moreover, should protect the right of all workers, male and female, to join unions and bargain collectively.[32]

Its opposition to the ERA tied the Kennedy Commission to the previous forty years of federal public policy toward women wage earners. Its demand for comprehensive and effective federal and state legal guarantees of equal employment and educational opportunity for women prophesied the future and an enlarged federal role of inspection and promotion of work rights for women.

Several commissioners explicitly chose to emphasize the differences between Bureau and Commission purposes. Secretary of Labor Arthur Goldberg, a member of the Commission, emphasized: "The Commission will cover a much broader field of study than that covered by the Women's Bureau."[33] Another Commission member, Senator Maurine Neuberger of Oregon, went much further. The Bureau, she said, was "definitely a tool of the labor unions. . . . Women thought that they had a voice in government when they didn't because it wasn't initiating anything. That was the thing that got me. It was just perpetuating statistics. . . .They'd add another two zeros at the end of how many women were employed, how many women were divorced."[34]

Senator Neuberger was wrong. The members of the Women's Bureau were not tools of organized labor. They frequently sought to initiate programs. In fact, the Kennedy Commission owed its existence partially to Women's Bureau agitation. Esther Peterson, a woman with White House entree, played a pivotal role lobbying for its creation. Other staffers wrote important sections of its final report. Clearly, however, the Bureau could not publicize policy as effectively as could well-known Commission members.

The Kennedy Commission provided greater visibility for women's issues, not dramatic suggestions for a completely different policy. But the publicity signaled the beginning of a more active federal posture toward issues raised by working women. John Kennedy understood the symbolic importance of the Commission and used its ceremonies and prominent members to showcase government concern for women's problems. When Eleanor Roosevelt died in November 1962, he argued that no one could adequately replace her, dedicated the Commission's work to her memory, and asked Esther Peterson and Professor Richard Lester, a Princeton economist, to manage the leadership of the Commission. When the Commission gathered at the White House on October 11, 1963, Eleanor Roosevelt's birthday, to submit its final report, Kennedy engineered even more symbolism as picture-taking began. White House protocol officers had arranged the Commission for the official photos. When President Kennedy entered the room he noticed that the entire first row, most apparent to the camera, was filled by males. Without saying a word, he motioned to Senator Maurine Neuberger and Congresswoman Edith Green to move into the first row.[35]

John Kennedy's successor, Lyndon Johnson, had delivered an address to the President's Commission in 1962, which began, "It is a great pleasure for me to come before this group this morning and I dare say [it is] the only group which can frankly and candidly and without any fear of criticism admit that the only thing on its mind is girls."[36] Such infelicities of phrase did not alter the fact that Lyndon Johnson presided over major changes in federal perception of women's status. A series of laws and executive orders stressed equality for women, not segregated protection. The Equal Pay Act, Title VII of the Civil Rights Act, Title IX of the Education Acts Amendment, and Executive Order 11246 mandating the beginning of federal Affirmative Action programs were elements of the new federal approach. The political and social turbulence of the decade helped spur this dramatic shift in policy. The 1960s witnessed the rebirth of organized and vocal feminist protest by thousands of women. New national women's organizations such as the National Organization for Women and the Women's Equity Action League were born. Older moderate women's organizations joined federal labor officials and reversed their long-standing opposition to the Equal Rights Amendment. By so doing, they began to remake four decades of policy centered on protective labor legislation. In 1970, the Women's Bureau itself finally endorsed the Equal Rights Amendment. Economics and the women's movement prompted these changes in position. Of equal importance was the fact that the cause of protective labor legislation became less compelling. Concessions granted labor during the New Deal and after meant that protective legislation for men became feasible. The forty-hour week became standard. Unions agitated for and won safety regulations for all workers. "Equal Rights," moderates began to concede, no longer had to mean dismantling basic protection for women workers.

The vast majority of working women still labored long hours for low wages and won little prestige. Nonetheless, an important change of perception had occurred. The prosperity of the postwar period and the energy of the women's movement had given many moderate feminists a sense of great expectations. It was a similar sense of buoyantly optimistic great expectations in the face of far more ambiguous social realities that had led a tiny minority in the militant and isolated Woman's Party decades earlier to demand the Equal Rights Amendment. The ERA required faith that women would benefit and not suffer from complete legal equality and equal access to all types of work. It also required a different definition of women's proper place, a repudiation of the Progressive canonization of motherhood, an emphasis on women as individuals. The optimism of the social protest movements of the 1960s, with their visions of an egalitarian America implemented by a changed legal structure, proved infectious.

Society seemed to be changing rapidly; divorce rates skyrocketed, and so did remarriage rates. Formal employment and occupational barriers fell.[37] Fewer social activists publicly argued that they and their organizations had a major commitment to protect the downtrodden working woman. By the early 1960s, even the politics of the Women's Bureau had changed. Federal policy for forty years had focused on the need to protect a young, politically weak woman worker. By 1963, change was in the wind.

NOTES

1. Eli Ginzberg, "Paycheck and Apron—A Revolution in Woman Power," vol. 7, *Industrial Relations* (May 1968), pp. 193-203; for a review of the 1930s, see Winifred Wandersee, "The Economics of Middle-Income Family Life: Working Women During the Great Depression," *Journal of American History*, 65 (June 1978), pp. 60-74.

2. Green quoted in George Martin, *Madam Secretary: Frances Perkins, A Biography of America's First Woman Cabinet Member* (Boston: Houghton Mifflin, 1976), p. 3.

3. "My Eight Years as Madame Secretary," 24, *Fortune* (September 1941), pp. 78, 94.

4. Even Jonathan Grossman, who as historian of the Department of Labor portrays the Department of Labor in a favorable light, admits the truth of many of her claims. *The Department of Labor* (New York: Praeger, 1973), pp. 30-50.

5. George Martin, *Madam Secretary*, pp. 409-419.

6. Grossman, *The Department of Labor*, pp. 58-61.

7. Clara Beyer, interview with the author, January 19, 1976, Washington, D.C. (hereafter cited as Beyer interview).

8. Mary Anderson to Frances Perkins, September 1932, Folder 28, Mary Anderson Paper, Schlesinger Library (hereafter cited as SL).

9. See files on letters to Perkins (some with carbon replies) in the Records of the Women's Bureau (R.G. 86), National Archives Bx. 840-848 (hereafter cited as WB, NA); see also Secretary Perkins' General Subject File, 1933-40, (Records of the Secretaries of the Department of Labor, R.G. 174) (hereafter cited as Labor, NA).

10. Anderson to Elizabeth Magee, November 10, 1943, Anderson Papers, Folder 38, SL.

11. *The New York Times*, March 13, 1947; *The Christian Science Monitor*, March 28, 1947. Among the organizations that sent representatives to lobby for the maintenance of the Women's Bureau were the American Association of University Women, the League of Women Voters,

the General Federation of Women's Clubs, the Women's Trade Union League, and the YWCA. For further evidence of the organizational campaign to keep the Women's Bureau, see Hilda Smith to Rose Terlin, March 31, 1943, Bx. 20, Hilda Smith Papers, Franklin Roosevelt Presidential Library, Hyde Park, N.Y. (hereafter FDR Lib.)

12. These last named agencies had been transferred to the Federal Security Administration. See Vincent Lapomarda, *Maurice Tobin, 1901-1953: A Political Profile and an Edition of Selected Papers* (Boston: Houghton Mifflin, 1969), pp. 25-67.

13. "Memorandum: Miss Miller to Mr. Moran" (typescript marked confidential), August 17, 1945, Bx. 1723, WB, NA.

14. *Ibid.*

15. Summary of Action, Secretary's Policy Committee, Meeting #38, August 2, 1954, James P. Mitchell Files, Bx. 54, Labor, NA.

16. The Oral History Transcript of Millard Cass, July 14, 1970, Oral History Collection, John F. Kennedy Presidential Library (hereafter cited as KL).

17. Anderson to Mary Van Kleeck, April 12, 1959, Mary Van Kleeck Papers, Bx. 9, Sophia Smith Collection, Smith College (hereafter cited as SS).

18. Address by James O'Connel, press release, June 3, 1960 (typescript), Press Releases File, WB, NA.

19. Women's Bureau *Bulletin #243*, "Report of the National Conference on Equal Pay, March 31 and April 1, 1952" (Washington, D.C.: Government Printing Office, 1952), p. 1.

20. Alice Leopold, Speech to Norwalk, Conn., Luncheon of Business and Professional Men, April 29, 1955 (speech typescript), pp. 11-12, Women's Bureau Information Office, Speech File, WB, NA.

21. The following *Bulletins* are representative of the new tone of the 1950s. For complete list, see Appendix. Women's Bureau *Bulletin #258*, "Employment Opportunities for Women in Professional Accounting" (Washington, D.C.: Government Printing Office, 1955); Women's Bureau *Bulletin #264*, "College Women Go To Work: Report on Women Graduates, Class of 1956" (Washington, D.C.: Government Printing Office, 1958); Women's Bureau *Bulletin #265*, "Employment Opportunities for Women in Legal Work" (Washington, D.C.: Government Printing Office, 1958); Women's Bureau *Bulletin #270*, "Careers for Women in the Physical Sciences" (Washington, D.C.: Government Printing Office, 1959); Women's Bureau *Bulletin #268*, "First Jobs of College Women—Report on Women Graduates, Class of 1957" (Washington, D.C.: Government Printing Office, 1959); Women's Bureau *Bulletin #262*, "Employment Opportunities for Women Mathematicians and Statisticians" (Washington, D.C.: Government Printing Office, 1956).

22. Alice K. Leopold to Secretary of Labor James Mitchell, April 18, 1955, "Memorandum on Conference," carbon copy, Bx. 99, Labor, NA.

23. Summary: Purposes of the Commission. Report of the Conference on the Status of Women Around the World, March 30, 1959, Washington, D.C., typescript of proceedings, p. 22, WB, NA.

24. Women's Bureau *Bulletin #244,* "Women Power Committees in World War II" (Washington, D.C.: Government Printing Office, 1953), p. 40.

25. See "Materials: Minutes of Meetings, October 24, 1960- January 19, 1962," The President's Commission on the Status of Women (hereafter cited as PCSW), KL. Cynthia Harrison argues that Peterson, a long-time and influential Kennedy advisor on labor issues, acted as the catalyst that prompted the establishment of the Commission. Peterson, in effect, differed from other presidential "spokespersons" for women's interests by focusing on a commission and equal pay legislation rather than on appointments for women to government posts. See Cynthia Harrison, "A 'New Frontier' For Women: The Public Policy of the Kennedy Administration," *The Journal of American History* (December 1980), pp. 630-646.

26. Joseph Lash, *Eleanor: The Years Alone* (New York: 1972), p. 321.

27. Members of the President's Commission on the Status of Women are listed: Eleanor Roosevelt, Chairman; Dr. Richard A. Lester, professor of economics, Princeton University; Esther Peterson, Director of Women's Bureau, assistant secretary of labor; Attorney General Robert F. Kennedy; Secretary of Agriculture Orville L. Freeman; Secretary of Commerce Luther H. Hodges; Secretary of Labor Arthur J. Goldberg; Secretary of Health, Education and Welfare Abraham A. Ribicoff; Chairman, United States Civil Service Commission, John W. Macy, Jr.; Senator George D. Aiken, Republican, of Vermont; Senator Maurine B. Neuberger, Democrat, of Oregon; Congresswoman Edith Green, Democrat, of Oregon; Congresswoman Jessica M. Weis, Republican, of New York; Ellen Boddy, civic leader, rancher, Henrietta, Texas; Dr. Mary I. Bunting, president, Radcliffe College; Mary R. Callahan, member, Executive Board, International Union of Electrical, Radio and Machine Workers, AFL-CIO; Dr. Henry David, president, New School for Social Research; Dorothy Height, president, National Council of Negro Women; Margaret Hickey, lawyer, contributing editor, *Ladies' Home Journal;* Viola H. Hymes, national president, National Council of Jewish Women; Edgar F. Kaiser, corporation executive; Margaret J. Mealey, executive director, National Council of Catholic Women; Marguerite Rawalt, lawyer, member of Bar of the District of Columbia, State of Texas, and United States Supreme Court; William F. Schnitzler, secretary-treasurer, American Federation of Labor and Congress of Industrial Organizations; Dr. Caroline Ware, sociologist, historian for UNESCO, former professor at Vassar; and Dr. Cynthia C. Wedel, psychologist, president, United Church Women. List from: PCSW Document 5, February 8, 1962, PCSW, KL.

28. Quoted in Thomas Wolanin, *Presidential Advisory Commissions* (Madison: University of Wisconsin Press, 1975), p. 35. See Wolanin, *Presidential Advisory Commissions;* Elizabeth Drew, "On Giving Oneself a Hotfoot: Government by Commission," *Atlantic Monthly,* 221 (May, 1968); Thomas Cronin and Sanford Greenberg, eds., *The Presidential Advisory System* (New York: Harper and Row, 1969).

29. *Progress Report on the Status of Women,* First Annual Report of the Interdepartmental Committee and the Citizens' Advisory Council on the Status of Women, November, 1964, copy in Pamphlet File, WB, NA.

30. Mead was not a member of the Commission but edited the officially sanctioned Scribner's edition of the final report: Margaret Mead, ed., *American Women: The Report of the President's Commission on the Status of Women* (New York: Scribners, 1965), p. 181.

31. Mead, *American Women,* p. 191.

32. *Ibid.,* pp. 20-73; "Commission Reports on Status of Women," *IUE News Chicago,* October, 1963.

33. Memorandum from Esther Peterson (typescript), no date, "Back ground Information: Why a Commission on the Status of Women," PCSW, KL.

34. Oral History Transcripts, Oral History of Maurine Neuberger (February 12, 1970), pp. 15, 16, PCSW, KL.

35. The incident is recounted in Oral History Transcripts, Oral History of John Macy (May 23, 1964), p. 60, PCSW, KL.

36. "Remarks of Vice President Lyndon Johnson," September 24, 1962 (typed transcript), Bx. 4, PCSW, KL.

37. For discussion of the status of women during this period, see Patricia Zelman, *Women, Work and National Policy: The Kennedy-Johnson Years* (Ann Arbor: UMI Research Press, 1981); James Kenneally, *Women and American Trade Unions* (Quebec: Eden Press, 1978); Valerie Oppenheimer, *The Female Labor Force in the United States* (Westport, Conn.: Greenwood Press, 1976); Milton Cantor and Bruce Laurie, *Class, Sex, and the Woman Worker* (Westport, Conn.: Greenwood Press, 1977); William Chafe, *The American Woman: Her Changing Social, Economic, and Political Role, 1920-1970* (New York: Oxford, 1972).

The "Outsider as Insider": The Woman-Worker Issue and Government Reform, 1920-1963

8

What had these forty years of federal programs focused on the woman worker accomplished? The history of federal reaction to the phenomenon of female work from 1920 to 1963 is a history of the uses and exercise of influence and persuasion, but not power. It would be wrong to call the efforts of the Women's Bureau and its allies failures, but the reforms achieved were limited, the goals such as protective labor legislation debated and debatable, the victories cheated of much significance.

A summary of federal involvement with the woman-worker issue during these decades should list achievements and probe reasons for failures. Certainly, the publications of the Women's Bureau are an achievement.[1] The writers and researchers of the Women's Bureau—ever without sufficient money to stage large-scale surveys or undertake complicated statistical analyses—nonetheless completed and distributed hundreds of pamphlets, books, bulletins, and newsletters. Many reports written in the 1920s or 1930s remain standard essays on the subjects. Without the Women's Bureau, it is unlikely that researchers would now have the same wealth of information about injury rates in the textiles industry, the living conditions of women tobacco workers, changing employer attitudes about hiring women over age thirty-five, high disease rates among women shoe workers in New Hampshire, and a host of other topics. The published reports combined with the hundreds of boxes of unpublished records housed in the National Archives form a valuable resource for historians.

The *Bulletins* published by the Women's Bureau were not white-washes. Many delivered hard-hitting attacks, citing dangerous working conditions and discriminatory pay as the average working woman's lot. However, no union or factory official had to let a Bureau agent see his records. No agent could enter a work place uninvited. Not surprisingly, given the reality that Bureau agents could not afford to alienate those whose acquiescence was vital if they were to do their jobs, many of the most damning survey and interview materials never saw print. Voluminous files of confidential materials still exist, useful to any attempt to reconstruct the history of working women from 1920 to 1960.

A 1928 directive on interview techniques advised Women's Bureau agents to: "take *full* notes, not only on schedule questions, but on matters which may seem to them pertinent to the study, as *no* schedule can indicate all the significant points which may be revealed in the survey. The investigator stands a good chance of discovering valuable and significant points of view not even *hinted* at in the schedule."[2]

Women's Bureau agents regularly took such "full notes." Ethel Erickson's observations were often withering. For instance, she prefaced her transcript of an interview with John Mullar of the California Cotton Mills with the notation that "Mullar was a glib, three-variety liar."[3] The Bureau's unpublished summaries of work conditions were often critical: Typical of unpublished Bureau comments are the notes compiled during a 1944 Bureau survey of female migrant farm workers in New York state. The Floyd Olney Cannery at Lee Center housed its single male and single female workers in the same building: an old bar "with gaping holes in one wall . . . the men and women had only a low cardboard partition for privacy . . . this is a disgrace." The David Harum Camp in Homer furnished "bedding alive with bugs." The women workers at the migrant camp at Randalsville had lice infestations: "No wonder since they had no access to bathing or laundry facilities." The Comstock Canning Company in Rushville provided wooden shacks "thick with flies." The manager of the Keuka Cooperative Association Camp at King Ferry assured the Women's Bureau that a local doctor came to the camp regularly and that a health nurse came twice a week. "Maybe," Helen Sater of the Bureau commented, "But I saw one girl 22 years old; she lay on a bench by the hour, her eyes closed, one swollen shut. . . . No one paid attention to her. And no doctor had been to see her."[4]

While its most stinging analyses remained hidden in confidential memoranda, the published Bureau reports often used words like "shocking conditions," "unscrupulous employer abuse," and "a national shame" to describe conditions facing women workers.[5] These reports were not the objective unbiased investigations the Bureau purported, however. An examination of these documents reveals not only a wealth of information useful to scholars but also a great deal about government efforts to influence perceptions of women workers. Students reading only the hundreds of Women's Bureau reports would learn a great deal, but they would not receive a completely accurate impression of the American female work force in any particular decade. If they read every *Bulletin* published in the 1930s they would believe that most women workers toiled in sweatshops and dangerous factories. No doubt, the Depression was a very difficult time for women workers, but the Bureau totally neglected the increasing percentages of middle-class women, even middle-class married women, working for pay, which historian Winifred Wandersee has documented.[6] Clearly, the Bureau, in the thick of a fight for protective labor legislation, wished to emphasize that women were exposed to gross exploitation and danger and picked for its investigations places most likely to provide damning evidence, places like laundries and slaughterhouses.[7] Bureau agents did not exaggerate the situations they found, but they did focus their lenses narrowly.

In keeping with Progressive rhetoric, Bureau *Bulletins,* until the late 1950s, emphasized stereotyped notions of special and separate female abilities. For example, when in 1936 the Boston Chamber of Commerce requested the agency's advice on ways to reemploy New England women, the Bureau suggested that New England industries retool. New England merchants had in early days built a whaling industry. When that had disappeared, they had built a cotton industry. Since the cotton and textiles industries had begun to migrate to the South, New England industries should once again reassess opportunities. Bureau agents argued that potential regional markets could be found for low-priced canned fish in all parts of the nation where fresh fish was unavailable. Many immigrant women with fish-processing experience, such as the Portuguese, had settled in New England. The Bureau advocated that the fish canning emphasize salt and spiced fish products: "Because this is primarily a hand industry and requires ingenuity and infinite care in preparation of products, it is a skilled woman's industry."[8]

This emphasis on low-paid women's work in factories finally changed with dramatic swiftness in the mid-1950s, coincident with the reorganization of the Department of Labor, which altered the status of the Women's Bureau in important ways. Students who persevered and continued to read all the *Bulletins* one by one would be utterly startled to start reading after 1956 about career opportunities for women professional accountants, women mathematicians, women physicians, and women chemists. Again, if they had utilized only the Bureau *Bulletins* as research documents and knew nothing else about American economic history, they would believe some miraculous transformation in the female labor force had taken place between 1949 and 1955. Of course, no such thing happened. The average woman worker during the Depression was certainly not a woman mathematician, but neither was the average woman worker during the Eisenhower era. She was still minding the office files, serving up food in cafes, and selling shirts in department stores. Once again, a government wish to influence perceptions of women workers provides an explanation. With *Sputnik* in orbit and studies circulating indicating that women students eschewed technical fields and training in the sciences, government officials eagerly sought to channel more women into nontraditional jobs. Arthur Fleming, one-time secretary of Health, Education and Welfare, in 1962, looked back on his career and argued, "The number of trained women workers must increase 25 percent between now and 1970 as compared with 15 percent for men—if we are to capitalize on our opportunities for economic growth."[9] Thus, the legacy of published and unpublished documentation is a rich one, providing all kinds of information, some unintentionally revealed, about government perceptions of and reactions to women workers.

Another achievement marking these four decades of government reaction to women workers was the creation of an enduring alliance between government experts in the Women's Bureau and moderate women's organizations interested in publicizing the problems of women wage earners. In 1923, Mary Winslow wrote to Mary Anderson:

Our reputation as a scientific organization has not increased the interest of the average woman who would not think of reading any of our formal bulletins. It is very important that we should reach these women with some of the fundamental facts and ideas about this subject. . . . It cannot be done by showing them statistical reports from a government bureau. We must reach out.[10]

And the Bureau did reach out. During these decades, dozens of national leaders of such organizations as the League of Women Voters and the YWCA were involved with Bureau projects, and, through them, hundreds of their members passed out questionnaires at factory gates, compiled surveys, and petitioned unions, employers, and legislators.[11] In that sense, the Women's Bureau existed as a civics lesson in participatory democracy. People connected to the Bureau's network of allies filled jobs when the FERA, the NYA, or the President's Commission called for experts in women's work patterns. However, the collaborators and sponsors of government programs for women workers rarely included those groups that could have exercised the most influence. Women's clubs, not unions or employer associations, cheered on the Women's Bureau.

But a lack of powerful sponsorship was not the only problem with federal policy. The federal woman-worker experts of these decades rarely managed to act as effective advocates of working women. Haphazard planning exacerbated problems caused by the absence of necessary support among unions and management. Federal reaction to women workers lacked coherence. Administrative superiors often ignored the advice of their own specialists. As early as 1925, the Women's Bureau predicted the critical role women would have to play in any future war. Yet as late as 1941, no organized government effort to mobilize and train large numbers of women war workers existed. Many officials assumed Rosie the Riveter would go happily home after the war. The Women's Bureau, with greater insight, argued that she would stay on the job, taking lower status, lower paying work. Almost two decades passed before the Kennedy Commission accepted the reality of the working wife and the two-income family.

The Women's Bureau had warned since its inception that it needed funds and legal authority if it was truly to "investigate and improve conditions for women workers." Instead, during the ensuing years, succeeding Congresses denied its requests, while government agencies, some of them also concerned with problems of women wage earners, proliferated. Neither the Women's Bureau not any other federal agency coordinated or supervised all federal efforts, although the Bureau remained the only agency whose central concern was working women.

Problems of interpretation and viewpoint compounded problems of bad planning. A small staff of women economists, journalists, social workers, writers, and statisticians came to join the Women's Bureau in 1920 as reform-minded Progressives intent on protective labor legislation. Many of these same women retired from government service in the late 1940s or early 1950s, still intent on protective labor legislation. The extremely low job turnover in the Bureau meant that the federal investigators of women's work were, for decades, women with their minds already made up. Often their predictions were accurate, if ignored. But just as often their analyses were filtered through the Progressive screen that, in a sense, equated woman labor with child labor. The American family could suffer grave damage if helpless working women and helpless working children did not receive special protection. Federal reactions to women workers saw them first as family members, even though the federal bureaucrats writing the reports with this viewpoint were women. Of course, the agents of the Women's Bureau were mostly single women. But, different from the self-perceptions they claimed for the single women workers they wrote about, they seemed not to see themselves first as family members or potential family members. While worrying about women workers as people more likely to fall prey to stress, physical accidents, and job-related illnesses like tuberculosis, they themselves walked city streets at night searching out illegal sweatshops, repaired their cars on back country roads when stranded in the midst of investigations, or shouted down factory bosses. Their obstinate demand for protective legislation probably helped employers justify wage differentials between men and women. It also probably encouraged union leaders to think that women workers were too much trouble to organize. As a result of protective laws, tens of thousands of women workers escaped dangerous contact with poisons or escaped potential physical injury, but the price paid in restricted job opportunities was too high. This fact was especially true by the mid-1930s, when New Deal social welfare legislation provided basic guarantees like minimum wage and maximum hour legislation and unemployment and old age insurance for both men and women workers. Despite the passage of Social Security and the Fair Labor Standards Act, the Women's Bureau continued to assert that women needed additional protections. By the 1940s, those protections proved more burden than comfort. The poor planning and lack of powerful sponsorship inside or outside government that characterized federal reaction to women workers during these decades, therefore, were not entirely to blame for a government policy that largely failed to meet the needs of women workers. More money or better planning alone would not have solved what was a classic Progressive problem. Government definitions of what constituted reform for women workers were not arrived at collaboratively but were dictated by middle-class women, thinking that they were acting in the best interests of working-class women. Not surprisingly, the reforms advocated produced uneven results. In fact, they stimulated debates even among women about whether they helped at all. However, if the members of the Women's Bureau had agitated during the 1920s, 1930s, and 1940s for a government perception of women workers that saw them as individuals first, and secondarily as pillars of family stability, they not only would have performed a monumental feat of transcending their own values and culture but they would also have been so far ahead of their colleagues and sponsors that they would have been fired. A woman like Alice Paul had no chance of holding a government post during these years. As it was, the Bureau survived as a separate, autonomous agency for almost forty years. To do so, its agents made many, some undoubtedly unconscious, compromises. They were Outsiders as Insiders.

For forty years, federal public policy saw women workers as temporary workers, crisis workers, working until marriage, working to stave off family disaster. Of course, on an individual level, that perception was largely correct. Most women, working class as well as middle class, did quit the labor force upon marriage; not until the 1960s did the average wife work. Federal policy makers responded to the aggregate female work force as if it, too, were a temporary phenomenon, not meriting sustained, coordinated planning. In the decades between 1920 and 1960, those who wished a federal government energetically promoting the expansion and improvement of work opportunities for women were to be disappointed.

Those long decades of government apathy ended dramatically during the Kennedy-Johnson years. The names of many of the actors remained on the playbills, but even those who had studied their speeches for decades could no longer predict the script by 1961. In that year, for instance, the AFL-CIO sponsored a major conference held at the Department of Labor on the problems of working women. Assistant Secretary Esther Peterson, away in Geneva attending meetings of the ILO, sent Department of Labor official Aryness Wickens in her stead. Wickens exhorted the assembled unionists to take women workers seriously, to plan training programs for them, and to lobby for their rights. Wickens said:

> Oh to be sure, the League of Women Voters, the infinite number of women's clubs, are doing an intelligent, lady-like job to make local improvements in our faulty social structure. But these voluntary groups have never made enough effort to make life easier for working women . . . labor union women will have to do the lobbying. For the women's clubs are not sufficiently concerned. This is an age of revolution, and nice, lady-like efforts are not going to win the battle either for day-care nurseries or for equal opportunity and equal pay for the working woman.[12]

Who could have imagined Mary Anderson or any other Department of Labor official debunking the League of Women Voters and its efforts to help the working woman? It simply would not have happened in an earlier decade.

To use Wickens' dramatic phrase, the changes in government policy toward working women begun during the Kennedy years did constitute a kind of revolution. After 1963, new, aggressive government programs demanded that unions enroll women and that employers open jobs. The balancing act between management, labor, and women's organizations required for so long of the Women's Bureau lost its importance. Threats of withheld federal funds, not sweet persuasion, marked the new federal policies.

In striking ways, the average woman worker of 1963 differed from her counterpart of 1920. She was much older, age forty-two compared to age twenty-eight for the woman worker of 1920. No longer a small minority within the larger female population, as was the case in 1920 when one in four women worked for wages, she composed a majority in some age cohorts. More than one in two women between the ages of twenty-nine and sixty-five worked. Almost two out of three women between the ages of seventeen and twenty-eight worked outside their homes. By 1963, 24 million women worked, slightly more than one of every three workers. In 1920, eight million women, one of every five workers, earned wages. By the mid-1960s, the number of married women at work exceeded the number of single women for the first time in American history: Three out of five women workers were wives. Although now married and older, the average woman worker in 1963 still had something in common with her earlier counterpart: her job. In 1920, the four most common occupations for women were, in order: factory work, domestic service, secretarial and clerical work, and teaching. Forty years later the four were: factory work, secretarial and clerical work, teaching, and domestic service. Maids were no longer common; by 1963 their numbers were almost matched by waitresses, cooks, and saleswomen. Nevertheless, the four largest occupational groupings for women had remained unchanged for four decades, though percentages of female workers within groups had changed.[13]

Although significantly better educated, the average woman worker by the 1960s had not entered the middle class by virtue of higher job status or better wages. Instead, she had entered it when she combined her wages with her husband's, and the flood of wives into the labor force led to spectacular increases in average family earnings during the years 1947-1963. In 1947, one-tenth of the nation's families earned at least $10,000. By 1963, one-fifth earned that amount, and more than two-thirds of these $10,000 plus families depended on two breadwinners, usually the husband and wife.[14]

For decades, the Labor Department and the Women's Bureau had paid homage to the housewife and had defended the work of most married women as the result of dire financial need. Such family poverty, in an ideal world, would no longer exist. By 1963, Esther Peterson, touring to publicize the Kennedy Commission's report, saw a different relationship between work, marriage, and ideal worlds. The American woman, in effect, could no longer in good conscience stay home. "Interrelationships between home and community impel her to go beyond the home, either as worker or as community volunteer, in order to complete the framework of a full and satisfying life for herself and her family."[15] In an interesting way, Peterson echoed the message of a book that was a surprise best seller in 1963. Betty Friedan in *The Feminine Mystique* argued that paid work was the new "life plan for women."[16] Satisfying work, not marriage alone, helped guarantee fulfillment.

During the years 1920-1963, however, the federal administrative response to working women was not based on the assumption that they were leaving the home to enjoy full and satisfying lives. Rather, that response emphasized protection of a female labor force motivated predominately by economic necessity. Agencies and government committees created to protect, investigate, and improve the prospects of a group whose average member was young, single, not highly educated or skilled, and nonunionized, predictably received small budgets and little attention. The members of these agencies, commissions, and committees were bureaucrats and government consultants seeking to bring about change from within the established order. However, the federal government structure responded most quickly to demands backed up by powerful, well-organized constituencies. Women workers, despite their growing numbers, could not, before 1963, act as an effective pressure group to buttress the agencies established to champion their welfare. Politicians rarely feared that women workers would organize and vote them out of office. There seemed little chance that they would march in mass protest or engage in violent riot. Governmental apathy toward them threatened neither individual jobs nor social stability. As reformers in government, the bureaucrats within agencies that championed the woman worker were Outsiders as Insiders. As "Outsiders," they had contact with genuinely radical ideas. As "Outsiders," they stood wrongly accused of subversive activities. As "Outsiders," they frequently encountered condescension and indifference from their own administrative superiors. As "Insiders," they were hostage to the traditional view of ideal women as helpmates and homemakers. Their resolute dedication to restrictions meant to protect women workers, such as bans on night work, contributed to the problems of some working women even as they sought solutions for others. A study of federal reaction to women workers during the years spanning the passage of the Nineteenth Amendment and the Equal Pay Act illustrates the restricted nature of reform achievable by those who held this Outsiders as Insiders status.

NOTES

1. For a complete list of publications, 1920-1963, see Appendix B.

2. Emphasis in the original. "Instructions to Field Agents—Schedule Inquiry," Cooperative study done by Women's Bureau and Children's Bureau of Philadelphia Working Mothers, 1928 (typescript copy, p. 3), "Correspondence—Field Agents," Records of the Women's Bureau (R.G. 86), National Archives, Washington, D.C. (hereafter cited as WB, NA).

3. Interview transcripts (compiled July-August, 1926), Bx. 45, WB, NA: All interviews by Ethel Erickson in this transcript set.

4. Sater to Manning, December 31, 1943, Bx. 1407, WB, NA.

5. For examples, see Women's Bureau *Bulletin #108,* "The Effects of the Depression on Wage Earning Families" (Washington, D.C.: Government Printing Office, 1935); Women's Bureau *Bulletin #140,* "Reemployment of New England Women in Private Industry" (Washington, D.C.: Government Printing Office, 1936); Women's Bureau *Bulletin #152,* "Differences in the Earnings of Women and Men" (Washington, D.C.: Government Printing Office, 1937); Women's Bureau *Bulletin #109,* "The Employment of Women in the Sewing Trades of Connecticut" (Washington, D.C.: Government Printing Office, 1935); Women's Bureau *Bulletin #141,* "Piecework in the Silk Dress Industry" (Washington, D.C.: Government Printing Office, 1935).

6. Winifred Wandersee, *Women's Work and Family Values, 1920-1940* (Cambridge, Mass.: Harvard University Press, 1981).

7. See, for example, Women's Bureau *Bulletin #88,* "The Employment of Women in Slaughterhouses and Meat Packing" (Washington, D.C.: Government Printing Office, 1932); Women's Bureau *Bulletin #77,* "A Study of Laundries" (Washington, D.C.: Government Printing Office, 1930).

8. Women's Bureau *Bulletin #140,* "Reemployment of New England Women in Private Industry" (Washington, D.C.: Government Printing Office, 1936).

9. Arthur Fleming quoted in Sheila Rothman, *Women's Proper Place: A History of Changing Ideals and Practices, 1870 to the Present* (New York: Basic Books, 1978), p. 230.

10. Winslow to Anderson, memorandum (unpaginated), Bx. 1281, WB, NA.

11. Women's Bureau agents claimed only to show factory managers sample blank questionnaires. A sample questionnaire distributed to management follows: (1) Number of women and men by occupation in plant; (2) Present scheduled hours—scheduled hours in each year covered; (3) Were hours changed for entire plant—for both men and women; (4) If hours were changed, why; (5) Are departments balanced? Is overtime necessary in some departments; (6) Does the need for overtime make necessary the use of men on some occupations for which women would otherwise be

used; (7) Enumerate changes in organization which have occurred during the period—i.e.: private, corporation, part of chain, etc.; (8) What articles are produced; (9) What changes have been made in product; (10) Has machinery for making the same product been radically changed; (11) Have changes been made in method of operation; (12) Is plant or any part of it organized; (13) When was such organization recognized; (14) Does organization include men and women; (15) History of agreements—character and duration; (16) Do they include women as well as men; (17) Who does hiring. Published in *Bulletin #65*, Bx. 49, WB, NA.

12. A summary report of a Conference on the Problems of Working Women, Industrial Union Department, AFL-CIO, p. 20, Report Copy in "Union Materials," Bx. 1491, WB, NA.

13. See "Working Wives," *The Wall Street Journal,* October 30, 1963; United States Department of Labor, Bureau of Labor Statistics, *Handbook of Labor Statistics, 1920-1971* (Washington, D.C.: Government Printing Office, 1972), pp. 30-51; Eli Ginzberg, "Paycheck and Apron—Revolution in Woman Power," v. 7, *Industrial Relations* (May, 1968), pp. 193-203.

14. In 1940, two-fifths of all working women had at least a high school education—by 1960, more than three-fifths had high school diplomas. See "Educational Attainment of Women in the Labor Force," Women's Bureau Special Pamphlet, Press Release File, August, 1960, WB, NA; "Working Wives," *The Wall Street Journal,* October 30, 1963.

15. Quoted in *Detroit News,* October 25, 1963. The Esther Peterson Papers that are housed at the Schlesinger Library include an extensive press clipping file of reaction to the Commission during 1963-1964. See press clippings, Kennedy Commission on the Status of Women, Esther Peterson Papers, Schlesinger Library.

16. Betty Friedan, *The Feminine Mystique* (New York: Dell, 1963), p. 332.

An Act to Establish in the Department of Labor a Bureau to be Known as THE WOMEN'S BUREAU

Appendix A

Be it enacted by the Senate and House of Representatives of the United States of America in Congress assembled, That there shall be established in the Department of Labor a bureau to be known as the Women's Bureau.

Sec. 2. That the said bureau shall be in charge of a director, a woman, to be appointed by the President, by and with the advice and consent of the Senate, who shall receive an annual compensation of $5,000.* It shall be the duty of said bureau to formulate standards and policies which shall promote the welfare of wage-earning women, improve their working conditions, increase their efficiency, and advance their opportunities for profitable employment. The said bureau shall have authority to investigate and report to the said department upon all matters pertaining to the welfare of women in industry. The director of said bureau may from time to time publish the results of these investigations in such a manner and to such extent as the Secretary of Labor may prescribe.

Sec. 3. That there shall be in said bureau an assistant director, to be appointed by the Secretary of Labor, who shall receive an annual compensation of $3,500* and shall perform such duties as shall be prescribed by the director and approved by the Secretary of Labor.

Sec. 4. That there is hereby authorized to be employed by said bureau a chief clerk and such special agents, assistants, clerks, and other employees

---

*Amounts increased by Reclassification Act of March 4, 1923, as amended and supplemented.

Source: U.S., Statutes at Large, XLI, 987.

at such rates of compensation and in such numbers as Congress may from time to time provide by appropriations.

Sec. 5. That the Secretary of Labor is hereby directed to furnish sufficient quarters, office furniture, and equipment for the work of this bureau.

Sec. 6. That this act shall take effect and be in force from and after its passage.

Approved, June 5, 1920.

Public No. 259, 66th Congress (H. R. 13229).

The Bulletins and Special Bulletins of the Women's Bureau, United States Department of Labor, 1920-1963

Appendix B

All Printed by Government Printing Office, Washington, D.C.

1. *Proposed Employment of Women During the War, in the Industries of Niagara Falls, N. Y., 1918.* 16 pp. (1919).
2. *Labor Laws for Women in Industry in Indiana.* 29 pp. (1919).
3. *Standards for the Employment of Women in Industry.* 8 pp. Four editions (1918, 1919, 1921, 1928).
4. *Wages of Candy Makers in Philadelphia in 1919.* 46 pp. (1919).
5. *The Eight-Hour Day in Federal and State Legislation.* 14 pp. (1921).
6. *The Employment of Women in Hazardous Industries in the United States, 1919.* 8 pp. (1920).
7. *Night-Work Laws in the United States, 1919.* 4 pp. (1920).
8. *Women in the Government Service.* 37 pp. (1920).
9. *Home Work in Bridgeport, Connecticut.* 35 pp. (1920).
10. *Hours and Conditions of Work for Women in Industry in Virginia.* 32 pp. (1920).
11. *Women Street Car Conductors and Ticket Agents.* 90 pp. (1921).
12. *The New Position of Women in American Industry.* 158 pp. (1920).
13. *Industrial Opportunities and Training for Women and Girls.* 48 pp. (1920).
14. *A Physiological Basis for the Shorter Working Day for Women.* 20 pp. (1921).
15. *Some Effects of Legislation Limiting Hours of Work for Women.* 26 pp. (1921).
16. *State Laws Affecting Working Women.* 51 pp. Charts and maps (1921).

17. *Women's Wages in Kansas.* 104 pp. (1921).
18. *Health Problems of Women in Industry.* 11 pp. (1921) (Revised in 1935. See Bull. 136.)
19. *Iowa Women in Industry.* 73 pp. (1922).
20. *Negro Women in Industry.* 65 pp. (1922).
21. *Women in Rhode Island Industries.* 73 pp. (1922).
22. *Women in Georgia Industries.* 89 pp. (1922).
23. *The Family Status of Breadwinning Women.* 43 pp. (1922).
24. *Women in Maryland Industries.* 96 pp. (1922).
25. *Women in the Candy Industry in Chicago and St. Louis.* 72 pp. (1923).
26. *Women in Arkansas Industries.* 86 pp. (1923).
27. *The Occupational Progress of Women.* 37 pp. (1922).
28. *Women's Contributions in the Field of Invention.* 51 pp. (1923).
29. *Women in Kentucky Industries.* 114 pp. (1923).
30. *The Share of Wage-Earning Women in Family Support.* 170 pp. (1923).
31. *What Industry Means to Women Workers.* 10 pp. (1923).
32. *Women in South Carolina Industries.* 128 pp. (1923).
33. *Proceedings of the Women's Industrial Conference.* 190 pp. (1923).
34. *Women in Alabama Industries.* 86 pp. (1924).
35. *Women in Missouri Industries.* 127 pp. (1924).
36. *Radio Talks on Women in Industry.* 34 pp. (1924).
37. *Women in New Jersey Industries.* 99 pp. (1924).
38. *Married Women in Industry.* 8 pp. (1924).
39. *Domestic Workers and Their Employment Relations.* 87 pp. (1924).
40. *State Laws Affecting Working Women.* 51 pp. Charts (1924). (See Bull. 63.)
42. *Family Status of Breadwinning Women in Four Selected Cities.* 145 pp. (1925).
42. *List of References on Minimum Wage for Women in the United States and Canada.* 42 pp. (1925).
43. *Standard and Scheduled Hours of Work for Women in Industry.* 68 pp. (1925).
44. *Women in Ohio Industries.* 137 pp. (1925).
45. *Home Environment and Opportunities of Women in Coal-Mine Workers' Families.* 61 pp. (1925).
46. *Facts About Working Women.* 64 pp. (1925).
47. *Women in the Fruit-Growing and Canning Industries in the State of Washington.* 223 pp. (1926).
48. *Women in Oklahoma Industries.* 118 pp. (1926).
49. *Women Workers and Family Support.* 10 pp. (1925).
50. *Effects of Applied Research Upon the Employment Opportunities of American Women.* 54 pp. (1926).

51. *Women in Illinois Industries.* 108 pp. (1926).
52. *Lost Time and Labor Turnover in Cotton Mills.* 203 pp. (1926).
53. *The Status of Women in the Government Service in 1925.* 103 pp. (1926).
54. *Changing Jobs.* 12 pp. (1926).
55. *Women in Mississippi Industries.* 89 pp. (1926).
56. *Women in Tennessee Industries.* 120 pp. (1927).
57. *Women Workers and Industrial Poisons.* 5 pp. (1926).
58. *Women in Delaware Industries.* 156 pp. (1927).
59. *Short Talks About Working Women.* 24 pp. (1927).
60. *Industrial Accidents to Women in New Jersey, Ohio, and Wisconsin.* 316 pp. (1927).
61. *The Development of Minimum-Wage Laws in the United States, 1912 to 1927.* 635 pp. (1928).
62. *Women's Employment in Vegetable Canneries in Delaware.* 47 pp. (1927).
63. *State Laws Affecting Working Women.* 51 pp. Charts (1927). (See Bull. 98.)
64. *The Employment of Women at Night.* 86 pp. (1928).
65. *The Effects of Labor Legislation on the Employment Opportunities of Women.* 495 pp. (1928).
66. *History of Labor Legislation for Women in Three States and Chronological Development of Labor Legislation for Women in the United States.* 288 pp. (1929). (Later published as Bull. 66-I and Bull. 66-II.)
67. *Women Workers in Flint, Michigan.* 79 pp. (1929).
68. *Summary: The Effects of Labor Legislation on the Employment Opportunities of Women.* (Reprint of Chapter II of Bull. 65.) 22 pp. (1928).
69. *Causes of Absence for Men and for Women in Four Cotton Mills.* 22 pp. (1929).
70. *Negro Women in Industry in 15 States.* 72 pp. (1929).
71. *Selected References on the Health of Women in Industry.* 8 pp. (1929).
72. *Conditions of Work in Spin Rooms.* 39 pp. (1929).
73. *Variations in Employment Trends of Women and Men.* 141 pp. Charts (1930).
74. *The Immigrant Woman and Her Job.* 179 pp. (1930).
75. *What the Wage-Earning Woman Contributes to Family Support.* 20 pp. (1929).
76. *Women in 5- and 10-cent Stores and Limited-Price Chain Department Stores.* 56 pp. (1930).
77. *A Study of Two Groups of Denver Married Women Applying for Jobs.* 10 pp. (1929).
78. *A Survey of Laundries and Their Women Workers in 23 Cities.* 164 pp. (1930).

79. *Industrial Home Work.* 18 pp. (1930).
80. *Women in Florida Industries.* 113 pp. (1930).
81. *Industrial Accidents to Men and Women.* 46 pp. (1930).
82. *The Employment of Women in the Pineapple Canneries of Hawaii.* 28 pp. (1930).
83. *Fluctuation of Employment in the Radio Industry.* 63 pp. (1931).
84. *Fact Finding With the Women's Bureau.* 35 pp. (1931).
85. *Wages of Women in 13 States.* 211 pp. (1931).
86. *Activities of the Women's Bureau of the United States.* 13 pp. (1931).
87. *Sanitary Drinking Facilities, With Special Reference to Drinking Fountains.* 26 pp. (1931).
88. *The Employment of Women in Slaughtering and Meat Packing.* 208 pp. (1932).
89. *The Industrial Experience of Women Workers at the Summer Schools, 1928 to 1930.* 60 pp. (1931).
90. *Oregon Legislation for Women in Industry.* 37 pp. (1931).
91. *Women in Industry: A Series of Papers to Aid Study Groups.* 79 pp. (1931). (See Bull. 164.)
92. *Wage-Earning Women and the Industrial Conditions of 1930: A Survey of South Bend.* 81 pp. (1932). (See Bull. 108)
93. *Household Employment in Philadelphia.* 85 pp. (1932).
94. *State Requirements for Industrial Lighting: A Handbook for the Protection of Women Workers, Showing Lighting Standards and Practices.* 62 pp. (1932).
95. *Bookkeepers, Stenographers and Office Clerks in Ohio, 1914 to 1929.* 31 pp. (1932).
96. *Women Office Workers in Philadelphia.* 14 pp. (1932).
97. *The Employment of Women in the Sewing Trades of Connecticut—Preliminary Report.* 13 pp. (1932). (See Bull. 109.)
98. *Labor Laws for Women in the States and Territories.* 67 pp. Charts. Supplement. 4 pp. (1933). Revised ed. 67 pp. (1934).
99. *The Installation and Maintenance of Toilet Facilities in Places of Employment.* 86 pp. (1933).
100. *The Effects on Women: Changing Conditions in the Cigar and Cigarette Industries.* 184 pp. (1932).
101. *The Employment of Women in Vitreous Enameling.* 61 pp. (1932).
102. *Industrial Injuries to Women in 1928 and 1929 Compared With Injuries to Men.* 33 pp. (1933).
103. *Women Workers in the Third Year of the Depression—A Study of Students in the Bryn Mawr Summer School.* 13 pp. (1933).
104. *The Occupational Progress of Women, 1910 to 1930.* 87 pp. (1933).
105. *A Study of Change from 8 to 6 Hours of Work.* 14 pp. (1933).

106. *Household Employment in Chicago.* 62 pp. (1933).
107. *Technological Changes in Relation to Women's Employment.* 39 pp. (1935).
108. *The Effects of the Depression on Wage Earners' Families: A Second Survey of South Bend.* 31 pp. (1936).
109. *The Employment of Women in the Sewing Trades of Connecticut.* 45 pp. (1935).
110. *The Change from Manual to Dial Operation in the Telephone Industry.* 15 pp. (1933).
111. *Hours, Earnings, and Employment in Cotton Mills.* 78 pp. (1933).
112. *Standards of Placement Agencies for Household Employees.* 68 pp. Charts (1934).
113. *Employment Fluctuations and Unemployment of Women, 1928-1931.* 236 pp. (1933).
114. *State Reporting of Occupational Disease, Including a Survey of Legislation Applying to Women.* 99 pp. (1934).
115. *Women at Work.* 60 pp. (1933). (See Bull. 161.)
116. *A Study of a Change From One Shift of 9 Hours to Two Shifts of 6 Hours Each.* 14 pp. (1934).
117. *The Age Factor as It Relates to Women in Business and the Professions.* 66 pp. (1934).
118. *The Employment of Women in Puerto Rico.* 34 pp. (1934).
119. *Hours and Earnings in the Leather-Glove Industry.* 32 pp. (1934).
120. *The Employment of Women in Offices.* 126 pp. (1934).
121. *A Survey of the Shoe Industry in New Hampshire.* 100 pp. (1935).
122. *Variations in Wage Rates Under Corresponding Conditions.* 57 pp. (1935).
123. *Employment in Hotels and Restaurants.* 105 pp. (1936).
124. *Women in Arkansas Industries.* 45 pp. (1935).
125. *Employment Conditions in Department Stores in 1932-33: A Study in Selected Cities of Five States.* 24 pp. (1936).
126. *Women in Texas Industries.* 81 pp. (1936).
127. *Hours and Earnings in Tobacco Stemmeries.* 29 pp. (1934).
128. *Potential Earning Power of Southern Mountaineer Handicraft.* 56 pp. (1935).
129. *Industrial Injuries to Women in 1930 and 1931 Compared With Injuries to Men.* 57 pp. (1935).
130. *Employed Women Under N.R.A. Codes.* 144 pp. (1935).
131. *Industrial Home Work in Rhode Island, With Special Reference to the Lace Industry.* 27 pp. (1935).
132. *Women Who Work in Offices: I. Study of Employed Women. II. Study of Women Seeking Employment.* 27 pp. (1935).

133. *Employment Conditions in Beauty Shops.* 46 pp. (1935).
134. *Summaries of Studies on the Economic Status of Women.* 20 pp. (1935).
135. *The Commercialization of the Home Through Industrial Home Work.* 49 pp. (1935).
136. *The Health and Safety of Women in Industry.* 23 pp. (1935).
137. *Summary of State Hour Laws for Women and Minimum-Wage Rates.* 54 pp. (1936).
138. *Reading List of References on Household Employment.* 15 pp. (1936).
139. *Women Unemployed Seeking Relief in 1933.* 19 pp. (1936).
140. *Reemployment of New England Women in Private Industry.* 118 pp. (1936).
141. *Piecework in the Silk Dress Industry.* 68 pp. (1936).
142. *The Economic Problems of the Women of the Virgin Islands of the United States.* 24 pp. (1936).
143. *Factors Affecting Wages in Power Laundries.* 82 pp. (1936).
144. *State Labor Laws for Women.* 93 pp. Charts (1937).
144. *Summary of 1937 Labor Laws for Women.* (45 pp.). Charts. Revised (no date). (See Bull. 156.)
145. *Special Study of Wages Paid to Women and Minors in Ohio Industries. Prior and Subsequent to the Ohio Minimum-Wage Law for Women and Minors.* 83 pp. (1936).
146. *A Policy Insuring Value to the Woman Buyer and a Livelihood to Apparel Makers.* 22 pp. (1936).
147. *Summary of State Reports of Occupational Diseases, With a Survey of Preventive Legislation, 1932 to 1934.* 42 pp. (1936).
148. *The Employed Woman Homemaker in the United States: Her Responsibility for Family Support.* 22 pp. (1936).
149. *Employment of Women in Tennessee Industries.* 63 pp. (1937).
150. *Women's Employment in West Virginia.* 27 pp. (1937).
151. *Injuries to Women in Personal Service Occupations in Ohio.* 23 pp. (1937).
152. *Differences in the Earnings of Women and Men.* 57 pp. (1938).
153. *Women's Hours and Wages in the District of Columbia in 1937.* 44 pp. (1937).
154. *Reading List of References on Household Employment.* 17 pp. (1938).
155. *Women in the Economy of the United States of America.* 137 pp. (1937).
156. *State Labor Laws for Women. As of Dec. 31, 1937.* 16 pp. (1938). *Part I. Summary. As of Dec. 31, 1940.* 18 pp. (1940). *Part II. Analysis of Hour Laws for Women Workers.* 45 pp. Charts (1938). (See Bull. 202-I.)
157. *The Legal Status of Women in the United States of America. Jan 1, 1938. United States Summary.* 89 pp. (1941). Separate reports for

each state and the District of Columbia. *The Legal Status of Women in the United States of America. U.S. Summary: Supplement I.* 16 pp. (1943).

157A. *The Legal Status of Women in the United States of America. Cumulative Supplement, 1938-1945.* 31 pp. (1946).

157. *The Legal Status of Women in the United States of America. January 1, 1948. United States Summary.* 105 pp. Revised (1951). Separate reports for each state and the District of Columbia.

157. *The Legal Status of Women in the United States of America. January 1, 1953. United States Summary.* 103 pp. Revised (1956). Separate reports for each state and the District of Columbia.

157-1 through 157-52. *The Legal Status of Women in the United States of America.* Revised reports, as recent as 1966, for individual states, the District of Columbia, and territories and possessions. (Dates of revisions vary from state to state.)

158. *Unattached Women on Relief in Chicago, 1937.* 84 pp. (1938).

159. *Trends in the Employment of Women, 1928-36.* 48 pp.

160. *Industrial Injuries to Women and Men, 1932 to 1934.* 37 pp. (1938).

161. *Women at Work: A Century of Industrial Changes.* 80 pp. (1942).

162. *Women in Kentucky Industries, 1937.* 84 pp. (1938).

163. *Hours and Earnings in Certain Men's Wear Industries:*

163-1. *Work Clothing, Work Shirts, Dress Shirts.* 27 pp. (1938).

163-2. *Knit Underwear, Woven Cotton Underwear.* 10 pp. (1938).

163-3. *Seamless Hosiery.* 8 pp. (1938).

163-4. *Welt Shoes.* 9 pp. (1938).

163-5. *Raincoats, Sports Jackets.* 29 pp. (1940).

163-6. *Caps and Cloth Hats, Neckwear, Work and Knit Gloves, Handkerchiefs.* 22 pp. (1939).

164. *Women in Industry: A Series of Papers to Aid Study Groups.* 85 pp. (1938).

165. *The Negro Woman Worker.* 17 pp. (1938).

166. *The Effect of Minimum-Wage Determinations in Service Industries: Adjustments in the Dry-Cleaning and Power-Laundry Industries.* 44 pp. (1938).

167. *State Minimum-Wage Laws and Orders: An Analysis.* 34 pp. Charts (1939). Two Supplements. 15 pp. (1940); 13 pp. (1941). (See Bull. 191.)

168. *Employed Women and Family Support.* 57 pp. (1939).

169. *Conditions in the Millinery Industry in the United States.* 128 pp. (1939.)

170. *Economic Status of University Women in the U.S.A.* 70 pp. (1939).

171. *Wages and Hours in Drugs and Medicines and in Certain Toilet Preparations.* 19 pp. (1939).

172. *The Woman Wage Earner: Her Situation Today.* 56 pp. (1939).

173. *Standards for Employment of Women in Industry: Recommended by the Women's Bureau.* 9 pp. (1939).
174. *Job Histories of Women Workers at the Summer Schools, 1931-34 and 1938.* 25 pp. (1939).
175. *Earnings in the Women's and Children's Apparel Industry in the Spring of 1939.* 91 pp. (1940).
176. *Application of Labor Legislation to the Fruit and Vegetable Canning and Preserving Industries.* 162 pp. (1940).
177. *Earnings and Hours in Hawaii Woman Employing Industries.* 53 pp. (1940).
178. *Women's Wages and Hours in Nebraska.* 51 pp. (1940).
179. *Primer of Problems in the Military Industry.* 47 pp. (1941).
180. *Employment in Service and Trade Industries in Maine.* 30 pp. (1940).
181. *The Nonworking Time of Industrial Women Workers.* 10 pp. (1940).
182. *Employment of Women in the Federal Government, 1923 to 1939.* 60 pp. (1941).
183. *Women Workers in Their Family Environment.* 82 pp. (1941).
184. *The Occurrence and Prevention of Occupational Diseases Among Women, 1935 to 1938.* 46 pp. (1941).
185. *The Migratory Labor Problem in Delaware.* 24 pp. (1941).
186. *Earnings and Hours in Pacific Coast Fish Canneries.* 30 pp. (1941).
187. *Labor Standards and Competitive Market Conditions in the Canned-Goods Industry.* 34 pp. (1941).
188. *Office Work and Office Workers in 1940.* Introduction, 4 pp.
188-1. *Office Work in Houston, 1940.* 58 pp. (1942).
188-2. *Office Work in Los Angeles, 1940.* 64 pp. (1942).
188-3. *Office Work in Kansas City, 1940.* 74 pp. (1942).
188-4. *Office Work in Richmond, 1940.* 61 pp. (1942).
188-5. *Office Work in Philadelphia, 1940.* 102 pp. (1942); *Wages of Office Workers, 1940.* 31 pp. (1941); *Chart. Women Office Workers: Salary Rates in Five Cities, 1940.* 2 pp. (1942).
189-1. *Women's Factory Employment in an Expanding Aircraft Production Program.* 12 pp. (1942).
189-2. *Employment of Women in the Manufacture of Small-Arms Ammunition.* 11 pp. (1942).
189-3. *Employment of Women in the Manufacture of Artillery Ammunition.* 17 pp. (1942).
189-4. *The Employment of and Demand for Women Workers in the Manufacture of Instruments—Aircraft, Optical and Fire-Control, and Surgical and Dental.* 20 pp. (1942).
190. *Recreation and Housing for Women War Workers: A Handbook on Standards.* 40 pp. (1942).

191. *State Minimum-Wage Laws and Orders: 1942. An Analysis.* 52 pp. Charts (1942).

192. *Reports on Employment of Women in Wartime Industries:*

192-1. *Women's Employment in Aircraft Assembly Plants in 1942.* 23 pp. (1942).

192-2. *Women's Employment in Artillery Ammunition Plants, 1942.* 19 pp. (1942).

192-3. *Employment of Women in the Manufacture of Cannon and Small Arms in 1942.* 36 pp. (1943).

192-4. *Employment of Women in the Machine-Tool Industry, 1942.* 42 pp. (1943).

192-5. *Women's Employment in the Making of Steel, 1943.* 39 pp. (1944).

192-6. *Employing Women in Shipyards.* 83 pp. (1944).

192-7. *Women's Employment in Foundries, 1943.* 28 pp. (1944).

192-8. *Employment of Women in Army Supply Depots in 1943.* 33 pp. (1945).

192-9. *Women's Wartime Jobs in Cane-Sugar Refineries.* 20 pp. (1945).

193. *Women's Work in the War.* 10 pp. (1942).

194. *Your Questions as to Women in War Industries.* 10 pp. (1942).

195. *Women Workers in Argentina, Chile, and Uruguay.* 15 pp. (1942).

196. *"Equal Pay" for Women in War Industries.* 26 pp. (1942).

197. *Women Workers in Some Expanding Wartime Industries—New Jersey, 1942.* 44 pp. (1944).

198. *Employment and Housing Problems of Migratory Workers in New York and New Jersey Canning Industries, 1943.* 35 pp. (1944).

199. *Successful Practices in the Employment of Nonfarm Women on Farms in the Northeastern States, 1943.* 44 pp. (1944).

200. *British Policies and Methods in Employing Women in Wartime.* 44 pp. (1944).

201. *Employment Opportunities in Characteristic Industrial Occupations of Women.* 50 pp. (1944).

202. *State Labor Laws for Women, With Wartime Modifications, Dec. 15, 1944:*

202-1. *Analysis of Hour Laws.* 110 pp. (1945). (See Bull. 250.)

202-2. *Analysis of Plant Facilities Laws.* 43 pp. (1945).

202-3. *Analysis of Regulatory Laws, Prohibitory Laws, Maternity Laws.* 12 pp. (1945).

202-4. *Analysis of Industrial Home-Work Laws.* 26 pp. (1945).

202-5. *Explanation and Appraisal.* 60 pp. (1946).

203. *Medical and Other Health Services Series. The Outlook for Women:*

203-1. *As Physical Therapists.* 24 pp. (1944).

203-1. *As Physical Therapists.* 51 pp. Revised (1952).

203-2. *As Occupational Therapists.* 15 pp. (1944).
203-2. *As Occupational Therapists.* 51 pp. Revised (1952).
203-3. *In Professional Nursing Occupations.* 66 pp. (1950).
203-3. *In Professional Nursing Occupations.* 80 pp. Revised (1953).
203-4. *As Medical Technologists and Laboratory Technicians.* 10 pp. (1944).
203-4. *As Medical Technologists and Laboratory Technicians.* 54 pp. Revised (1954).
203-5. *As Practical Nurses and Auxiliary Workers and on the Nursing Team.* 20 pp. (1945).
203-5. *As Practical Nurses and Auxiliary Workers and on the Nursing Team.* 62 pp. Revised (1953).
203-6. *As Medical Record Librarians.* 9 pp. (1945).
203-7. *As Women Physicians.* 28 pp. (1945).
203-8. *As Medical X-Ray Technicians.* 14 pp. (1945).
203-8. *As Medical X-Ray Technicians.* 53 pp. Revised (1954).
203-9. *As Women Dentists.* 21 pp. (1945).
203-10. *As Dental Hygienists.* 17 pp. (1945).
203-11. *As Physicians' and Dentists' Assistants.* 15 pp. (1946).
203-12. *Trends and Their Effect upon the Demand for Women Workers.* 55 pp. (1946).
204. *Women's Emergency Farm Service on the Pacific Coast in 1943.* 36 pp. (1945).
205. *Negro Women War Workers.* 23 pp. (1945).
206. *Women Workers in Brazil.* 42 pp. (1946).
207. *The Woman Telephone Worker.* 38 pp. (1946).
207-A. *Typical Women's Jobs in the Telephone Industry.* 49 pp. (1947).
208. *Women's Wartime Hours of Work—The Effect on Their Factory Performances and Home Life.* 187 pp. (1947).
209. *Women Workers in Ten War Production Areas and Their Postwar Employment Plans.* 56 pp. (1946).
210. *Women Workers in Paraguay.* 16 pp. (1946).
211. *Employment of Women in the Early Postwar Period, With Background of Prewar and War Data.* 14 pp. (1946).
212. *Industrial Injuries to Women.* 20 pp. (1947).
213. *Women Workers in Peru.* 41 pp. (1947).
214. *Maternity Benefits Under Union Contract Health Insurance Plans.* 16 pp. (1947).
215. *Women Workers in Power Laundries.* 67 pp. (1947).
216. *Women Workers After VJ-Day in One Community—Bridgeport, Connecticut.* 34 pp. (1947).
217. *International Documents on the Status of Women.* 113 pp. (1947).
218. *Women's Occupations Through Seven Decades.* 260 pp. (Reprinted

1951). (See Bull. 253.)
219. *Earnings of Women in Selected Manufacturing Industries, 1946.* 14 pp. (1948).
220. *Old-Age Insurance for Household Workers.* 17 pp. (1947).
221. *Community Household Employment Programs.* 70 pp. (1948).
222. *Women in Radio.* 30 pp. (1947).
223. *Science Series. The Outlook for Women in:*
223-1. *Science.* (General introduction to the series.) 78 pp. (1949).
223-2. *Chemistry.* 62 pp. (1948).
223-3. *Biological Sciences.* 87 pp. (1948). (See Bull. 278.)
223-4. *Mathematics and Statistics.* 21 pp. (1948). (See Bull. 254.)
223-5. *Architecture and Engineering.* 85 pp. (1948). (See Bull. 254.)
223-6. *Physics and Astronomy.* 32 pp. (1948).
223-7. *Geology, Geography, and Meteorology.* 48 pp. (1948).
223-8. *Occupations Related to Science.* 30 pp. (1948).
224. *Women's Bureau Conference, 1948. The American Woman—Her Changing Role as Worker, Homemaker, Citizen.* 207 pp. (1948).
224. *Women's Bureau Conference, 1948. The American Woman—Her Changing Role as Worker, Homemaker, Citizen.* 207 pp. (1948).
225. *Women's Bureau Handbook of Facts on Women Workers.* 76 pp. (1948). (See Bull. 237.)
226. *Working Women's Budgets in Twelve States.* 33 pp. (1948).
226. *Working Women's Budgets in Thirteen States.* 41 pp. Revised (1951).
227. *State Minimum-Wage Laws and Orders, July 1, 1942-January 1, 1949.* Supplement to Bull. 191. 58 pp. (1949). (Multilithed supplements.)
227. *State Minimum-Wage Laws and Orders July 1, 1942-July 1, 1950.* Revised supplement to Bull. 191. 68 pp. (1950). (See Bull. 247.)
228. *The Industrial Nurse and the Woman Worker.* 48 pp. (1949). Revision of Special Bull. 19.
229. *Occupations for Girls and Women—Selected References. July 1943-June 1948.* 102 pp. (1949).
230-I. *Women in the Federal Service, 1923-1947: Trends in Employment.* 79 pp. (1949).
230-II. *Women in the Federal Service: Occupational Information.* 84 pp. (1950).
231. *The Outlook for Women in Police Work.* 31 pp. (1949).
232. *Women's Jobs—Advance and Growth.* Popular version of Bull. 218. 88 pp. (1949).
233. *Night Work for Women in Hotels and Restaurants.* 56 pp. (1949).
234. *Home Economics Occupations Series. The Outlook for Women:*
234-1. *In Dietetics.* 77 pp. (1950).
234-2. *As Food-Service Managers and Supervisors.* 54 pp. (1952).

235. *Social Work Series. The Outlook for Women In:*
235-1. *Social Case Work in a Medical Setting.* 55 pp. (1950).
235-2. *Social Case Work in a Psychiatric Setting.* 56 pp. (1950).
235-3. *Social Case Work With Children.* 69 pp. (1951).
235-4. *Social Case Work With Families.* 80 pp. (1951).
235-5. *Community Organization in Social Work.* 37 pp. (1951).
235-6. *Social Work Administration, Teaching, and Research.* 79 pp. (1951).
235-7. *Social Group Work.* 41 pp. (1951).
235-8. *Social Work. General Summary.* 93 pp. (1952).
236. *Women in Higher-Level Positions.* 86 pp. (1950).
237. *Women's Bureau 1950 Handbook of Facts on Women Workers.* 102 pp. (1950). (See Bull. 242.)
238. *Part-Time Jobs for Women—A Study in 10 Cities.* 82 pp. (1951).
239. *Women Workers and Their Dependents.* 117 pp. (1952).
240. *Maternity Protection of Employed Women.* 50 pp. (1952). (See Bull. 272.)
241. *Employment of Women in an Emergency Period.* 12 pp. (1952).
242. *Women's Bureau 1952 Handbook of Facts on Women Workers.* 121 pp. (1952). (See Bull. 255.)
243. *Report of the National Conference on Equal Pay, March 31 and April 1, 1952.* 25 pp. (1952).
244. *Womanpower Committees During World War II—United States and British Experience.* 73 pp. (1953).
245. *A Short-Term Training Program in an Aircraft Engine Plant.* 11 pp. (1953).
246. *Employed Mothers and Child Care.* 92 pp. (1953).
247. *State Minimum-Wage Laws and Orders, July 1, 1942-March 1, 1953.* 84 pp. Charts (1953). (Multilithed supplements.) (See Bull. 267.)
248. *"Older" Women as Office Workers.* 64 pp. (1953).
249. *The Status of Women in the United States, 1953.* 26 pp. (1953).
250. *State Hour Laws for Women.* 114 pp. (1953). (See Bull. 277.)
251. *Progress Toward Equal Pay in the Meat Packing Industry.* 16 pp. (1953).
252. *Toward Better Working Conditions for Women.* 71 pp. (1953).
253. *Changes in Women's Occupations, 1940-1950.* 104 pp. (1954).
254. *Employment Opportunities for Women in Professional Engineering.* 38 pp. (1954).
255. *1954 Handbook on Women Workers.* 75 pp. (See Bull. 261.)
256. *Training Mature Women for Employment.* 46 pp. (1955).
257. *The Effective Use of Manpower—Report of the Conference, March 10 and 11, 1955.* 113 pp. (1955).
258. *Employment Opportunities for Women in Professional Accounting.* 40 pp. (1955).

259. *State Minimum-Wage Order Provisions Affecting Working Conditions, July 1, 1942 to June 1, 1955.* 75 pp. (1955). (See Bull. 269.)

260. *Employment Opportunities for Women in Beauty Service.* 51 pp. (1956).

261. *1956 Handbook on Women Workers.* 96 pp. (1956). (See Bull. 266.)

262. *Employment Opportunities for Women Mathematicians and Statisticians.* 37 pp. (1956).

263. *Employment Opportunities for Women as Secretaries, Stenographers, Typists, and as Office-Machine Operators and Cashiers.* 30 pp. (1957).

264. *College Women Go to Work: Report on Women Graduates, Class of 1956.* 41 pp. (1958).

265. *Employment Opportunities for Women in Legal Work.* 34 pp. (1958).

266. *1958 Handbook on Women Workers.* 153 pp. (1958). (See Bull. 275.)

267. *State Minimum-Wage Laws and Orders, July 1, 1942 to July 1, 1958* (1958). *Part I-Historical Development and Statutory Provisions.* 31 pp. *Part II-Analysis of Rates and Coverage.* 145 pp.

267. *State Minimum-Wage Laws and Orders, July 1, 1942 to January 1, 1963. Part II-Analysis of Rates and Coverage.* 107 pp. (1963). (See Bull. 291.)

268. *First Jobs of College Women—Report on Women Graduates, Class of 1957.* 44 pp. (1959).

269. *State Minimum-Wage Law and Order Affecting Working Conditions, July 1, 1942 to April 1, 1959.* 141 pp. (1959). (See Bull. 280.)

270. *Careers for Women in the Physical Sciences.* 77 pp. (1959).

271. *Careers for Women in Retailing.* 52 pp. (Reprinted 1963).

272. *Maternity Benefit Provisions for Employed Women.* 50 pp. (1960).

273. *Part-Time Employment for Women.* 53 pp. (Reprinted 1960).

274. *Training Opportunities for Women and Girls.* 64 pp. (Reprinted 1961).

275. *1960 Handbook on Women Workers.* 160 pp. (1960). (See Bull. 285.)

276. *Today's Woman in Tomorrow's World.* 138 pp. (1960).

277. *State Hour Laws for Women.* 105 pp. (1961).

278. *Careers for Women in the Biological Sciences.* 84 pp. (1961).

279. *Life Insurance Selling—Careers for Women as Life Underwriters.* 35 pp. (1961).

280. *State Minimum-Wage Law and Order Provisions Affecting Working Conditions, July 1, 1942 to January 1, 1961.* 147 pp. (1961). (See Bull. 293.)

281. *Day Care Services—Form and Substance.* 55 pp. (1961).

282. *Careers for Women as Technicians.* 28 pp. (1961).

283. *Fifteen Years After College—A Study of Alumnae of the Class of 1945.* 26 pp. (1962).

284. *Women Workers in 1960: Geographical Differences.* 17 pp. (1962).

285. *1962 Handbook on Women Workers.* 202 pp. (1963). (See Bull. 290.)
286. *Women Telephone Workers and Changing Technology.* 46 pp. (1963).
287. *Negro Women Workers in 1960.* 55 pp. (1963).

SPECIAL BULLETINS

1. *Effective Industrial Use of Women in the Defense Program.* 22 pp. (1940).
2. *Lifting and Carrying Weights by Women in Industry.* 12 pp. (Revised 1946).
3. *Safety Clothing for Women in Industry.* 11 pp. (Revised 1946).
4. *Washing and Toilet Facilities for Women in Industry.* 11 pp. (1942).
5. *Women's Effective War Work Requires Time for Meals and Rest.* 4 pp. (1942).
6. *Night Work for Women and Shift Rotation in War Plants.* 8 pp. (1942).
7. *Hazards to Women Employed in War Plants on Abrasive-Wheel Jobs.* 6 pp. (1942).
8. *Guides for Wartime Use of Women on Farms.* 11 pp. (1942).
9. *Safety Caps for Women in War Factories.* 4 pp. Supplement, 4 pp. (1942).
10. *Women's Effective War Work Requires Good Posture.* 6 pp. (1943).
11. *Boarding Homes for Women War Workers.* 6 pp. (1943). Supplement: *Wartime Reminders to Women Who Work.* 8 pp. (1943).
12. *Choosing Women for War-Industry Jobs.* 10 pp. (1943).
13. *Part-Time Employment of Women in Wartime.* 17 pp. (1943).
14. *When You Hire Women.* 16 pp. (1944).
15. *Community Services for Women War Workers.* 11 pp. (1944).
16. *The Woman Counselor in War Industries: An Effective System.* 13 pp. (1944).
17. *Progress Report on Women War Workers' Housing, April 1943.* 10 pp. (1944).
18. *A Preview as to Women Workers in Transition from War to Peace.* 26 pp. (1944).
19. *The Industrial Nurse and the Woman Worker.* 47 pp. (1944). Revised and reprinted as Bull. 228 (1949).
20. *Changes in Women's Employment During the War.* 29 pp. (1944).

Essay on Sources

PERSONAL PAPERS

Schlesinger Library

The Schlesinger Library provided a rich storehouse of useful papers. The most vital to this study were the personal papers of women employed by the Women's Bureau or the Department of Labor: Mary Anderson, Frieda Miller, Mary Winslow, Esther Peterson, and Alice K. Leopold of the Women's Bureau; and Clara Beyer of the Department of Labor, Division of Labor Standards. The papers of members and leaders of women's and reform organizations provided insights into interactions between those interested in the question of female labor and the government. Women whose papers were reviewed were Caroline Lexow Babcock, Alma Lutz, Jane Norman Smith, Katherine Norris, Doris Stevens of the Woman's Party (the Stevens Papers are especially useful in outlining WP-WB conflict over international issues); Mary Beard of the Women's Charter, who provided an analysis of women's position in society; Marguerite Wells, Belle Sherwin, Dorothy Kirchwey Brown of the NLWV (the Dorothy Brown Papers contain a series of interviews with NLWV leaders and discussions of cooperation with the WB which were especially helpful); Maud Nathan of the NCL; and Mary Dingham of the YWCA. Women government officials whose papers proved most helpful included Florence Allen, the first woman state supreme court justice, United States Circuit Court (see for women in the New Deal, concern for the WB); Elinore Herrick, regional director for National Labor Relations Board, New York, New Jersey, Connecticut, who was deeply involved with WB minimum wage compaign; and Ellen Woodward, director, Women's Division, FERA (see for women in the

New Deal). Two very useful sets of papers are scattered between the Schlesinger and the FDR libraries, those of Mary Dewson (SL materials emphasize her early work with the NCL) and Hilda Smith (SL materials emphasize her work with the women's worker school movement).

Franklin Roosevelt Presidential Library

The Franklin Roosevelt Presidential Library provided material on Mary Dewson, which concentrates on her central role in organizing women for the Democratic Party (see for women in the New Deal); on Hilda Smith, which deals with her work with FERA, women worker camps, and WPA; on Katherine Ellickson, lobbyist with AFL-CIO, whose papers (scattered, also at Wayne State University) are useful for an examination of Women's Bureau interaction with unions; on Frances Perkins, 1932-1944, which relates to her work with the Department of Labor (scattered, also at Columbia); and on Eleanor Roosevelt, a key figure, who lobbied for federal programs for women workers during and after the New Deal.

The Wisconsin Historical Society

The Wisconsin Historical Society collection of personal papers includes the papers of Maude Swett of the Division of Women and Children, Wisconsin Bureau of Labor; Helen Sumner Woodbury, economist and assistant chief of the Children's Bureau, Department of Labor; Elizabeth Gurley Flynn, Communist organizer, whose papers demonstrate an interesting use of Women's Bureau *Bulletins;* and Morris Hillquit, whose papers are useful for an analysis of federal reactions to female labor in World War II and for information about union policy throughout the period.

Wayne State Labor Archives

The Wayne State Labor Archives contains material on Katherine Ellickson, CIO lobbyist (and Mary Van Kleeck, whose Woman-in-Industry Service, Russell Sage Foundation, and women in industry papers are scattered— the majority are at Smith).

Southern History Collection, University of North Carolina at Chapel Hill

The Southern History Collection includes material on Olive Arnold Campbell, who worked with the Russell Sage Foundation, organized the conference of Southern Mountain Workers, and worked with the Women's Bureau; and on Eva Sumner Bryant. (See for women in the New Deal— Democratic Party organizing.)

Perkins Library—Duke University

The Perkins Library provided information on Lucy Randolph Mason's CIO-organizing activities in the South and was useful in examining the Women's Bureau's relationship with labor.

Sophia Smith Collection, Smith College

The Sophia Smith Collection contains material on Mary Van Kleeck, the first director of the Woman-in-Industry Service. Although Van Kleeck resigned from government service in 1920, she continued a lifelong interest in the WB. Her papers throw valuable light on a wide variety of topics.

Butler Library, Columbia University

The Butler Library was useful in providing information on Frances Perkins. The Perkins collection is in subject file boxes, especially in boxes labeled "Unemployment," "United States Congress," and "International Labor."

Library of Congress

The Library of Congress was most useful here for details on Sophonisba Breckinridge's work with the Pan-American Conference of 1933, and her work with the Women's Bureau during the 1930s. The material on Mary Church Terrell, who campaigned for a Colored Women's Division in the WB, was useful for assessing Bureau attitudes toward blacks.

ORGANIZATIONAL ARCHIVES

Schlesinger Library

Organizational papers often provided valuable information about Women's Bureau contacts and relationships with private groups interested in the problems of women workers. At the Schlesinger Library, I made limited use of American Association of University Women papers, Institute of Women's Professional Relations papers, and International Federation of

Working Women papers. The papers of the National Women's Trade Union League are scattered. Those at the Schlesinger Library are most helpful in understanding Bureau-WTUL relationships in the early 1920s.

Franklin Roosevelt Presidential Library

Papers of the Women's Division of the National Committee of the Democratic Party provided insight into Women's Bureau involvement with Democratic politics in the 1930s and 1940s, women government professionals, and the issue of patronage for women. Records of the Presidents' Interdepartmental Committee to Coordinate Health and Welfare Activities, 1935-1941, were of limited use in investigating the question of the Bureau's advisory role with other government agencies.

The John F. Kennedy Presidential Library

A key collection used in completing this study is housed at the Kennedy Library, in the records of the President's Commission on the Status of Women.

Library of Congress

The material on the National Women's Trade Union League in the Library of Congress was more valuable than were the WTUL papers located in the Schlesinger Library. Also useful was the extensive correspondence of the WTUL with the Bureau, especially on the International Congress of Working Women, the Inter-American Program of the WB, the Workers' Summer Summer Schools, and the separate file on the WB. The material on the Women's Joint Congressional Committee was helpful in understanding the forces that organized to establish the WB, and the files of the minutes of meetings provided good summaries of women's reform work in the 1930s and 1940s. Containers of speech files of the National Consumers' League were quite useful, especially in investigating the Women's Charter, the WB Advisory Committee Structure, and the conferences of the WB. The papers of the National League of Women Voters, together with the WTUL papers, were the most valuable organizational papers used, providing extensive correspondence with the WB on a wide variety of topics.

Labor Management Documentation Center, Cornell University

Papers of the American Association for Labor Legislation, which constantly supported Bureau projects, were useful, especially for the correspondence between Mary Anderson and AALL Executive Secretary John Anderson. Papers of the New York Women's Garment Industry and International Ladies' Garment Workers Union were of limited use, except for some correspondence with the WB.

Sophia Smith Collection, Smith College

The records of the YWCA were useful because they contain preliminary drafts and research materials for cooperative studies done under Bureau aegis, and extensive correspondence with WB.

The Wisconsin Historical Society

Extremely useful for perceptions of labor's attitudes about working women were the papers of the AFL, housed here. Also used among organizational papers were the papers of the Advertising Women of New York, the papers for the Wisconsin Society for the Equal Rights Amendment, and the papers of the Women's International League for Peace and Freedom, Madison Chapter.

GOVERNMENT ARCHIVES

National Archives

This study relies heavily on government records. It makes the first extensive use of the voluminous and to date largely uncataloged records of the Women's Bureau (Record Group 86). The Social and Industrial Division of the National Archives staff, which is responsible for the WB records, worked during 1977-1979 on an inventory of the records, but for the purposes of this study, R.G. 86 existed as a large body of material with only the most meager of finding aids available. In 1981, some parts of R.G. 86 remained uninventoried in Federal Records Center transport containers. Since 1975, the National Archives has been moving the WB records from the Federal Records Depository in Suitland, Maryland, into the main Archives building in Washington, D.C. While R.G. 86 provided a wealth of information for this study, much of that information was painfully retrieved, because most of the records had not yet been very carefully arranged, either in chronological or topical order. While R.G. 86 is the backbone of this study, I also made use of the following, listed in order of importance to this study: Records of the National Youth Administration (R.G. 11), especially Series 321-325 (useful for looking at federal involvement with the Women's Summer School movement); Records of the President's

Committee on Fair Employment Practices (R.G. 228) (the files of the Division of Review and Analysis utilize Bureau services on questions of black female employment); Records of the Office of Education (R.G. 12) (files relating to the Lanham Act and Bureau involvement with the Lanham Act); Records of the Committee on War Services (R.G. 215) (information on Bureau involvement with WW II day-care planning); Records of the Secretaries of Labor (R.G. 174) (the records of Secretary Frances Perkins were more helpful than those of other secretaries of labor, arranged as they were with separate files on the Women's Bureau and women); Records of the President's Organization on Unemployment Relief (R.G. 73) (files of the Women's Division of POUR provide useful insights into informal use of Bureau services); Records of the Works Progress Administration (R.G. 69) (files in the Division of Women and Professional Projects contain much information about Bureau work during the Depression); Records of the War Manpower Commission (R.G. 211) (information about the work of the Women's Advisory Committee, and women workers in World War II); Records of the Department of State (R.G. 59) (useful in investigating the WB's international involvements as well as its relationship with the State Department); Records of the National War Labor Board, World War II (R.G. 202) (of limited use, but the records of Board members representing labor such as George Meany and Carl Shipley reveal expressed attitudes about women war workers).

PERSONAL INTERVIEWS

Between 1975 and 1976, the following people kindly took the time to talk with me, many on more than one occasion: Clara Beyer, Mary Cannon, Ethel Erickson, Jonathan Grossman, Mary Hilton, Mary Keyserling, Esther Peterson, and Selma Rein.

ORAL HISTORY INTERVIEWS

The Wayne State Labor Archives houses an extensive series of oral history interviews with women workers. I read through many, hoping to find worker perceptions of the Women's Bureau, but found them of little use.

The Office of Information in the Women's Bureau has a file of transcripts of interviews conducted in 1962-1964 with women government and labor leaders. Both tapes and transcripts exist for the following persons, although it should be mentioned that many of the tapes contain long inaudible sequences: Mary Pidgeon, Louis Stitt, Elizabeth Christman, Maude Swett, Pauline Newman, Frieda Miller. The Women's Bureau Files at the Department of Labor contain a copy of a letter from Mary Keyserling to Mrs. William Moran, curator of manuscripts at the Schlesinger Library, dated November 24, 1965, discussing plans to send transcripts of the above-mentioned tapes to the library. However, I have checked with curators at the SL, who say that the promised transcripts never arrived.

At the Columbia University Oral History Collection, I made use of the oral history transcripts for Alice Paul, John Philip Frey, Katharine Lenroot, and Frances Perkins. The Kennedy Library's Oral History Collection is rich. Among the most useful Oral Histories are transcripts of conversations with John Macy, Millard Cass, and Maurine Neuberger.

OFFICIAL PROCEEDINGS AND GOVERNMENT PUBLICATIONS

The official proceedings of the National League of Women Voters (1920-1948) and the National Women's Trade Union League (1913-1944) proved very helpful in assessing the public positions that these organizations took with regard to the Women's Bureau.

The Office of War Information, the War Manpower Commission, and the Bureau of the Budget published studies during the 1940s that were useful both in assessing government attempts to woo women into the war labor force and in examining these agencies' use of Bureau information. Especially useful were the studies of the Office of War Information, *Women and the War* (Washington: Government Printing Office, 1942); the War Manpower Commission, *America at War Needs Women at Work* (Washington: Government Printing Office, 1943); and the Bureau of the Budget, *The United States at War* (Washington: Government Printing Office, 1946).

Publications of the Bureau of the Census provided necessary background information about size and characteristics of the female population useful in understanding occupational shifts. I found the following especially helpful: United States Bureau of the Census, *1930 Census of Population: v. 5. General Report on Occupations* (Washington: Government Printing Office, 1931); *1940 Census of Population: The Labor Force (Sample Statistics),* "Employment and Family Characteristics of Women" (Washington: Government Printing Office, 1941); 1950 Census of Population: v. 4, Special Reports, Part 1, Chapter B, "Occupational Characteristics," (Washington: Government Printing Office, 1951); *Historical Statistics of the United States: Colonial Times to 1957* (Washington: Government Printing Office, 1957); *Current Population Reports:* Series P-50, No. 39, "Marital and Family Characteristics of the Labor Force in the United States: April, 1951" (Washington: Government Printing Office, 1951).

The printed *Bulletins* of the Women's Bureau proved to be a very important resource. Those published between 1919 and 1960 have been chronologically organized and listed in Appendix B.

UNPUBLISHED MATERIAL

The interactions between women's organizations and the government received attention in several useful dissertations. Valborg Fletty's "Public Services of Women's Organizations" (Ph.D. dissertation, Syracuse University, 1952) provides a great deal of largely undigested information about the activities of women's groups, especially during the 1920s. She argues that World War I was a major turning point in orienting private women's organizations toward involvement with government; Dorothy Johnson, "Organized Women and National Legislation, 1920-1941" (Ph.D. dissertation, Case Western Reserve University, 1960), discusses the interwar political activities and legislative goals of five major women's groups. She devotes little attention, however, to the fact that legislative goals often involved lobbying for the Women's Bureau; Paul Taylor's "Women in Party Politics, 1920-1940" (Ph.D. dissertation, Harvard University, 1966) is a sophisticated analysis of female involvement in political parties, emphasizing Mary Dewson's role in the Democratic Party; Susan Deubel Becker, "An Intellectual History of the National Woman's Party 1920-1941" (Ph.D. dissertation, Case Western Reserve University, 1975), carefully outlines the ideological underpinnings of the Woman's Party. Her dissertation is quite helpful in understanding the Party's position on the ERA, protective labor legislation, and the position of women; Louise Stitt's "A Study of the Woman's Party Position on Special Labor Laws for Women" (M.A. thesis, Ohio State University, 1925) vigorously attacks the Party. Since Stitt graduated from Ohio State to begin a lengthy career with the Bureau, her master's paper provides insight into the negative attitudes toward the Party she carried with her into government service; Lucille LeGanke, "The National Society of the Daughters of the American Revolution: Its History, Policies, and Influences, 1890-1940" (Ph.D. dissertation, Case Western Reserve University, 1951) discusses the DAR shift from social feminism to conservatism. Her work provides a basis for understanding DAR attacks on the Bureau. Also helpful were Robert Shanley, "The League of Women Voters—A Study of Pressure Politics in the Public Interest" (Ph.D. dissertation, Georgetown University, 1955) and Nancy Schrom, "New York Women's Trade Union League and the Organization of New York Women Workers, 1906-1930" (Ph.D. dissertation, University of Wisconsin, 1972).

Two dissertations written concerning women in federal government service proved to be of limited use. Sister John M. Daly, "Mary Anderson, Pioneer Labor Leader" (Ph.D. dissertation, Georgetown University, 1968), discusses the Women's Bureau only as a somewhat triumphant culmination of Mary Anderson's upwardly mobile life. Elsie George's study, "Women Appointees of the Roosevelt and Truman Administrations" (Ph.D. dissertation, American University, 1972), presents useful thumbnail biographies of several female government officials whose work may have brought them into repeated contact with the Bureau. However, such possible contact is not discussed in this dissertation, nor are any Women's Bureau members included in George's list of sketches.

Several dissertations provided insights into the structure of the Labor Department: James Russell Anderson, "The New Deal Career of Frances Perkins, Secretary of Labor" (Ph.D. dissertation, Case Western Reserve University, 1968); Joan Curlee, "Some Aspects of the New Deal Rationale: The Pre-1936 Writings of Six of Roosevelt's Advisers" (Ph.D. dissertation, Vanderbilt University, 1957), discusses social policy and labor philosophies of Berle, Perkins, Moley, Ickes, Tugwell, and Wallace; Hilda Gilvert, "The United States Department of Labor in the New Deal Period" (Ph.D. dissertation, University of Wisconsin, 1942); J. William MacEachron, "The Role of the United States Department of Labor" (Ph.D. dissertation, Harvard University, 1953); Francis Rourke, "The Reorganization of the Department of Labor" (Ph.D. dissertation, University of Minnesota, 1952). These three theses, while somewhat dated, provide a great deal of information about the changing position of the Department of Labor, 1913-1950. Especially useful were the interviews with Perkins, Wyzanski, and others included in the MacEachron manuscript. Edgar Shor's "The Role of the Secretary of Labor" (Ph.D. dissertation, University of Chicago, 1954) also utilizes interviews but is not very perceptive.

Mary Margaret Fonow's "Women in Steel: A Case Study of the Participation of Women in the Trade Union" (Ph.D. dissertation, The Ohio State University, 1977) provides an interesting case study of efforts by women workers to participate in and influence one trade union.

Several papers and dissertations focusing on government involvement with questions of female labor force participation proved quite helpful: Sarah Schramm, "Section 213: Woman Overboard," paper delivered at the Second Berkshire Conference on the History of Women, Radcliffe College, Cambridge, 1974; Eleanor Straub, "United States Government Policy Towards Civilian Women During World War II" (Ph.D. dissertation, Emory University, 1973); Patricia Anne White Tanabe, "Views of Women's Work in Public Policy in the United States: Social Security and Equal Pay Legislation, 1935-69" (Ph.D. dissertation, Bryn Mawr College, The Graduate School of Social Work and Social Research, 1973); Harvey S. Rosen, "The Impact of United States Tax Laws on the Labor Supply of Married Women" (Ph.D. dissertation, Harvard University, 1974); Kate Avery Arbogast, "The Procurement of Women for the Armed Forces: An Analysis of Occupational Choice" (Ph.D. dissertation, The George Washington University, 1974); Richard John Leaper, "Female Labor Force Attachments: An Analysis of Unemployment Rates in the United States and Canada" (Ph.D. dissertation, Duke University, 1976);

Aline Olson Quester, "The Labor Force Behavior of Wives: Effect of the Federal Tax Structure" (Ph.D. dissertation, University of Illinois at Urbana-Champaign, 1975).

Good overviews of changing occupational patterns for women's work in the late nineteenth and twentieth centuries appear in Josephine Chandler Holcomb's "Women in the Labor Force in the United States, 1940-1950" (Ph.D. dissertation, University of South Carolina, 1976); Rachel Ann Rosenfeld's "Women's Employment Patterns and Occupational Achievements" (Ph.D. dissertation, The University of Wisconsin-Madison, 1976); and Elyce Jean Rotella's "Women's Labor Force Participation and the Growth of Clerical Employment in the United States, 1870-1930" (Ph.D. dissertation, University of Pennsylvania, 1977.)

Useful in understanding interactions between public attitude and public policy toward women workers are Betty Stirling's "The Interrelation of Changing Attitudes and Changing Conditions with Reference to the Labor Force Participation of Wives" (Ph.D. dissertation, University of California at Berkeley, 1963) and Ed Russell Coover's "Status and Role Change Among Women in the United States, 1940-1970: A Quantitative Approach" (Ph.D. dissertation, University of Minnesota, 1973).

Useful dissertations on protective labor legislation include: G. M. Horne's "Mary Anderson and the Development of Protective Legislation for Women in the United States, 1890-1938" (Ph.D. dissertation, London School of Economics, 1976); Susan Lehrer's "Origins of Protective Labor Legislation for Women, 1900-1925" (Ph.D. dissertation, State University of New York at Binghamton, 1980).

Scholars in related disciplines such as political science, economics, and sociology have produced a wealth of information in dissertation studies on the general topic of women and work. The following dissertations, written from the perspectives of non-historians on social, economic, political, and family issues relating to female employment in the twentieth century, provided valuable background information. These dissertations were especially helpful for discussions of the impact of work by married women, although they illuminate other topics as well: Barbara Ann Pasey Jones, "The Contribution of Black Women to the Incomes of Black Families; An Analysis of the Labor Force Participation Rates of Black Wives" (Ph.D. dissertation, Georgia State University, School of Business Administration, 1973); Michael Duke Hurd, "Changes in Labor Force Participation" (Ph.D. dissertation, University of California, Berkeley, 1972); Jack Allan Meyer, "Labor Supply of Women Potentially Eligible for Family Assistance" (Ph.D. dissertation, The Ohio State University, 1972); Geraldine Bryant Terry, "The Interrelationship Between Female Employment and Fertility: A Secondary Analysis of the Growth of American Families Study" (Ph.D.

dissertation, The Florida State University, 1973); Elizabeth Gardner Maret Havens, "Female Labor Force Participation and Fertility" (Ph.D. dissertation, The University of Texas at Austin, 1973); Peter Ymen DeJong, "Factors Instrumental in Female Occupational Status: A Comparison to Factors Instrumental in Male Occupational Status" (Ph.D. dissertation, Western Michigan University, 1972); James Gregory Williams, "Occupational Differentiation By Sex in the United States Labor Force, 1900-1960" (Ph.D. dissertation, The University of Texas at Austin, 1972); Harry Michael Rosenberg, "The Influence of Fertility Strategies in the Labor-Force Status of American Wives" (Ph.D. dissertation, The Ohio State University, 1972); Allen Rupert Thompson, "Comparative Occupational Position of White and Non-White Females in the United States" (Ph.D. dissertation, The University of Texas at Austin, 1973); Ellen Shapiro Fried, "Female Labor Force Participation and Fertility: A Life Cycle Model" (Ph.D. dissertation, The University of Chicago, 1975); Kimball P. Marshall, "Female Participation in the Labor Force and Fertility: Cross-sectional and Longitudinal Perspectives" (Ph.D. dissertaion, The University of Florida, 1975); John F. Cogan, "Reservation Wages, Labor Force Participation, and Hours of Work of Married Women" (Ph.D. dissertation, University of California, Los Angeles, 1976); Lucille Olive Sherman, "Women in the Labor Force: Relationships Among Occupational Attachments, Family Statuses, and Poverty" (Ph.D. dissertation, University of Georgia, 1973); Evelyn Ruben Rosenthal, "Structural Patterns of Women's Occupational Choice" (Ph.D. dissertation, Cornell University, 1974); Sue Goetz Ross, "The Timing and Spacing of Births and Women's Labor Force Participation: An Economic Analysis" (Ph.D. dissertation, Columbia University, 1975); Carolyn Palmer Thomas, "Social Participation of Women: Labor Force, Formal, Informal" (Ph.D. dissertation, Michigan State University, 1974); Elizabeth Ness Nelson, "Women's Work—Jobs and Housework" (Ph.D. dissertation, University of California, Los Angeles, 1975); Jerome James Schmelz, "The Fertility Swing: An Investigation of U.S. Fertility Trends in Relation to Income, Housing, Socioeconomic Aspirations, and Female Labor Force Activity" (Ph.D. dissertation, University of Minnesota, 1975); Judith Huff Fox, "Women, Work, and Retirement" (Ph.D. dissertation, Duke University, 1976); Henry Allen Gordon, "Employment of Women with Pre-School Age Children" (Ph.D. dissertation, University of Maryland, 1976); Gerry Mitchell Arthur, "Employment and Fertility Among Women in the United States" (Ph.D. dissertation, University of Kentucky, 1975); Patricia R. McAlister, "Changes in Employment Status of Women Between the Parental and Postparental Periods" (Ph.D. dissertation, The Pennsylvania State University, 1975); Patricia Yvonne Anderson, "Women and Work: A Study of Female Labor Utilization in the

United States" (Ph.D. dissertation, The University of Chicago, 1977); Daniel Henry Hill, "A Dynamic Analysis of the Labor Force Participation of Married Women" (Ph.D. dissertation, The University of Michigan, 1977).

PUBLISHED MATERIAL

Some of the women who worked in or with the Women's Bureau have written autobiographies or have been the subject of biographies. Mary Anderson's *Woman at Work: The Autobiography of Mary Anderson as Told to Mary Winslow* (Minneapolis: University of Minnesota Press, 1951) is certainly required reading for a history of the Women's Bureau. However, Anderson's late-in-life reminiscences to her friend Mary Winslow contain many factual errors and oversimplifications and are primarily useful for understanding the viewpoints and personality of the Bureau director. Both Rose Schneiderman's and Margaret Dreier Robins' connections with the WTUL brought them into repeated contact with the Women's Bureau. However, Schneiderman's *All for One* (New York: Paul Eriksson, 1967) emphasizes her early work as an organizer for the ILGWU rather than her presidency of the WTUL. Mary Dreier's biography of her sister, *Margaret Dreier Robins: Her Life, Letters, and Work* (New York: Doran, 1923), is an autobiographical account that comments on Bureau international activities in the early 1920s.

I have indicated in the footnotes the secondary interpretive works that have helped me place this analysis in proper social, economic, and political contexts. The body of literature analyzing the changing roles of American women has recently expanded greatly. In making my way through much of this literature, I have been most impressed by the following works.

Sound historical, economic, and sociological explanations for changes in economy and government and concomitant changes in social values and labor force participation by women appear in Ferriss Abbott, *Indicators of Trends in the Status of American Women* (New York: Russell Sage Foundation, 1971); Glenn Cain, *Married Women in the Labor Force* (Chicago: University of Chicago Press, 1966); Rosalyn Baxandall, Linda Gordon, Susan Reverby, *America's Working Women* (New York: Vintage Books, 1976); Theodore Caplow, *Sociology of Work* (Minneapolis: University of Minnesota Press, 1954); Eva Mueller, *Technical Advance in an Expanding Economy, Its Impact on a Cross Section of the Labor Force* (Ann Arbor: University of Michigan Press, 1969); Alva Myrdal and Viola Klein, *Women's Two Roles* (New York: Humanities Press, 1968); Valerie Oppenheimer, *The Female Labor Force in the United States: Demographic and Economic Factors Governing Its Growth and Changing Composition* (Westport, Conn.: Greenwood Press, 1976); Herbert Parnes, *Research on Labor Mobility* (New York: Social Science Research Council, 1954); Robert

Smuts, "The Female Labor Force: A Case Study in the Interpretation of Historical Statistics," *Journal of the American Statistical Association,* 55 (March 1960), pp. 71-79; George Stigler, *Trends in Employment in the Service Industries* (Princeton: Princeton University Press, 1956); Richard Edwards, Michael Reich, David Gordon, *Labor Market Segmentation* (Lexington, Mass.: D.C. Heath, 1973); Milton Cantor and Bruce Laurie, eds., *Class, Sex, and the Woman Worker* (Westport, Conn.: Greenwood Press, 1977); David Katzman, *Seven Days A Week: Women and Domestic Service in Industrializing America* (New York: Oxford University Press, 1978); James Kenneally, *Women and American Trade Unions* (St. Albans: Eden Press, 1978); Susan Kleinberg, "Technology and Women's Work: The Lives of Working Class Women in Pittsburgh, 1870-1900," *Labor History,* 17 (Winter 1976), pp. 58-72; Alice Kessler-Harris, "Women's Wage Work as Myth and History," *Labor History,* 19 (Spring 1978), pp. 287-307; Sheila Rothman, *Woman's Proper Place: A History of Changing Ideals and Practices, 1870 to the Present* (New York: Basic Books, 1978); Martha Blaxall and Varvara Reagan, eds., *Women and the Workplace: The Implications of Occupational Segregation* (Chicago: University of Chicago Press, 1976); Barbara Garson, *All the Livelong Day: The Meaning and Demeaning of Routine Work* (Garden City, N.Y.: Doubleday and Company, Inc., 1975); Eli Ginzberg and Hyman Berman, *The American Worker in the Twentieth Century: A History Through Autobiographies* (New York: The Free Press, 1963); Fabian Linden and Helen Axel, *Women: A Demographic, Social, and Economic Presentation* (New York: The Conference Board, 1973).

Good overviews of women's history that help place the history of changing work patterns in context include William Chafe's *The American Woman: Her Changing Social, Economic, and Political Role, 1920-1970* (New York: Oxford University Press, 1972). Chafe utilizes some of the Bureau's materials in making his conclusions but provides no comprehensive discussion of its activities. Chafe's book does, however, provide an excellent introduction to public and government attitudes about women's place, and the impact of events like economic depression and war on both those attitudes and women's actual status. Carl Degler's *At Odds, Women and the Family in America From the Revolution to the Present* (New York: Oxford University Press, 1980) provides an excellent synthesis of secondary writing on American family and women's history. *At Odds* surveys female roles within the family and helps explain changing patterns for female labor force participation.

Susan Estabrook Kennedy, *If All We Did Was to Weep at Home: A History of White Working Class Women in America* (Bloomington: Indiana University Press, 1979), provides a readable survey of changing work patterns among working-class women. Winifred Wandersee's excellent *Women's Work and Family Values, 1920-1940* (Cambridge, Mass.: Harvard University Press, 1981) provides insights into changing patterns of work

among married and middle-class women as does Frank Stricker's "Cook-books and Law Books: The Hidden History of Career Women in Twentieth Century America," *Journal of Social History*, 10 (Fall 1976), pp. 1-19.
Among historical works analyzing the Progressive era and suffrage are Anne Firor Scott and Andrew Scott's *One Half the People: The Fight for Woman Suffrage* (New York: Lippincott, 1975), which provides both a brief, well-argued discussion of the campaign for the Nineteenth Amendment and a collection of edited documents. Eleanor Flexner's *Century of Struggle, The Woman's Rights Movement in the United States* (Cambridge: Belknap Press, 1959) and Aileen Kraditor's *Ideas of the Woman Suffrage Movement* (New York: Columbia University Press, 1965) are still standards, helpful in understanding the motivations of female Progressives as are Eileen Lagemann's *A Generation of Women—Education in the Lives of Progressive Reformers* (Cambridge, Mass.: Harvard University Press, 1981); Nancy Schom Dye's "Creating a Feminist Alliance: Sisterhood and Class Conflict in the New York Women's Trade Union League, 1903-1914," *Feminist Studies*, 2 (1975), pp. 24-38; and James J. Kenneally's "Women and Trade Unions, 1870-1920: The Quandary of the Reformer," *Labor History*, 14 (1973), pp. 42-55.

Investigations of women's political and economic activities during the New Era and New Deal include *Leslie Woodcock Tentler, Wage-Earning Women Industrial Work and Family Life in the United States, 1900-1930* (New York: Oxford University Press, 1979); Patricia M. Hummer, *The Decade of Elusive Promise: Professional Women in the United States, 1920-1930* (Ann Arbor: UMI Research Press, 1979); Barbara Klaczynska, "Why Women Work: A Comparison of Various Groups—Philadelphia, 1910-1930," *Labor History* 17 (1976), pp. 73-86; Estelle Freedman, "The New Woman: Changing Views of Women in the 1920's," *Journal of American History*, 61 (September 1974), pp. 372-93; Winifred Wandersee, "The Economics of Middle Income Family Life; Working Women During the Great Depression," *Journal of American History*, v. 65, 1 (June 1978), pp. 66-74; Rosylyn L. Foldberg, "'Union Fever': Organizing Among Clerical Workers, 1900-1930," *Radical America* (1980), pp. 53-70; Margary Davies, "Woman's Place is at the Typewriter: The Feminization of Clerical Workers and Changes in Clerical Work in the United States, 1879-1930," *Radical America*, 8 (1974), pp. 1-28; Lois Scharf, *To Work and to Wed: Female Employment, Feminism, and the Great Depression* (Westport, Conn: Greenwood Press, 1980); and Elizabeth Baker, *Protective Labor Legislation* (New York: AMS Press, 1969).

There has been an explosion of recent publications that investigate the roles played by women in both World Wars. Among the most useful are Alan Clive, "Women Workers in World War II: Michigan as a Test Case,"

Labor History, 20 (1979), pp. 44-72; Valerie J. Conner, "'The Mothers of the Race' in World War I: The National War Labor Board and Women in Industry," *Labor History,* 21 (1979-80), pp. 31-54; Chester W. Gregory, *Women in Defense During World War II: An Analysis of the Labor Problem and Women's Rights* (New York: Exposition Press, 1974); Marc Miller, "Working Women and World War II," *New England Quarterly,* 53 (1980), pp. 42-61; Mary M. Schweitzer, "World War II and Female Labor Force Participation Rates," *Journal of Economic History,* 40 (1980), pp. 89-97; Joan E. Trey, "Women in the War Economy, World War II," *Review of Radical Political Economics,* 4 (July 1972), pp. 40-57; Nancy Gabin, "Women Workers and the UAW in the Post World War II Period," *Labor History* (Winter 1979-80), pp. 5-31; D'Ann Campbell, "Was the West Different? Values and Attitudes of Young Women in 1943," *Pacific History Review* (August 1978), pp. 453-463; Karen Anderson, *Wartime Women: Sex Roles, Family Relations, and the Status of Women During World War II* (Westport, Conn.: Greenwood Press, 1981); Sheila Tobias and Lisa Anderson, *What Really Happened to Rosie the Riveter—Demobilization and the Female Labor Force—1944-47* (New York: Modular Press, 1973); Leila Rupp, *Mobilizing Women for War: German & American Propaganda 1939-45* (Princeton: Princeton University Press, 1978); and Susan M. Hartmann, "Prescription for Penelope: Literature on Women's Obligations to Returning World War II Veterans," *Women's Studies,* 5:3 (1978), pp. 223-240.

Many of the books in women's history mentioned as good surveys of the twentieth century have final chapters analyzing the postwar period. Among specific works I found useful are Peter Henle and Paul Ryscavage, "The Distribution of Earned Income Among Men and Women, 1958-77," *Monthly Labor Review,* 103 (1980), pp. 3-10; Patricia Zelman, *Women, Work and National Policy, The Kennedy-Johnson Years* (Ann Arbor: UMI Research Press, 1981); and Linda J. Waite, "Working Wives: 1940-1960," *American Sociological Review,* 41 (February 1976), pp. 65-79.

An overview of the American labor movement was also useful to establish background and context for this study. Milton Derber's *The American Idea of Industrial Democracy, 1865-1965* (Urbana: University of Illinois Press, 1970) provides a framework for understanding the collective bargaining system crystallized in the labor violence of the 1890s, the employer-dominated welfare capitalism of the 1920s, and with the New Deal and World War II, the elimination of employer-dominated labor systems and the assumption by the federal government of a new and complicated role. Also useful: Irving Bernstein, *The Lean Years: A History of the American Worker, 1920-1933* (Boston: Houghton Mifflin, 1960); Milton Derber and Edwin Young, eds., *Labor and the New Deal* (Madison: University of Wisconsin

Press, 1957); Phillip Taft, *Organized Labor in American History* (New York: Harper and Row, 1964); Walter Galenson, *The CIO Challenge to the AF of L: A History of the American Labor Movement, 1935-1941* (Cambridge: Harvard University Press, 1960); Bruno Stein, "Labor's Role in Government Agencies During World War II," *Journal of Economic History,* 17 (September 1957), pp. 389-408; Colston E. Warne, ed., *Labor in Post-War America* (Brooklyn: Remsen Press, 1949); James Green, *The World of the Worker: Labor in Twentieth Century America* (New York: Hill and Wang, 1980).

There are no really good studies of the Department of Labor. Of those written, the following provide biased, relatively nonanalytical discussions of the department. Jonathan Grossman, *The Department of Labor* (New York: Praeger, 1973); James Leiby, *Carroll Wright and Labor Reform: The Origin of Labor Statistics* (Cambridge: Harvard University Press, 1960); John Lombardi, *Labor's Voice in the Cabinet: A History of the Department of Labor, from its Origins to 1921* (New York: Columbia University Press, 1942); John Terrell, *The United States Department of Labor: A Story of Workers, Unions, and the Economy* (New York: Meridith Press, 1968); although dryly written, Thomas Wolanin's *Presidential Advisory Commissions* (Madison: University of Wisconsin Press, 1975) provides information about the bureaucratic institution of the Presidential Commission, useful in evaluating the character of the Kennedy Commission on Women.

The only published study of the Women's Bureau itself is a twenty-five page leaflet written in 1923 under the auspices of the Johns Hopkins Institute of Government Research: Gustavus Weber, *The Women's Bureau* (Baltimore: Johns Hopkins, 1923). The pamphlet merely summarizes the 1920 legislative hearings held to consider the formal establishment of the Bureau and provides a five-page summary of the Woman-in-Industry Service.

Index

About the Author

JUDITH SEALANDER is Associate Professor of History at Wright State University in Dayton, Ohio, where she specializes in American social and business history. Her articles have appeared in numerous scholarly journals, and she is now at work on a book-length study of the changing nature of the turn-of-the-century American business corporation.